Praise for *Army Wife*

"Timeless, poignant, moving, and inspirational, Vicki Cody's *Army Wife* reads like a can't-put-it-down thriller. Having sent a husband and two sons to combat as Apache pilots, Vicki's 33 years of marriage to Dick Cody and her selfless leadership as an Army spouse at every command level provide lessons in faith, endurance, love, marriage, and decision making. *Army Wife* should be required reading in every boardroom and classroom."

—A.J. Tata, national bestselling author of
Three Minutes to Midnight

"*Army Wife* is a unique—yet unsurprisingly common—perspective from a young wife 'coming of age' through the years, the fears, and a deepening faith. Deep within a culture all its own, the Army refines both the Soldier and the soldier's family, and the reader is given a window into this world of strength—from the beginnings of young love, to the constant moves, the realities of death and mortality, the challenges of reintegration after deployments, the unknowns. It's rare to have such personal insight from a wife's perspective as she takes us on their journey through the Army ranks."

—Sharlene Hawkes, Miss America 1985,
President of Remember My Service

"Vicki Cody shares her life experiences with the grace and dignity befitting an Army spouse and mother of soldiers. The unsung heroes of America's 21st-Century War finally get their long overdue day in the sun as Vicki takes readers on an Army family journey. *Army Wife* is a must read. The American people deserve to truly understand the commitment and sacrifice that all military spouses selflessly give."

—Jimmy Blackmon U.S. Army (Ret.) and author of
*Pale Horse: Hunting Terrorists and Commanding
Heroes with the 101st Airborne Division*

Army

Wife

Army
Wife

A Story of Love and Family
in the Heart of the Army

Vicki Cody

SHE WRITES PRESS

Published 2016

Printed in the United States of America

ISBN: 978-1-63152-127-0 pbk

ISBN: 978-1-63152-128-7 ebk

Library of Congress Control Number: 2016935740

For information, address:

She Writes Press

1563 Solano Ave #546

Berkeley, CA 94707

She Writes Press is a division of SparkPoint Studio, LLC.

Names and identifying characteristics have been changed to protect the privacy of certain individuals.

Cover photo courtesy US Army

Contents

Prologue 1

1: Burlington, Vermont 5

2: Wedding-Bell Blues . . . and a Thing Called Deployment . 17

3: Educating Vicki, Brand-New Army Wife 22

4: Sweet Home Alabama 28

5: We're Having a Baby . . . and a Short Tour, Too! 36

6: Savannah, Georgia, 1979 44

7: Life Takes a Sharp Turn 49

Thoughts on Faith and Trust 58

8: A Fork in the Road 61

9: The Year We All Went to School 66

10: A Rendezvous with Destiny 76

Thoughts on Moving 85

11: Summer 1990 90

12: Operation Desert Shield/Desert Storm 100

Thoughts on Reintegration 109

13: The Best Year of Our Lives 114

Photo Insert 121

14: Welcome to Texas, Y'all! 137

15: A Time of Transition 144

16: The First Star 148

17: Washington, DC, 1999–2000 158

Thoughts on Just Being Me 164

18: A Final Rendezvous with Destiny 169

19: September 11, 2001 179

20: A New "Band of Brothers" 190

Thoughts on Deployments 201

21: Inside the E-Ring 205

22: Operation Iraqi Freedom 213

Thoughts on What Goes Around Comes Around 227

23: A Fourth Star 231

24: More Deployments 237

Thoughts on the Nature of the Business 248

25: The Last Chapter 253

Epilogue 264

Acknowledgments 267

About the Author 269

Prologue
Fort Campbell, Kentucky, February 2004

It is four in the morning, and a cold rain is falling at Campbell Army Airfield as I stand on the tarmac, juggling an umbrella and a handmade WELCOME HOME sign, trying to stay dry. I am in a crowd of hundreds of other families, all of us waiting for the chartered 747 that is bringing our soldiers home from combat. I can see tiny lights in the distance; it's hard to tell how far out the plane is because of the darkness and the rain, but it looks like it's on a long final approach.

I'm thinking, *Thank God he's almost home!*

Both of our sons, serving in the same aviation brigade with the 101st Airborne Division, have been deployed to Iraq; the oldest one, Clint, has been gone for twelve months and will hopefully come in next week. Our youngest, Tyler, arriving on this plane, has been gone for six months.

I am oblivious to the rain, to the cheering crowd, to everything except my husband on one side and our daughter-in-law on the other. I look at Brooke and am overcome with emotion for what she has been through this past year. She and Tyler had been married just three months when he left for Iraq. She is not only a newlywed but also a brand-new Army wife. An Army wife myself, I know exactly what she is feeling, for I, too, have experienced deployments as a young wife—though in a different war, a different time in history. But this time, as the mother of two soldiers, I'm in uncharted territory.

Dick, my husband of almost thirty years, gray now, but still the

1

handsome man I fell in love with so many years ago, is in uniform, just like his sons. And those stars on his beret . . . I can clearly remember when he had a gold lieutenant's bar on a green field cap instead. I adore this man beside me—so stoic, yet I feel his excitement and see the emotion on his face and the pride in his eyes. We are soul mates and always have been. There's never been a day in these past thirty years when I haven't felt his love for me and he my love for him. We've become even closer these past couple of years, when he's been "stuck" back at the Pentagon while his sons were deployed. It has been difficult for both of us, but especially for Dick, in part because as he moved up in rank and position and became the vice chief of staff of the Army, our sons, just beginning their careers, began deploying. To be not just the number-two guy in the Army, making decisions that affect hundreds of thousands of soldiers, but also the father of two of those soldiers, puts Dick in a tough position. Where he really wants to be is in the combat zone with all of them, flying an Apache helicopter, like he did in the first Gulf War. But that's not meant to be this time. Instead, in this war, his sons are flying Apache helicopters in his old brigade in the legendary 101st. Even as Dick sits this one out, though, he knows that he and his two sons will be forever linked by the Screaming Eagle combat patch that each wears on the right shoulder of his uniform.

I'm flooded with memories of standing on this tarmac, at this airfield. So many times, the boys and I waited here for their dad to return home. Now, I think, *There's nothing better than welcoming your husband home from war—nothing except welcoming your sons.* It feels almost strange to have Dick by my side, waiting for the boys.

The plane touches down, and the crowd erupts in cheers. Tyler and a few hundred soldiers are home safe, at last! Tears stream down my cheeks, and I wonder if the people around me can hear my heart pounding.

We watch as the plane taxis toward us in slow motion. After what seems like an eternity, the soldiers start walking down the steps of the plane to the exuberant, flag-waving crowd. Brooke and I stand on tiptoe to try to get a glimpse of Tyler. It takes forever, as he is toward the back of the plane. And then we see him! All I can think is, *I don't ever want to forget this feeling. It's pure joy. Tyler is home, and in one more week Clint will be home and I will feel whole again, my family complete.*

The next minutes are chaos as families run up to greet their soldiers. We find Tyler in the crowd, and as I watch our son with his wife, I can't help but feel blessed, wondering how we got so lucky. How did Dick and I manage to stay in love all these years, raise two wonderful sons, and never lose sight of what is important to us and what is important in life? We've been through a lot in our thirty years of marriage, yet I wouldn't change a thing or trade places with anyone.

So I begin my journey back in time, with the luxury of hindsight: to find out how and why my marriage and family have survived, when so many around me have failed. How did we make it through not only what life in general threw at us but also what Army life dumped on us? As a brand-new Army wife, heading to Hawaii to begin my life with Dick, I was so naive—not so much about marriage as about being married to a soldier and all that meant. Then again, aren't we all naive when we're young and in love?

I had no idea how the Army would dictate and determine our fate, pull us in different directions, and test our relationship, over and over again. That it would be the source of some of our biggest stresses and fears and, at the same time, our greatest joys. That for all of the challenges we faced, we would experience great satisfaction; for every downside, we would find an upside; for every separation, there would be a reunion. Over time, I would learn to embrace Army life, with all of its unique qualities, idiosyncrasies, flaws, and difficulties, because those very things made me stronger as a wife, as a mother, and as a woman. It made us stronger as a couple and as a family. We would experience the adventures together, and on my own I would learn independence and self-discovery. I would learn to feel pride that I never knew was possible—pride in my husband, our sons, our Army, and our country. Army life would teach me not only how to live in the moment but also to cherish and relish the ordinary moments as much as the extraordinary ones. Army life—the people, the places, and the experiences—was what helped shape all four of us.

It seems like only yesterday . . .

1

Burlington, Vermont

The summer of 1969 was tumultuous and eventful for the United States. We put our first man on the moon. One of the newest teams in baseball, the New York Mets, was having its best season ever and was nicknamed the Miracle Mets as the team worked its way to winning the World Series. In Los Angeles, the gruesome murders of actress Sharon Tate and her friends dominated the headlines, and Charles Manson became a household name. The Vietnam War was escalating on the other side of the world, and the controversy over it seemed to be dividing our country. I didn't really understand what the war was about; it seemed so far away from the peace and quiet of the Green Mountain State. I didn't know anyone in the Army, and there were no military installations in Vermont, just the Vermont Air National Guard. There were also no twenty-four-hour news shows with instant coverage, and there was no Internet, so we Vermonters were somewhat sheltered from the ravages of the war; most of what I knew about it was what I heard my parents talking about or what I saw on the evening news.

It was also a summer of peace, love, and rock 'n' roll. That August, the Woodstock Music Festival in Bethel, New York, brought together the biggest names in the industry for four days of music, drugs, and sex, as an estimated five hundred thousand people converged on Max Yasgur's farm. Anyone from the 1960s generation who remembers Woodstock will never forget the iconic phrase "The New York State Thruway is closed, man!" The shutdown of the major north–south artery between New England and New York City was a truly amazing feat and gave us all a visual on just how many people attempted to get to the festival. Woodstock became a symbol of the hippie culture that defined the music for my generation. But all of the big news stories that summer were a mere blip on my radar screen, because for me, the biggest event was meeting the guy whom I would love for the rest of my life.

Burlington was a great place to grow up. Known for its winter sports, gorgeous fall foliage, Green Mountains, and beautiful Lake Champlain, it is the quintessential small New England city. At sixteen, I had just finished my sophomore year of high school, and my life was pretty simple. My world consisted of babysitting, going to my brother's Little League baseball games, and hanging out at the beach with my best friend. Becky and I were inseparable and spent countless afternoons in her bedroom or mine. With the radio tuned to the Top 40 hits, we heard the 5th Dimension's "The Age of Aquarius," Zager and Evans's "In the Year 2525," and Barry McGuire's sobering ballad, "Eve of Destruction." We listened to any kind of music: the Beatles, Bob Dylan, James Taylor, the Grassroots, the Mamas & the Papas, Simon & Garfunkel; their songs served as the backdrop for our young and innocent lives. We tried on clothes, tested makeup and the latest shades of Revlon frosted lipstick, all the while discussing who was going out with whom, who had been kissed, and the various other sexual exploits of anyone we knew who had actually done anything. We pored over issues of *Photoplay* (the tabloid of the day), reading about Hollywood stars and the latest gossip and movie reviews. We thought we were worldly and sophisticated.

I had gotten my driver's license that year—a huge deal—and my braces removed, so, in my mind, I was mature enough for romance. Becky and I dreamed of finding the perfect boyfriend. I hadn't had one yet—a couple of movie dates, a few crushes on boys from school, some make-out sessions with said boys, but nothing serious. I was hoping that would change.

I had heard the name Dick Cody from my sister, Chris, and her boyfriend, Jim, who was Dick's cousin. Dick was a superstar in Vermont high school sports—an All-American honorable mention in basketball who set scoring records in the state, and a West Point cadet who drove a new Corvette every summer when he came home on leave. And, according to Jim, he had *tons* of girlfriends. Dick was from Montpelier, about forty-five miles from Burlington, so I had never met him. Little did I know that I was about to come face-to-face with the legendary Dick Cody, and nothing could have prepared me for how I would feel about him.

On the night of June 21, 1969, Chris and I were babysitting our younger brother, Dicky. Jim had gone out with his cousin, Dick, which was why Chris was home with me on a Saturday night. At about 10:30 p.m., we headed upstairs. We were lying in our white French provincial twin beds, talking. It was warm, and the windows were open.

All of a sudden, we heard a very loud car pull into the driveway. We were out of our beds in seconds and scrambled into Dicky's room, where we had a view of our driveway. Oh my God! There was this beautiful, shiny aquamarine Corvette, and out of the driver's side emerged this hunk of a guy. I had to strain to get a good look at him: muscular body; short, dark hair; handsome face, from what I could see.

Once we realized it was Jim and his famous cousin, Dick Cody, Chris and I tripped over each other trying to get back into our room to put some clothes on. We threw on cutoffs and T-shirts and bounded down the stairs and out the front door in seconds. I tried to be nonchalant during the introductions, but my heart was pounding and I felt something I had never felt before—weak in the knees. He was *so* good-looking! While Chris and Jim sat on the porch, talking, Dick stared at me. Because I was nervous, I picked up a basketball and started shooting on our garage hoop. What was I thinking, doing that in front of an All-American athlete? Thankfully, he put me out of my misery when he asked, "Do you want to go for a ride in my car?"

Holy shit, do I want a ride in your car! I thought. But I simply replied, ever so calmly, "Sure."

It was one of those perfect summer evenings in Vermont. Dick had the T-top off the 'Vette, and we decided to drive the few blocks to the beach at Lake Champlain. He parked the car, and as we walked the path through the woods to the beach, it was almost pitch black. I said, "I can't see where I'm going."

He took my hand and led me along, explaining that he had just finished his summer training at West Point's Camp Buckner. "They taught us all these neat navigational skills and how to use the darkness. Don't look back at the street lights; just look into the dark, and once your eyes adjust, you'll be able to find your way."

My eyes did adjust, but I sure liked having him hold my hand. As we sat on the sand, the stars and the moon were so bright, I had no trouble seeing the young man sitting next to me. I thought he was the cutest guy I had ever seen, like a movie star right out of *Photoplay*. We chatted about Chris and Jim's relationship, what grade I was in, just the usual small talk of two people who had just met. Then he leaned over and kissed me. I felt as if my insides were melting.

When we stopped, he looked me in the eyes and said, "You're really cute." He was so smooth. I was so turned on by this guy who had walked into my life just thirty minutes before. Then he kissed me again and I wanted it to go on forever. Kissing Dick felt different from any kissing I had done with boys my age. I sensed right away that something important had just happened to me: I had met the man of my dreams.

But my dreams would have to wait, as reality crept into my consciousness and I remembered my curfew. Suddenly, Dick and I both said at the same time, "We'd better go back." My parents would be getting home soon, and I didn't know how they would react to my going to the beach at night with someone they had never met, which was out of character for me. To this day I think about the randomness of that night and how fate changed the course of my life and Dick's.

He let me drive his car back to my parents' house. My driver's license was just six months old, and there I was, driving a Corvette. I could feel his eyes on me as I gripped the steering wheel and concentrated on the road. I don't know what was more exciting to me at that point: Dick Cody or his Corvette. Either way, by the time we got to the house, the crush of the century had begun. But a popular song was playing in my head: *Come back when you grow up, girl. You're still livin' in a paper doll world. . . .* He had used the word *cute*; maybe I was too young for him. I convinced myself he would never call me. (Sure enough, whenever Dick later recounted the story of our first meeting, he said, "There was Vicki, in pigtails and on roller skates." I wasn't *that* young!)

But he did call, a few days later, and I almost fainted when my mom handed me the phone. He asked me out on a date. My parents were hesitant, not just because of our three-year age difference but because Dick was more mature; he was already in college. They agreed only because Chris and Jim would be going with us. We went to the drive-in to see *Romeo and Juliet*, but we watched little of the movie. There was an awful lot of kissing going on, and not just on the big screen. I didn't want the date to end. Later that night, as I lay in my bed, and for days after that, Dick was all I could think about.

We had one more date that summer before Dick returned to West Point. My parents thought it was just a schoolgirl crush, and in the beginning, that's exactly what it was. After all, my first encounter with him was based purely on physical attraction. His good looks, the whole West Point cadet image—it was all very sexy. I knew very little about Dick Cody the person but was hoping I would get the chance to learn more.

As I began my junior year in high school, I continued thinking about Dick a lot. Young and inexperienced in the ways of love, I wasn't really sure where it was going with him or if it was even going anywhere. At that point, our age difference seemed significant, and he didn't hide the fact that he was dating girls from the various girls' schools near West Point. But letters and an occasional phone call from him kept the spark alive as we got to know each other. While I could tell from our phone conversations that he liked me and thought I was fun and "cute," I sometimes wondered if I was just a pen pal to him. After all, I was a lanky, flat-chested, inexperienced high school girl and didn't think I could compete with the girls he dated, who, in my mind, were blond, voluptuous, and worldly.

Meanwhile, I led a typical teenager's life: studying; going to football, basketball, and hockey games; attending parties; and hanging out with friends. Becky and I were on the ski team and spent weekdays training and Saturdays racing. Skiing was a way of life in Vermont; when we weren't racing, we were skiing with our families. I dated a guy in my high school for something to do, but it was over by the end of the school year.

Later that year, the reality of the Vietnam War came into my safe little world when a young man from my school was killed in Vietnam. Harmie Bove was a legend in high school sports; he and Dick had faced each other on the baseball field. Becky had been dating Harmie before he left for basic training. In less than a year, I had gone from knowing very little about war and the US military to personally knowing someone who had been killed in the war, and to dating a guy who was a cadet at the United States Military Academy. Up until that point, I hadn't made the connection between Dick's being a cadet and Dick's being in the Army. Now, I suddenly looked at him and the career he had chosen in a different light.

★ ★ ★

Those first two years of our courtship, I saw Dick whenever he came home on leave. It was sporadic, since cadets, especially underclassmen, don't get a lot of time off. When he was able to come home for the big winter holidays, we spent most of our time snow-skiing, and in the summer, we water-skied on Lake Champlain. No matter what we did, we had fun and made each other laugh. But it seemed like we never had enough time together.

I made my first trip to West Point during my senior year of high school, with Dick's parents. I was thrilled to finally get to see Dick in his element. He looked so handsome in his cadet uniform. West Point was fascinating to me, and it gave me some insight into another facet of Dick Cody—the one that was committing himself to a career in the Army. I was getting past his superficial layers; I saw how he respected and revered his parents, the close relationship he had with his mother, what a good big brother he was to his siblings, and what a loyal friend he was to his West Point buddies. As I watched him play sports, I saw his drive and energy.

We came from slightly different backgrounds. Dick was from a large Catholic family of seven kids; his grandparents had immigrated from Lebanon and made a small fortune in real estate and various businesses in Montpelier. I was from a small, middle-class, nonpracticing Episcopalian family; my relatives were from the Midwest. Yet what we had in common were the most important things in life: our values and our sense of family. We both came from very loving and happy families, with parents whom we viewed as our role models.

As our relationship grew, our time apart and the geographical distance between us worked to our advantage. I began to get to know the real Dick Cody even more through his letters. In person, he was very sure of himself—some even called him cocky—but in his letters to me, he showed a softer side, vulnerable and sweet but never too sappy. The fact that he knew what he wanted to do with his life was one of the reasons he captured my heart and excited me in a way no one else had. He was like a magnet that I was drawn to.

Still, while I was falling all over him in my mind, I was careful not to show too much of that to him. He had enough girls doing that, and I didn't want to be yet another one. If he was a little hard to get, then I was, too. And because we didn't get to see each other on a regular basis and often went months in between dates, there was no reason for either of us to expect the other not to have a social life when we weren't together. At that point, I didn't feel threatened by or jealous of other girls he dated—they were just dates. But just when I thought I didn't know where I stood with him, he would surprise me. While we were driving around in his Corvette one summer evening, he turned to me and said, very simply, "You're probably the girl I'm going to marry." Just like that, it was out there.

I didn't even respond, because it was such a matter-of-fact statement and caught me so off guard. But my stomach was doing backflips as I thought, *That* must *mean he loves me!*

I began my freshman year at the University of Vermont (UVM) in the fall of 1971. UVM was (and still is) a fine academic institution, but it also had the distinction of being number three on *Playboy* magazine's list of Top Ten Party Schools. Partying and skiing were my top priorities; academics came in third. Still, I managed to do well in my courses while having fun; I joined a sorority my first semester and loved every aspect of college life. My four years at UVM were some of the best of my young life.

When I was a college freshman, Dick was in his last year at West Point. As a "firstie," he had more free time (when he wasn't in confinement or walking tours for misconduct), so we were able to see more of each other. It was the first time I felt like we were on equal footing, like our age difference didn't matter. Our college campuses and experiences couldn't have been more different, though. Mine had beautiful, ivy-covered brick buildings; long-haired, sandal-wearing hippies lounging on the campus greens; ponytailed professors; a free-spirited, freethinking culture; peace rallies, drugs, and drunken frat parties—a typical New England college campus in the early 1970s. Compare that with the historic gray stone of the United States Military Academy, with its uptight, high-and-tight, regimented, all-male, overachieving corps of cadets—a culture that breeds future Army leaders, a place where every young man looked the same in his uniform. My uniform was bell-bottom blue jeans (preferably hip-huggers), a peasant blouse, and sandals. There was no lollygagging, no free spirits, on Dick's campus; the cadets marched or ran everywhere they went, and with a sense of purpose. When you walked into my coed dorm, the smell of incense and marijuana and blaring rock music filled the air. Dick's barracks smelled of disinfectant and shoe polish, and all you could hear were cadence chants and underclassmen suffering a barrage of screaming insults.

What a contrast, and yet it worked. It was like we had the best of both worlds. I loved experiencing Dick's world at West Point: the football weekends, watching him march in parades, attending formal dances with him. I admired and respected him and his fellow cadets for what they stood for, what they endured, and what they would become. Plus, he was so cute in his uniform! Dick was always amazed at the laid-back, unstructured atmosphere when he came to visit me at UVM. He escorted me to an occasional sorority function and enjoyed experiencing normal college life. With his high-and-tight haircut, he was quite an enigma to my UVM friends.

That Christmas of 1971, "Your Song," by Elton John, became *our* song, and we listened to it constantly. I made a few more visits to West Point that winter for formal dances, including the Ring Hop, where he got his class ring. Then suddenly it was spring and June Week, a week of cadet activities and festivities leading up to the Graduation Ball and commencement ceremony. Dick's parents, grandparents, siblings, and I were all thrilled as we watched him get sworn in as a second lieutenant and receive his diploma. And then, in the time-honored tradition, Dick and his fellow cadets of the class of 1972 threw their hats into the air.

Dick had about a month off that summer before he had to report to Fort Eustis, Virginia, for the Transportation Basic Course, and we spent as much time as we could together. In January 1973, after six months at Fort Eustis, Dick left for his first duty assignment: the 25th Infantry Division, Schofield Barracks, Hawaii. As exciting as that was for him, we both knew his being so far away would affect our relationship. I wouldn't be able to just hop on a plane and visit him for the weekend. We would have to work even harder if we were going to keep our relationship going. We talked about my going to Hawaii that summer and began plotting. I was glad for my busy college life, which helped pass the time until I could visit him.

A few days after my last exam of the school year, I boarded a plane for Honolulu to spend a month with Dick, embarking on the biggest adventure of my life to date. I left Vermont a little apprehensive, not about the trip itself but because both sets of parents weren't exactly excited. Mine thought I was "following" Dick halfway around the world and that my doing so meant he would never commit to me. I didn't see it like that; I knew he loved me and that if our relationship was going to progress, we needed to spend time together. His parents, as devout Catholics, questioned the whole living-arrangements thing. But there wasn't much anyone could do—Dick was twenty-three years old and a lieutenant in the Army, I was almost twenty-one, we were adults, and we were in love. It was the first time in my life that I went against my parents' wishes, and that bothered me. *But* sometimes a girl has to follow her heart.

★ ★ ★

Hawaii was a place I had only read about or seen on TV or in movies. From the moment I stepped off the plane and got my first whiff of trop-ical air—a combination of ocean, flowers, and Hawaiian Tropic suntan oil, a smell so unique to the state—I fell in love with the islands. I could barely contain my excitement when I saw Dick waiting for me. We had a ball, doing all the things that you could do in such a paradise. Dick and two West Point buddies lived in a beach house on the North Shore. Someone was always in the field, so we were never all there at the same time. Dick and I shared his cramped little bedroom with palmetto bugs and geckos climbing up the walls. I got to meet many of Dick's bachelor buddies, and he showed me around Schofield Barracks and where he worked. The Army post felt like a foreign country to me. In our free time, I lay on the beach while Dick surfed, and I went to his basketball and baseball games. And then, before we knew it, it was time for me to return to Vermont, to the summer job that was waiting for me back in Burlington.

We talked about when we would see each other again. "I can

probably take leave during Christmas, so I'll come home to Vermont," Dick said. "That's only six months from now. That's not too bad."

"It's an eternity to me. I wish I could stay all summer."

"Maybe I can get you a job here next summer and you could spend the whole time here."

"Oh, Dick, do you think so? That would be perfect!"

At that, my spirits lifted and I knew that I could get through six months until Christmas. I boarded the plane with tears running down my face. Now that I had had a taste of paradise, everything from then on would pale in comparison.

★ ★ ★

Another school year for me meant months away from Dick. We talked on the phone, wrote letters, and planned my next visit. I missed him terribly, but while I was at school, it was easy to stay busy and time passed quickly. Kappa Alpha Theta sorority house provided me with a very active social life. Because I was younger than Dick and just beginning college, we both wanted me to experience college life to the fullest. Why should I sit home and miss out just because my boyfriend happened to be in Hawaii? I had plenty of friends, including guys who were just friends but could escort me to a fraternity party or sorority function. I did some casual dating (no benefits) with really nice and fun guys, but I never let it get serious; I always let them know up front that I had a boyfriend in Hawaii, and some were willing to put up with that.

By the same token, I never expected Dick to sit home by himself. I was realistic; he was a bachelor lieutenant stationed in paradise, not a priest! We were in love but not in a possessive way. I was never foolish enough to think that Dick was dating with no benefits, but I was so confident that he would never find anyone better for him than I was, I honestly didn't worry about the other girls. Plus, we still had two years to go before we could think about marriage.

True to his word, Dick got me a job in Hawaii the following summer, at his favorite restaurant, the Haleiwa Sands, on the North Shore. The Japanese family who owned the restaurant were wonderful and treated me like one of their own. That summer, I not only got to experience a little slice of Hawaiian culture but also got more insight into Army life. Dick and I had almost three months together, the most time we had ever spent one-on-one, and during that time we began to talk about our shared future. We had been dating for five years at that point. We had had our ups and downs (a couple of breakups, which hadn't lasted long), we had survived separations and a long-distance relationship, and we had each dated other people, enough to know that neither one of us wanted anyone else, so it was pretty obvious that we were meant for each other.

While we hadn't talked about specifics, I was getting close to my departure back to Vermont. One afternoon, while driving us from the North Shore down to Honolulu, Dick said, "So, Vick, I was thinking, since you're graduating next May, maybe it's time to think seriously about getting engaged."

Despite all the years we had spent together and my preexisting knowledge of where we were headed, I found myself absolutely thrilled when he brought up the subject and said those words on his own.

"Well, I think it's time," I replied. "I'm ready if you are. Besides, I think our parents have about had it with us and our living arrangements!"

We said nothing more right then, but in the coming days I could sense that something was up. The week before I left to go back to school, on a Monday night after bowling league, Dick, still wearing his bowling shoes and purple Hawaiian-print bowling shirt with his name embroidered on the pocket, proposed. He had been carrying the little black ring box in his pocket all night. We were shaking and laughing, and I cried as I said, "Of course I'll marry you!" We called our parents, who were thrilled for all the obvious reasons.

I headed back to UVM for my last two semesters with a ring on my finger. On the long plane ride home, I kept staring at and twisting the ring on my finger, and all I could think was, *I'm going to marry Dick Cody!*

PS: To some, our six-year courtship seemed ordinary and typical of any young couple. But to us, it was anything but. It was exciting and romantic. But as much as I adored Dick and loved being with him, I realized I could survive being away from him for long periods of time.

I loved him, but I didn't *need* him in order to be happy. I didn't know at the time that I already possessed one of the most important qualities in an Army wife—a trait that would serve me well in the coming years.

2

Wedding-Bell Blues . . .
and a Thing Called Deployment

During the second semester of my senior year in college, while I and many of my sorority sisters were making our wedding plans, the war in Vietnam was coming to an end. The last of the US troops were leaving, and the prisoners of war had been released, some of whom had been in captivity for seven years. The North Vietnamese made their way south to Saigon, and by April, the country was ready to implode. I was busy with thoughts of final exams, wedding plans, and some "issues" Dick and I were having about my not being Catholic. His parents wanted me to convert before the wedding; I wanted to make sure that was what Dick wanted. In early April, I flew to Hawaii so we could resolve the issue in person. We had been burning up the phone lines between Hawaii and Vermont, but we weren't getting anywhere.

I was a bundle of nerves when I saw him waiting for me at the gate at Honolulu International Airport. It had been eight months since we had seen each other, but one look at Dick and I felt our problems melting away. We started talking immediately as we left the airport. I had only four days to spend there, so we got right to it. Once Dick told me how important it was to *him* that I convert, I didn't have a problem with it.

Over the next few days, we discussed a lot of other issues, too. The summers I had spent with him had been more like vacations in paradise, and there were subjects that we had not really addressed, so my visit was good and much needed. We decided to postpone the wedding until later in the summer; in the meantime, I would become a Catholic.

Even though we were back on track, I couldn't help but notice how tired Dick looked. While I was there those few days, he worked really long hours and at times had a distracted look in his eyes. When I asked him about his packed duffel bags by the door, he mumbled something about "going to the field."

As I left to go back to Vermont and finish out my last semester, I didn't realize I was about to get my first lesson in Army life—about something called deployment. About two weeks after I returned to school, Dick called me at my sorority house and in a very serious voice said, "Vicki, cancel the wedding."

"What?" I asked shrilly.

"I'm deploying, and I can't tell you where or for how long. I don't really know the details myself."

I didn't even really understand the term *deployment*, but I sensed it was more significant than *going to the field*. The war in Vietnam was ending, so I couldn't figure out where the Army was sending Dick. I had a million questions, but he cut me off before I could ask any of them. He told me to trust him and that he would be in touch as soon as he could. Then he said something that would become his mantra throughout our marriage and his career: "Vicki, watch the news."

I was stunned and wasn't sure what to do. He had said he would call his parents, so I called mine. They were shocked and, I believe, on some level thought this was Dick's way of backing out of the wedding. None of us had any experience with the military or Army life. But, as confused as I was, I had to trust Dick.

Two days later, all hell broke loose in Vietnam. It was April 25, 1975, and as the United States was pulling the last of the troops and Americans out of the country, the North Vietnamese took control of Saigon. The city was in total chaos, and the images on the news were frightening: US soldiers trying to evacuate the American embassy, people trying to flee, helicopters lifting people off the roof. I began to think that maybe Dick's deployment had something to do with what was going on in Saigon and what I was seeing on TV, but I had no one to ask. I was scared, but it was also the first time I felt that little adrenaline rush mixed in with the fear. It was exciting, it was history in the making, and Dick was part of it.

As the events in Vietnam unfolded on the evening news, there was talk of refugees and orphans being evacuated to the island of Guam. The US Army was setting up camps to house the thousands of refugees who began arriving immediately after the takeover of Saigon. And then I got my first call from Dick, at my sorority house, no less! One of my sisters yelled up the stairs, "Vicki, you've got a call from an overseas operator!" I about wet my pants running down the stairs to grab the phone. I had no idea what to expect. An operator at the naval air station in Groton, Connecticut, was on the line and told me to hold for Second Lieutenant Cody.

"Hi, Vicki. I'm fine. I'm on the island of Guam, helping with the refugee effort. Over."

I giggled every time he said "over." It took a few minutes to get used to it. He explained that we were talking on a MARS radio and that the operator was on the line, too—hence the "over and out" thing.

That first conversation was short, but he sounded so good; he sounded like himself. He promised to write and then said, "I love you, and we'll get married when I return." That was all I needed to hear.

The days flew by, I finished my exams and graduated, and then I moved back home to my parents'. As time wore on and I attended friends' weddings that summer, I couldn't help feeling a little angry and frustrated at the Army for messing up *my* wedding plans. I was proud of Dick, and I understood the importance of the mission, but I missed him.

I watched the news and waited for letters and the occasional phone call from him. When it was obvious that he was not returning anytime soon, I got a job at the local Grand Union supermarket. I had a student loan to pay off and had not applied for teaching jobs in Burlington because I was supposed to be married and living in Hawaii by then. Every time someone said to me, "I thought you got married this summer!" I wanted to scream.

While I was checking groceries, Dick was making a name for himself on the island of Guam and within the military in one of the largest humanitarian efforts at that time in US history. The joint team of the Army, Navy, Air Force, and Marines had the huge task of setting up refugee camps for all the people fleeing Vietnam.

From April to September 1975, Operation New Life, along with Operation Babylift, would bring more than 110,000 refugees to the island of Guam to be processed. Approximately 93,000 of those refugees would receive asylum in the United States. At its peak, Camp Orote, Guam, housed 39,000 people on a daily basis.

Dick earned the nickname Mr. Transportation in those early days of
Operation New Life. As the transportation officer, he coordinated the
offloading of the planes and boats filled with refugees and the ground
transportation to get the refugees from the port or Anderson Air Force
Base to the makeshift camp at Orote Point. He also handled the incom-
ing soldiers (approximately ten thousand) and equipment flooding
onto the island from Hawaii and the US mainland.

In his letters and phone calls, he could barely contain his excitement. The deployment was the highlight of his young career. "Hey,
Vick, things are going great here in Guam. I have a huge responsibility,
and it's so exciting. Over."

"Wow, I'm really glad you're enjoying it. Over." (Dick Cody could
be neck deep in shit, in one-hundred-degree heat, flies swarming him,
and still claim to be having a good time. I really admired the guy for
that.)

★ ★ ★

The deployment had given Dick a convenient excuse to postpone
things, but it was time for me to take a stand. Around mid-July, Dick
called and I gave him an ultimatum, all of which, I'm embarrassed to
say, the Navy operator heard.

"Hi, Vick, how's everything going? Over."

"I'm getting just a little sick of sitting around here, working at the
Grand Union, with no real prospects, waiting for you to finish your gig
in Guam and tell me you want to get married. Over."

"Gee, Vick, I don't know what to say. Over."

"Let me put it this way: you have until the end of the summer to
marry me; otherwise, I'm movin' on. I've had some other offers. Over."
(I did have two former boyfriends who had been hanging around,
hoping that Dick and I wouldn't get married, so it wasn't a lie, but I
would never have seriously considered anyone else—I just needed to
make a point with Mr. Transportation.)

"Okay, let's pick a date. I think I'll be back in Hawaii by mid-August.
Over."

Checking my calendar, which was amazingly open, I suggested
August 30.

"That sounds good to me. I'll take leave and come home to Vermont. It's a date! Let's call our parents and get the ball rolling. Over."

Years later, Dick told me that after I hung up, the Navy operator said, "Lieutenant, you better marry that girl!"

Now, with the date set, my mom and I had six weeks to plan the wedding. Back then, we didn't have wedding planners and people in my world didn't spend tens of thousands of dollars on a reception. I had always been good at party planning, so, after I called each of my bridesmaids, everything else fell into place. But the most important thing was, we were getting married and beginning our life together as an Army couple.

Our wedding was simple and beautiful, everything I wanted it to be. As my dad walked me down the aisle and I saw Dick waiting for me, so handsome in his tuxedo, I did not think about the reality of being an Army wife. All I cared about that day, in St. Mark's Church, was that I was marrying the man of my dreams. I knew that he loved me as much as I loved him, and I was excited for whatever lay ahead and ready for where our journey might take us. After a small reception, my sorority sisters and I locked arms and ended the festivities with our traditional Kappa Alpha Theta song. I was leaving my sorority sisters and entering the sisterhood of Army wives.

PS: In the coming months, I began to realize that the man I had married didn't just *wear* a uniform and *work* in the Army. His uniform defined him, and his job was his life. He had taken an oath to defend our country, and he meant every word of that oath. When you marry a soldier, you pretty much marry the Army and everything it stands for.

3

Educating Vicki, Brand-New Army Wife

Okay, so maybe Army life wasn't all fun and games in the beginning. The first year of marriage can be tricky for any couple. And as a brand-new Army wife, I was not only adjusting to marriage but had entered into a whole new way of life, with its own language, rules, expectations, and responsibilities. Add to that the fact that I was thousands of miles from home, with no family or friends nearby, and I had to navigate pretty much on my own. But at least I had Dick, my best and *only* friend, by my side.

In many ways, being so far from home that first year cemented our foundation. When we argued or got on each other's nerves, we had no one else to turn to. There was no running home from Hawaii to Mom and Dad. We faced adjustments and an occasional struggle, but never once did either of us think that we had made a mistake. From the beginning, we felt as if we complemented and brought out the best in each other.

I'm not sure what I expected married life to be. I was just one generation removed from the Betty Crocker image of a typical housewife, the woman who greets her husband when he comes in the door at 5:00 p.m., still wearing her apron, pots on the stove, delicious smells emanating from the kitchen. That's what Dick and I had each grown up with: a stay-at-home mom and a dad who was home every night for dinner. But I was naive to think that Army life would play out that way.

"I don't understand why you work such long hours," I complained to Dick.

"Vicki, it's not like I can help it. If there's work to be done, I can't just leave it."

"But I make dinner, and then I wait and wait and try to keep it warm for you. Plus, I'm bored and lonely. I live for you coming home each day."

"I know it must be hard right now. This is a big adjustment for you."

That was an understatement. I didn't want to resent Dick, but initially, that was exactly what happened. I didn't like that side of me—it was unlike me. I also didn't want to be the nagging wife. I wanted to be Betty Crocker!

I had so much to learn, and Dick was a willing teacher when it came to Army things. The problem was that we approached things differently. I was a hands-on learner, preferring to learn as I went, whereas Dick liked to jump right in and learn everything up front. He thought he could teach me everything the first week of our marriage, throwing facts and acronyms, of which there seemed to be thousands, at me. It was like a whole other language and so confusing.

"Vick, remember I told you that I'm the MCO in the DTO of the 25th ID. My job also encompasses the monthly OTJs to the Big Island" (movement control officer, division transportation office, 25th Infantry Division, opportune journey).

"All I know is, you work long hours, go to the Big Island for one week every month, and have to stay in the barracks at least one night a month."

"Well, because I'm the lowest-ranking officer on staff, I pull SDO a lot" (staff duty officer).

"Wow, that really explains things! Tell me, what's the acronym for 'brand-new Army wife with no friends, no job, and homesick as hell'?"

"You're funny, Vick."

"I'm a laugh a minute, Dick!"

As I understood more about Dick's job and the Army in general, I came to the realization that I was going to have to be comfortable with myself and being on my own. That was a fact of life in the Army. I couldn't blame Dick for the long hours and separations; that was just the nature of the Army. I decided it was easier to be angry with the Army than with Dick; I didn't want to jeopardize what he and I had, so I would just have to figure out how to get through it. I knew I could do it. I also knew then that we were probably not going to have a typical marriage like my friends back home. Still, I never once doubted our love for each other.

I began substitute-teaching in the elementary schools in central Oahu and on post at Schofield Barracks. I also got a job teaching high school English to soldiers working on their high school equivalency diplomas. I enjoyed the part-time teaching jobs—each so different, yet each providing learning experiences for me. It gave me something to do with my free time, and I began to feel like my old self again.

One thing I still had no clue about was the importance of being in the proper uniform, including the PT (physical training) uniform. Back then, the PT uniform was not standardized; soldiers wore shorts with their division logo (the 25th Infantry Division was the Tropic Lightning Division), their unit T-shirt, and white socks. I got behind on the laundry and innocently sent Dick off one morning with different socks packed in his gym bag. Because I didn't understand the uniform thing, I figured it was okay for him to wear socks with little red stripes at the top. Personally, I thought they looked cute with his red shorts. Big mistake!

When he came home later, he told me what had happened at PT. "My battalion commander singled me out in front of the whole formation and said I was out of uniform. He said, 'Can't your little wifey do the laundry?' I was so embarrassed."

"What a sexist and demeaning thing for him to say!" I said to Dick. "I'd like to give him a piece of my mind! I'm trying my best to learn the whole Army thing, and who cares about the socks, anyway?"

Eventually, I did learn to care about the socks and all the parts of Dick's uniforms. I learned that it was all about standards, about every soldier doing exactly what he was supposed to do and never, under any circumstances, being out of uniform. I bought Dick more socks—more of everything—and tried to be organized about the uniforms and all the other Army things that he needed, but I had to hold my tongue the next time I saw that lieutenant colonel.

We lived in a high-rise building just across the street from the main gate at Schofield Barracks. It was convenient for Dick but not the most picturesque location, let alone a condo on the beach. Our apartment was a roach-infested, one-bedroom unit with walls so thin we could hear the couple next door screaming and fighting night after night. Still, we fixed it up as best we could with our few belongings and some Army-issue quartermaster furniture. There was no point in buying a lot of furniture, since we would be moving within a year. I loved cooking and entertaining and reciprocated both for the couples who had been so good to Dick when he was a bachelor and for any of his bachelor buddies. At least once a week, we had some guys for dinner.

I went to the monthly coffee group for the wives of Dick's coworkers. Because Dick was the youngest on staff, everyone was quite a bit older, and I didn't have what I would have considered a day-to-day best friend. I longed for one—someone I could feel comfortable with and could talk to and confide in. I had just come from four years of college, living with sorority sisters, surrounded by more friends than I could count, but those first weeks in Hawaii, I couldn't *buy* a friend. At first I didn't know where I fit in, but some wonderful senior wives took me under their wing and, without even realizing it, became my first teachers. I was especially grateful to the lieutenant colonel's wife who took me to my first Officers' Wives Club (OWC) luncheon.

In the mid-1970s, the Army was suffering the effects of the decade-long war in Vietnam. There were budget cuts and a large reduction in forces (RIF), many of the NCOs and officers were worn out from multiple combat tours, and many soldiers didn't want to be in the Army but had been drafted. People were doing drugs and drinking, some were probably suffering from post-traumatic stress disorder (although we didn't use that term back then) as well as discipline problems, and there were even riots in the barracks. Many of the issues and social unrest that our society was experiencing had crept into the ranks of the Army. As much as Hawaii was a great place to be stationed, it was also wild and crazy back then. Happy hour at the Officers' Club featured topless dancers and excessive drinking. I was surprised to find a college campus mentality in the Army. Forgive me for not wanting to share my husband with the betasseled dancers and his beer-drinking, rugby-playing buddies, but, having just finished four years of college and lots of partying of my own, I wanted only to settle into married life. Dick was ready for that, too, so we started doing more on our own or with other married couples.

When Dick was around on the weekends, we went for long drives, exploring the island. I was always trying to get him to go to the beach, but his short attention span and lack of desire to sunbathe (he had to be doing something like surfing) made it a struggle. He liked the drive out to Waianae with the top off the Corvette, along with a stop for lunch at Pioneer Chicken. I figured that if he could tolerate excursions to the beach with me, then I could certainly endure the frequent trips to Hickam Field to check on the C-5A and C-141 cargo planes that were so much a part of his job. And if I gave him lectures on beach etiquette, then I deserved his tutorials on each type of plane and its load capacity.

A typical duty assignment back then was about two to three years. Since Dick had already been in Hawaii for three years when we got married, we knew that he would be getting new orders for a PCS (permanent change of station) move for the following summer.

One day that winter, Dick came home from work all excited and announced, "I got accepted to flight school!"

"Wait a minute—run that by me again. Flight school?"

"I've wanted to fly helicopters since I was a kid."

I prided myself on knowing just about everything there was to know about Dick Cody, but here was something I hadn't heard.

"Remember, I told you I applied before I graduated from West Point but got turned down because of my knee surgeries? I reapplied before I left for Guam. I can't believe I got accepted. It's a dream come true!"

Okay, maybe he *had* told me, but it had clearly gotten lost in the whole canceled-wedding-and-deployment shuffle.

"What type of helicopters, where exactly is flight school, how long is the course, and when do we move?"

"The Army's flight school is at Fort Rucker, Alabama, and my class begins June first. We'll leave here at the end of April so I can take my thirty days of leave."

I had my maps out before he could finish his sentence. I was a map reader from way back, having inherited this unusual attribute from my dad. (Some people keep magazines in the bathroom or by their favorite chair; my family kept US road maps.) I was poring over the map while he was talking to me, trying to explain stuff I wasn't yet ready for. "Please, Dick, first things first." It took me a few minutes to find Fort Rucker on my map. It was way down in lower Alabama, near the Florida border.

A helicopter pilot—I hadn't considered that one. I had finally started feeling as if I belonged in Hawaii, and now it was time to pack up and move on. However, that year I had begun to see why Dick loved being in the Army. It wasn't just a job; he was serving his country, he was working with soldiers every day, and he felt satisfied whatever his job was, never mind the long hours and low pay. Dick's passion was infectious, so I couldn't help but say, "I'm so excited for you!"

There were lots of farewell parties for Dick as we prepared to leave. At each one, I learned even more about what Dick Cody the soldier had done during his four years in the 25th Infantry Division, and I was in awe of and so very proud of him. We were both so excited for the next chapter in our Army life and all that was ahead of us.

PS: Before we were married, I was sure that Dick would do his time in the Army and then go back to Montpelier, Vermont, and help run his family businesses. I think his family thought the same. But after our first year of marriage, I knew differently. Dick was a soldier at heart.

4

Sweet Home Alabama

We picked up our car in Oakland, California, and began our long journey across the United States. We drove through the deserts of California and Nevada, deep into the canyons of Utah, and over the Colorado Rockies, before finally stopping in Denver.

While having the car serviced at a Chevy dealership, we found out that there was a ski area still open, a place called Arapaho Basin (A-Basin). We drove back up into the Rockies and found Keystone Lodge. For the next three days, we skied the trails and bowls at A-Basin, above the tree line, at an altitude of twelve thousand feet, with the sun shining and the bluest sky we had ever seen. A-Basin is like a spring-break party on the slopes, featuring blaring rock music and tailgates, complete with beach chairs and grills in the parking lot. That stop we made purely by chance on this trip would become one of our favorite family destinations for decades.

Back in the car and eastbound, we relived every detail of our ski adventure. I learned some things about Dick Cody on that long drive. He is a driving machine and likes to set land-speed records on every leg of a trip. I also learned that Dick is a good listener who will allow me to talk incessantly for hours on end. I liked that. In the confines of our small Corvette, we entertained each other and shared stories about funny, silly things we'd done and scary situations that we had found ourselves in. Even after all these years, just a word or two from one of us—"Reno," "Bryce Canyon," "Indianapolis"—can trigger a memory that causes us to burst into laughter, a memory that only the two of us share.

Our families in Vermont welcomed us with open arms, but, after traveling and living out of suitcases for a month, we were ready to begin the last leg of our journey, down the East Coast, across Georgia, and into Alabama. I was getting sick of the interior of the Corvette and couldn't wait to reach our destination. By the time we crossed the Georgia-Alabama border, I had pretty much memorized everything on my map and the anticipation was building.

Finally, we saw the sign for Fort Rucker, the home of Army Aviation. What struck me the most, as we drove onto the post that first time, were all the helicopters flying overhead. They were everywhere, like buzzing insects. We passed by one of the stage fields and could see student pilots doing maneuvers—takeoffs and landings, and auto-rotations (engine-off landings). Dick could barely keep his eyes on the road. We were both craning our necks, mouths open, trying to see out the windows. Like Dick, I, too, had a fascination with flying. I had taken my first plane ride in 1957, at age five, and I'd loved every minute of it, but I had never dreamed that one day I would be married to a pilot. The course of our lives and the path of Dick's career would change forever on June 1, 1976, the day he signed on for the rotary-wing officers' basic course at Fort Rucker.

After he did that, Dick got us on the waiting list for housing on post with most of the other student pilots and their wives. While we waited for our house to become available, we rented a furnished, one-bedroom efficiency apartment with an air conditioner protruding from the bedroom window.

Later that day, in a very brief and spottily attended ceremony, Dick and two of his West Point classmates were promoted to the rank of captain. I pinned on his captain's bars to commemorate his moving up another rung on chain of command.

That night, we went out to dinner to celebrate. As we pulled into the 1950s-looking Officers' Club, I couldn't help but think about what a stark contrast it was with what we had just left. I looked at Dick and said, "This sure is different from the Hilton Hawaiian Village."

"It was either this, the Daleville Inn, or the Tastee Freeze down Highway 231. Welcome to rural Alabama, Vick!"

★ ★ ★

While Dick began his classes, I set up our temporary apartment. He would literally burst through the door every afternoon with tales of everything that had happened in class that day. He had boxes of books and flight gadgets, and we pored over all of it. He was the most excited I had ever seen him. He couldn't wait to get out of the classroom and into the cockpit. It was such an exciting time, we felt like kids filled with anticipation—and for some reason, all our talk of school, books, and flying often led us into our tiny bedroom, where we experienced the best sex ever every afternoon, in the sweaty heat of southern Alabama. We'd turn the air conditioner on high to drown out our sounds. *Mm-mm-mm*—it was the best of times.

Because of his date of rank, Dick was the class leader, which meant he organized the class, held the formations, and was the conduit for information. (Every unit in the Army has a chain of command with a leader, even in a school setting.) Each class was designated a hat color that denoted their graduation date. Dick's class was Navy Blue Flight 03/77. Approximately eight to ten classes went through Fort Rucker each year; about every six weeks, a new class was beginning and another was graduating, so there was a continual flow of students in and out. The hat colors were necessary to distinguish the classes from one another.

When Dick and I went to the meeting for class leaders, we met Randy and Eleanor Young. Randy was second in date of rank after Dick and assisted Dick with class duties. Eleanor and I began talking that night and didn't stop for the next nine months. We talked about feeling unsure of what was ahead for our husbands and what was expected of us. We made plans to drive down to Panama City Beach the following weekend, and just like that, I had a new best friend, the very thing I had missed in Hawaii.

Our very first function as new student-pilot wives was a reception hosted by the commanding general's wife at their quarters. The reception and the other events that were planned for us that year were all part of the education process for new Army wives, to teach us proper etiquette and protocol. We were told to wear a dress or skirt and short white gloves for the receiving line. I thought, *Wow, I didn't know women still wore white gloves for daytime functions!* But Eleanor and I went into Enterprise, on our first shopping mission, in search of them. Enterprise, a neat little town with a statue of a boll weevil right in its center, consisted of a five-and-dime store, a hardware store, and a ladies' dress shop. It was like going back in time, but we found our little white gloves in the dress shop and were ready for our first ladies' function.

Dick and I moved into our house on post at the end of the summer, and I busied myself decorating our quarters—which were huge compared with our one-bedroom apartment in Hawaii—while Dick and his classmates were totally immersed in their studies and began to fly. Each class was made up of a cross-section of officers from all branches of the Army. The first female Army aviator had graduated from Fort Rucker earlier that year, and Dick's class had one female student. Her name was Vicki, too, and she was Dick's "stick buddy." (Stick buddies are two students assigned to each instructor pilot [IP]. "Stick" refers to the cyclic, the helicopter's control arm, which sits between the pilot's legs.) Dick's class had international students from Germany, Israel, Morocco, and Denmark. The foreign students were young, about nineteen to twenty years old on average, and for most of them it was their first time away from home. We invited them to our house frequently, and became especially close to Moha Oulidad from Morocco and Elan Frank from Israel.

After everyone in the class had soloed, we wives were allowed to go out to the airfield and watch our husbands fly. I watched Dick come in for a landing, and after he shut down the aircraft, he got out and helped me climb in. As I sat next to him in the tiny Plexiglas bubble of a cockpit, I looked at all the switches, knobs, and controls and couldn't believe he had learned to fly a helicopter in the short amount of time that we had been at Fort Rucker.

Once the first phase of flight school was done, Dick was definitely on his way. While he was a natural at flying and did really well academically, we never took that for granted. Each phase was different and progressively more difficult. Every flight was graded, so there was always the potential for a screw-up. A busted check ride would result in a dreaded pink slip; too many pink slips, and you were out of flight school. But Dick had more than pink slips to be concerned with, as I was awaiting the results of a pregnancy test.

The day I found out I was pregnant, Dick came home from class and told me that his assignment after graduation would be a short tour in Korea. I was in my usual position—hanging over the toilet, gagging—when he made his big announcement.

I looked up at him and said, "But I'm pregnant!" It wasn't how I'd envisioned revealing the news.

"Wow, Vicki, that's great!"

"It is, but would you please explain what a 'short tour' is?"

"It's a one-year, unaccompanied tour in Korea, meaning I'm not sponsored to bring dependents."

A quick calculation told me that my due date was approximately the same as his departure date. What should have been a joyous occasion was turning into a significant emotional event for me. That night over dinner, we discussed every possible scenario. I had to work extra hard to keep the whine out of my voice. "What if I come to Korea when the baby is a few months old and you've had time to settle in?"

"Maybe; we could think about that. But, Vicki, here's the reality: I will most likely live in the barracks at Camp Casey, up near the demilitarized zone (DMZ), so you would have to live in Seoul by yourself with a new baby. The Army will not pay for anything for you and the baby because you are not command-sponsored. I just think it's too risky."

It was so weird to be talking about a baby that we had just barely found out we were having.

"But what will I do? Where will I go? I can't stay here after graduation."

"I honestly think the best thing would be for you to go home to Vermont. Look, I know this isn't what we planned, but I will have to do a short tour sometime in the very near future. Don't you think it would be better to get it over with now, while the baby is too young to remember?"

For the next twenty-four hours, we discussed all the pros and cons and realized there were far too many reasons why I shouldn't go to Korea. I needed to wrap my head around the whole idea quickly, before I called my parents. I knew that my attitude would shape their reaction. Using what I thought was an unemotional voice, I called and told them the news. "Guess what? We're having a baby!"

"Oh, that's wonderful! Congratulations!"

Then I totally blew it when I started crying and blurted out the part about the short tour to Korea.

"What do you mean, Dick is going to Korea?" They were so shocked, they just kept asking why he had to go. "And where will you live?"

"Um . . . I was wondering if I could come home and live with you for the year."

"Well, of course you can. We would love to have you and the baby!"

Just like that, I felt better. I knew that I could get through the year with the love and support of my family and Dick's.

★ ★ ★

Excitement and nervousness over being pregnant (and the nausea) took over all my waking thoughts those first few months. I read books on natural childbirth and the Lamaze method, which was so popular in the '70s. We would have to teach ourselves, since the small hospital at Fort Rucker didn't offer the classes.

As had happened before, once I got busy with substitute teaching and the many planned social events for the wives, I didn't dwell on Dick's short tour quite as much. I still didn't like the idea, and it was always in the back of my mind (and always the subject of our planning discussions), but I was able to accept it. Once I did that, I could live in the moment and enjoy life.

After Christmas in Vermont with our families, Dick began the most difficult and final phases of flight school: tactics, instruments, and night flying. He continued to do well but had to spend a little more time studying. When he had to memorize his emergency procedures (there were at least fifty of them, written on little index cards), I was his quizzer. I would sit cross-legged on the bathroom floor, resting the index cards on my growing belly, while he soaked in the tub, nursing his latest basketball injury or sore muscles. I learned the emergency procedures right along with him, until I probably could have passed the exam, too. It was in those sweet little moments with Dick that I realized, *How wonderful my life is. I'm married to my best friend, and our love for each other is far more significant than any short tour.*

As my stomach grew, so did our excitement about the living being inside me that would enter the world and be our child. We were convinced it was a boy (no ultrasound, just my intuition), and we chose the name Clinton Richard—a combination of both of our fathers' middle names and Dick's name. Also, we were big Clint Eastwood fans.

Our upcoming move posed some challenges for us. I would be almost nine months pregnant, so, after much discussion, we decided that I would fly to Vermont and Dick would drive the Corvette there. His parents were coming for graduation, on their way back from Florida, and they would follow Dick and make the three-day drive to Vermont together.

Suddenly, it was time. Dick gave the speech at the formal ball the night before graduation, and each of the wives received our own diploma and a pair of miniature flight wings for having supported our husbands during flight school. As we left the Officers' Club, each student pilot stopped at the big wooden board in the lobby, where nine months before, on the first day of class, each had put up a pair of wings. If they made it through the training, the night before graduation, they retrieved their wings to be pinned on at graduation.

I sat with Dick's parents at the graduation ceremony, and the three of us couldn't have been prouder as we watched Dick receive his diploma. Then, in what would become a family tradition, I pinned his wings on him.

We took a lot of pictures that morning with all of our friends. As a class, we had become very close, not just the student pilots but the wives, too. It had been an intense nine months as we'd shared in one another's successes and failures. It was hard to imagine all of us going our separate ways, knowing that some of us might not see each other again, but we exchanged addresses and vowed to stay in touch.

PS: We wives learned a lot that year. We learned about flying while our husbands went through their training; we learned etiquette and Army protocol. But what Fort Rucker did not teach the wives of Navy Blue Flight 03/77 were the dangers of being an Army helicopter pilot. They didn't talk to us about the sleepless nights we would spend while our husbands were out flying with night-vision goggles, or the risks of flying in the mountains of Korea during a snowstorm or flying combat missions in the deserts of the Middle East. They didn't talk to us about mechanical failure. They didn't warn us that in an instant, we could lose a loved one or a close friend. Maybe it was just as well—maybe we didn't want or need to know any of that at that point. We were young, carefree, and on top of the world. We would learn those lessons on our own.

5

We're Having a Baby . . .
and a Short Tour, Too!

The flight from Dothan, Alabama, to Burlington was long and grueling, with stops in Atlanta and Boston. The last leg of the flight, in a small ten-seat plane, flying over the mountains in a blizzard, had me gripping my armrest for all it was worth. I was so glad to be safely on the ground.

Dick arrived two days later from his road trip up the East Coast, and we got settled into my parents' house. Dick, never one to sit around and wait for anything, decided to work at his dad's Chevrolet dealership in the parts room and washing cars. It was the kind of manual labor he was used to in the Army, and it kept him busy and out of my hair.

I busied myself putting away my baby shower gifts, washing and folding all our tiny newborn outfits, and setting up a nursery. I had so many conflicting emotions: joy over the upcoming birth of our first child, anxiety about what lay ahead, and dread over Dick's leaving for twelve months. Much as I tried to focus on the birth, not on Dick's departure, it was hard to do because the two were intertwined.

The clock kept ticking, but the few times I saw my obstetrician, he seemed so blasé that I could tell he didn't fully grasp our situation. I doubt that he had many patients who were Army wives whose husbands were going on a short tour to Korea. Finally, when my due date arrived and nothing had happened, the doctor agreed to induce me the following week. But then, as often happens, I went into labor on my own.

Clinton Richard was born on April 9. I was so lucky—it was just a few hours of labor and an easy delivery, he was healthy and beautiful, and the waiting was over. It was the best feeling in the world—nothing quite like it. I got out of the hospital on Monday, we christened him at St. Mark's Church on Tuesday, and Dick left two days later.

Those couple of days before he left, I was in a fog. Exhausted from childbirth and very little sleep, I felt numb. We both just wanted to get the good-bye over with. But then reality set in on the day Dick left. I was not feeling well enough to take him to the airport, so his parents and younger brother, Bobby, took him. I tried to muster a smile, but I don't think I succeeded.

★ ★ ★

The first few weeks were the hardest and yet the most joyous. Clint was fascinating, and I spent hours holding him, kissing him, and just staring at him. I couldn't get enough of him; he was my salvation. I hated that Dick was missing out on all these special moments with our son, but I was glad my mom and dad were there to share them with me.

Overseas phone calls from Korea were too expensive back then for us to talk more than once a week, and the seven-hour time difference and Dick's flight schedule sometimes made it difficult for him to find a good time to call me at all. So we got to back to letter writing, just like when we were dating. I sent lots of pictures of Baby Clint and tried to give Dick a glimpse into our lives back in Burlington. Eventually, we settled into a routine that worked for us—letters and a Sunday-evening phone call—and somehow, the weeks passed.

★ ★ ★

Spring turned into summer, and with that came a better frame of mind for me. Summer in Vermont is always a celebration after the long, cold winter and usually a very short spring. I spent most days with my sister, Chris, who lived just a block away from my mom's house. She had married Jim (Dick's cousin), and they had two little girls. Almost every afternoon that summer, Mom, Chris, and I took the kids, a cooler, and beach chairs to the lake. I put mosquito netting over the baby carriage, and Clint took his nap in the shade of a tree. About every other weekend, I packed up Clint and all the baby paraphernalia and drove to

Montpelier to visit Dick's family. It was nice to get away, and the short road trip provided a change of scenery. Three of Dick's younger siblings still lived at home, and his oldest sister, Diane, her husband, and their two sons lived across the street.

Clint and I never lacked for love and support that year. I knew I was fortunate in many ways: I was living with my parents and sleeping in the comfort of my old bedroom, my sister just a block away, Dick's parents nearby. However, as well cared-for as we were, I was often so tired I could barely hold my head up in the middle of the night, when I was up every few hours for feedings, and in those moments I felt so alone. I missed my soul mate, and no one could help me with that.

Fall is one of the most beautiful seasons in Vermont, but I still felt a little blue when it rolled around that year. My brother went back to college, and my sister started classes at UVM to finish her degree. She had a full plate, and she and Jim had a social life on the weekends. I felt like everyone had somewhere to go, someone to be with. I had no way of knowing whether there were any other Army wives in Burlington. The only thing that got me through was caring for Clint.

When Dick had left that April, he had not made any promises about coming home for midtour leave. At that time, a round-trip plane ticket cost about $900, which was a lot of money to us—more than half his monthly pay. But by September, I was hanging on by a thread.

"Dick, I really want you to come home. I don't think I can make it seven more months without seeing you."

"I know. I miss you and Clint. Let me put in for leave and see when I can come home."

The next time he called, he told me his two-week leave had been approved for mid-November. I counted down the days. Driving to the airport, I was shaking, and when I saw him walking toward me in his Army greens, I fell in love with him all over again.

We hugged, and then he looked at me and said, "You look beautiful! You're so thin!"

His words were music to my ears; the last time he had seen me, I'd been bloated, swollen, and sore from childbirth. "I've been exercising and taking Clint for long walks, so the weight came off easily," I said.

On the drive back to my parents' house, we fell right back into our rhythm and talked the whole way home.

"I can't wait for you to see Clint. He's amazing and doing all kinds of neat things. It seems like every day he gives me something new to marvel at. This is the perfect time for you to come home."

When Dick unpacked his bags, he had all kinds of treasures and gifts for me, Clint, and all of our parents. He had bought various sizes of tiny Nike sneakers for Clint to grow into. I loved watching him with our baby; Dick had just two weeks to see the wonders I had gotten to experience for the past seven months.

While having a seven-month-old and living with my parents didn't make for the most romantic setting, we managed to have some alone time. We celebrated my birthday with Chris and Jim with dinner at a nice restaurant. I had bought a new dress and wore the jewelry Dick had brought me from Korea. With my pre-pregnancy figure back and Dick's compliments, I felt like a million bucks. Dick always made me feel beautiful, but that night I felt like his girlfriend again, not just a wife and a diaper-changing mom.

Dick also talked endlessly of flying. "As soon as I got to Korea, I transitioned into the OH-58 Scout helicopter. It's a small, two-seat observation helicopter and really fun to fly. Now I'm rated in two different aircraft and I've flown over six hundred hours already." I loved listening to him and tried to envision his life in Korea, but at times I couldn't help but dwell on the fact that he inhabited a whole other world that I was not part of. I had been isolated from Army life for long enough that I felt as if my life was boring compared with his.

Finally, I told him, "*My* life revolves around bottle feedings, diaper changing, doing laundry, folding laundry, naptime, mealtime, and bedtime. Oh, I almost forgot—one evening a week, I go visit your sister Cathi for a cup of tea and girl talk." (His younger sister was single and living and working in Burlington.) "How's that for excitement?"

"My life in Korea may sound exciting to you," he retorted, "but, except for the flying and the occasional tennis or basketball game, it's lonely and the same routine day after day. I fly, eat dinner in the mess hall, go to bed, and wake up the next morning to the same thing. I have no TV and no car, and I share a bathroom with ten other guys. Sometimes I don't even know what day it is."

★ ★ ★

When Dick left to go back to Korea, it was hard to say good-bye, but we also knew that we were on the downhill side of the short tour, and I knew then that I could make it the rest of the way.

It was a typical Vermont winter: the snow piled up, the wind blew, temperatures dropped well below zero, and ice covered the sidewalks and my car. For the first time in my life, I understood the term *cabin fever*. I had never felt that growing up, because we had skied every possible day and loved the snow and the long winters. But that winter, living in such extreme conditions with a nine-month-old baby, was not fun. Flu season hit with a vengeance; I was cooped up inside for days on end and thought I would go crazy. My salvation was my mom and my sister who were always there for me.

And soon the snow was melting and the smell of spring was everywhere. One beautiful spring day, I went skiing by myself. I just wanted to get out on the slopes and feel the freedom and happiness that experience always brought me. But it just wasn't the same without Dick. Oh, how I missed him! Still, Clint's first birthday was approaching, along with Dick's return from Korea, and now that I knew that we had made it through the year and the sun was shining again, all was right with the world.

The closer we got to Dick's return date, the more we talked on the phone. We talked every couple of days, as we could barely contain our excitement. We no longer cared about the phone bill; we just wanted the connection. My hands shook as I drove to the Burlington airport that April day. It was an adrenaline rush for me because I was welcoming him home for good, not just for two weeks of leave. When we hugged after all those days, weeks, and months of waiting, I cried and laughed all at once, just as I did when we got engaged. Dick was more reserved with his emotions, especially in public and while in uniform, but I didn't care—I wanted everyone to know my captain was home.

★ ★ ★

Dick's next duty assignment was the Transportation Officer Advanced Course (TOAC) at Fort Eustis, Virginia. My parents babysat Clint while Dick and I drove down to Virginia so he could sign in and get on the housing list. To some, that may not sound romantic, but for us, three days alone in the car and in a hotel room were a little honeymoon. It didn't matter where it was—we were together again.

Dick had accrued over one thousand flight hours in Korea. It was an enormous amount of flight time for a brand-new pilot, but he had bigger plans, which he shared with me on our trip.

"Vick, I've decided to become a maintenance test pilot. I got accepted to the test-pilot course, which starts right after I finish TOAC. That means we'll be at Fort Eustis for about nine months."

"But isn't it kind of dangerous being a test pilot? Doesn't that mean you'll fly broken helicopters?"

"Well, yes, but I want to be the one fixing and flying them. And it will make me a better pilot."

I didn't really care where we were going, just that we were going there as a family.

For the past year, while I had been essentially a single parent, I had also slipped back into the role of daughter. I had become very close to my parents again, and they had become really attached to Clint, watching him grow and enjoying every milestone. I could not have gotten through that year without their love and support, yet I was ready to be on my own. It was time to go back to my other life as a wife and a mother. Our leaving Vermont was pretty emotional for all of us. It was almost like when I got married and left home for the first time.

After moving into quarters on post, we resumed our normal lives. I joined the Officers' Wives' Club, took Clint to the post nursery while I played tennis, and took him to the swimming pool every afternoon. Dick and I tried to play tennis, but it was hard with a fourteen-month-old toddler. More and more, Dick went out to play with his buddies and left me at home with Clint.

When my parents came to visit, it was my mother who noticed we were out of sync. When she commented on it, I said, "You're right, Mom. I thought because Dick and I love each other so much, I just assumed everything would fall back into place, like it always has. But this time is different. We have a baby, and I don't feel like he's connecting with us as a family of three."

No one had told me what to expect. At the time, I didn't know there was a term for what we were going through: *reintegration*. I had based my expectations on our early years, when our reunions had been pure bliss. But it was different once we had a baby. I didn't understand my conflicting emotions; I was happy to be together again but angry at Dick for not wanting to spend more time with me and Clint. When I tried to express my feelings to him, he said simply, "Jeez, Vick, I don't mean to act that way. I just like to play tennis. It's what I did in Korea; it's what I've always done."

"But we have a baby now, and I need to feel like Clint and I are priorities. I'm not asking you to spend every minute with us, but maybe give up a tennis match from time to time," I started. Then I blurted out what I was really thinking: "I want you to stop acting like a bachelor and act more like a husband and father!"

"Vicki, I'm trying, but I'm not always sure where I fit in. I feel like you're used to doing everything and that's how you want it."

I knew the year had been tough on each of us, for different reasons. Dick had just missed an important year in our marriage, as well as Clint's first year. I realized that maybe it would take some time for him to bond with his baby and feel like a parent—something that I had had a whole year to do.

Luckily, Clint was young, so it didn't take long for the bonding to happen. By the end of the summer and early fall, as we began to make memories, the three of us were back on track. We settled into a nice little routine: Dick came home every day for lunch (he even watched the soaps with me) and was home for dinner every night. Things were going so beautifully, in fact, that I was pregnant again by October. We didn't plan it, but when it happened we were excited that our kids would be just two years apart.

Clint was growing and thriving and starting to talk. Everything he said and did was fascinating to us. He was a strong-willed, independent, tantrum-throwing child, but he was the joy of our lives.

Dick finished his advanced course and, after a brief break, started the maintenance test-pilot course. He loved the course work, and especially the flying. He had found his niche. He got his follow-on orders for Hunter Army Airfield (HAAF) in Savannah, Georgia. We would move the following May. We decided it was time to buy our first house, and, after two trips to Savannah that winter, we picked out one that was being built in a new community near HAAF. We were elated at the prospect of living in Savannah, in our very own home.

We moved out of our quarters in mid-May and decided that Dick and Clint, who had just turned two, would drive a U-Haul truck with our belongings to Savannah. Since I was nine months pregnant, my doctor thought it was better for me to fly, so I would join them a day later. Just before they drove off into the sunset, I handed Dick our diaper bag and gave him last-minute instructions, reminding him that Clint was *almost* potty-trained but to stop periodically. It was hard for me to give up complete control of Clint and watch them ride off in that dirty, stinky, bouncing U-Haul.

PS: I will always be thankful for that year at Fort Eustis when Dick was in school. It gave us some much-needed time together to work through the redeployment blues and to become a family again. Over the next thirty-two years, we would experience many reunions and periods of transition and reintegration. There was never anything we couldn't handle, but those times would always test us.

6

Savannah, Georgia, 1979

I arrived in Savannah the day before Mother's Day. Dick and Clint greeted me at the airport. What caught my eye, as Clint ran to me, was the wad of chewing gum in his beautiful blond hair and his bare feet—in a public place! (Never mind the Kool-Aid stains on his shirt.) I also noticed his lack of a diaper. All of that ran through my mind those first few seconds. I had to bite my tongue, as I was still working on my control issues and trying to let Dick take part in coparenting, and save my burning questions for the ride home from the airport.

"So, Dick, how'd the potty training go?" I asked once we were in the car.

"What potty training? Whenever we stopped, I took him to the men's room and he went to the bathroom. There was nothing to it."

"How did he get gum in his hair? I don't let him chew gum; he's too young."

"Well, he chews gum now. I don't know how he got it in his hair; he must have fallen asleep with it in his mouth."

The Kool-Aid on the shirt was a no-brainer: there was no food in the house, so I'm sure they stopped at a 7-Eleven on their way to the airport for Twinkies and Slurpees (an Army aviator's idea of breakfast). I could live with that, I guess.

But after I'd spent months of trying every creative thing in the Dr. Spock book on potty training—countless hours of cajoling, begging, cheering, and clapping, and numerous accidents—Dick had come in at the last minute and finished the deed in twenty-four hours, on one road trip! I was curious how he'd done it. I envisioned the two of them driving down I-95 that night and at some point Dick saying something like, "Clint, you better not shit your pants, because I'm not cleaning up the mess." I guess there are some things in life that are meant to remain a mystery.

When we pulled into the driveway of our brand-new, beautiful house, after living in a roach-infested apartment in Hawaii and government quarters at Fort Rucker and Fort Eustis, we felt like the luckiest couple in the world.

We didn't have an overwhelming amount of household goods at that point. The boxes of kitchen items, dishes, china, and clothing were manageable, and I knew I could get everything unpacked in a day or two. We had about three weeks before my mom arrived and Dick would leave for Fort Rucker, for the Cobra transition course. And once the baby arrived on June 15, my life would be not just hectic but crazy.

I met some of the neighbors and learned the lay of the land. I was excited that there were three Army wives on our street and they all had small children, too. I especially liked my next-door neighbor Sarah, who had a little girl. We became best friends and remain friends to this day. My ob-gyn's office and the hospital were just minutes from our house, and that gave me comfort for when the big moment arrived. I had not gained much weight, so the doctor assured me I was at least a month away from delivering and that I might go past my due date. I met the wife of a friend of Dick's, who offered to babysit Clint if I went into labor before my mom arrived. Our game plan was all set.

In the evenings, we took Clint for rides in the car and explored Savannah. It was so different from any other city we had lived in. The trees that covered the boulevards with a canopy of hanging branches and moss, the squares lined with row houses, and the beautiful parks with fountains all created a setting of Southern charm that was truly unique. We already loved the city.

Amid all the activity and the excitement of settling in, I didn't pay much attention to the cramping and contractions I was experiencing on June 5, but by the time I went to bed, I knew I was in labor. As it turned out, our second baby, a son, arrived nine days early, on June 6. It all happened so fast, and, except for throwing a monkey wrench into our finely tuned game plan, Tyler James was healthy and beautiful. What a blessing, and once again, I was overcome with relief and joy.

That night, Dick and I ate our complimentary steak dinner in my hospital room. Picturing the pain of labor, still so fresh, and the image of him standing on the sidelines, eating my ice chips without a care in the world, I told him, "I think that's my quota for delivering babies."

Dick was in full agreement. "I know, Vick, that was pretty exhausting! We have two beautiful, healthy boys; that's good for me."

He was leaving early the next morning for Fort Rucker, and as we said our good-byes, I was reminded of his having left for Korea right after Clint was born. He would be gone only six weeks, which was nothing compared with the short tour, but it was still emotional for me. I put a smile on my face and sent him on his way to begin a new chapter in his aviation career: becoming a Cobra pilot. I knew how excited he was, but I missed him the minute he walked out the door.

I was so thankful that my mom was there with me. I don't know what I would have done without her those first days I was home from the hospital. She cooked delicious meals and was a big help with Clint, and it was just nice to have her companionship. Tyler, like Clint, was a good baby—he ate, he slept, and he was very easy to care for—but two kids at that age were a lot of work, no matter how you look at it. I counted the days until Dick returned and we would be a family again.

There were no reunion issues when Dick returned that time. I was learning that separations measured in weeks were a piece of cake compared with those measured in months. I had learned a lesson or two from the short tour, and when Dick returned from Fort Rucker, I immediately got him involved with the baby, giving bottles and sharing diaper duty. And when it was time for tennis, we took turns babysitting so the other one could play.

Dick signed into his new unit, the 2nd Squadron, 9th Cavalry Regiment (2/9 CAV), at Hunter Army Airfield. HAAF housed all the aviation assets for the 24th Infantry Division at Fort Stewart, about forty minutes from Savannah.

As the new service platoon leader, Dick began a new chapter and career path as a maintenance test pilot. His platoon had approximately 125 personnel and was responsible for maintaining the unit's twenty-seven helicopters. He had an interesting cast of characters in his platoon, including some endearingly crusty old NCO crew chiefs and warrant officer pilots—all Vietnam vets. They weren't much older than Dick; they just had more Army experience, specifically combat time, so they seemed older. They were like gods to Dick because they had flown missions and maintained Cobras in combat. They were tough, no-nonsense guys who had no tolerance for anyone who got in the way of their maintenance and/or flying. They pushed the limits in everything they did, from their uniforms and haircuts to their approach to maintenance tactics. Often seen wearing their CAV Stetsons, with long hair and sideburns, and a cigarette dangling from their lips, they partied as hard as they worked. Above all, they shared their love of maintenance with a brand-new captain who was right out of test-pilot school. They were the perfect teachers for Dick Cody.

At the time, Dick was the only commissioned officer to be a current test pilot in three different aircraft: the OH-1 Huey, the OH-58 Scout, and the AH-1 Cobra. That in itself earned him the respect of the veteran pilots and maintenance officers around the airfield. He was always in the hangar, turning wrenches and test-flying aircraft. There was nothing he wouldn't personally fix or fly himself. He showed no fear but at the same time was meticulous and obsessive about the rules and safety. His old nickname, Mr. Transportation, was replaced with Commander Cody—a moniker that would stay with him for the rest of his career.

We immediately felt the special camaraderie that is so unique to aviators and their spouses. We enjoyed every aspect: the social events, both planned and spur of the moment, the hail and farewells, the potlucks, happy hour at the Officers' Club, and all the traditions of a CAV squadron. My education continued as I gained a better understanding of the Army and Army aviation. I learned about the brave aviators and the extraordinary wives who waited, worried, supported, and loved them. I watched as they balanced the fun and joy with the fear and stress of being married to an aviator.

I was navigating my way through the trials and tribulations of being the mother of two preschoolers, whose husband worked long hours, usually six days a week, and was gone to the field a lot. It was exhausting, grueling, and oftentimes boring, but I loved being a mother and never took for granted the fact that I could stay home with my sons. My mission was to raise good kids. Along with my fellow Army-wife neighbors and my best friend Sarah, we managed to get through the long, sometimes monotonous days of being stay-at-home moms. With our husbands gone so much of the time, we really counted on one another. We spent our days at the playground and the pool and taking long walks through the neighborhood.

Dick became best friends with a fellow pilot named Ned Hubard, a chief warrant officer 2 (CW2), a highly decorated Cobra pilot with two tours in Vietnam. Ned and his wife, Carole, lived in our neighborhood. Dick and Ned were together every day at work and usually played tennis on the weekends. What started out as a typical friendship developed into a deep bond, born of mutual respect, that they carried with them wherever the Army sent them—a connection that would span three decades. It didn't matter whether they were serving in the same unit or in different parts of the world—Dick and Ned always kept track of each other, always knew what the other one was doing, and enjoyed each other's successes.

Savannah was the perfect place for all four of us. Clint and Tyler were growing and thriving. We enjoyed the mild climate and long, hot summers. They started preschool, which was good for them and gave me a much-needed break. I found a couple of teenage girls to babysit, and Dick and I started going out for an occasional date night. Even amid Dick's schedule—the relentless, long work weeks and frequent field exercises—we still made time for fun, romance, and our relationship.

PS: I always knew that Dick's and my relationship was every bit as important as raising kids. Too many young couples overlook their relationship while they are busy with small children. I think that Dick's comings and goings actually served as a reminder that we needed to make time for each other, and that kept the old spark alive for us.

7

Life Takes a Sharp Turn

L ife is full of surprises, but I don't think we fully understand and appreciate that until we are pushed out of our comfort zone, backed into a corner, and tested in ways we don't expect or anticipate. Two key events happened while we were in Savannah that would forever change both of us: a helicopter crash and the death of a friend, and a deployment for Dick. Each took us out of our safe little world and thrust us smack into the reality of Army life. They forced me to confront fears about death and mortality and to grow even more as a mother and as an Army wife. The events would take Dick to a higher level of proficiency as a test pilot and combat aviator, and would shape and develop the leadership style that became his trademark for the rest of his career. But it was a painful time for both of us as we learned some tough life lessons.

In November 1979, on the other side of the world, Iranian militants stormed the US embassy in Tehran and took approximately seventy Americans captive. A small number were released, a few escaped, and then there were fifty-three hostages, who remained in captivity for 444 days. The Iran hostage crisis was the biggest daily news story for a brand-new twenty-four-hour news network called CNN. It was the first time we had watched world events unfold on live TV.

In April 1980, there was a failed joint military operation to rescue the hostages, called Desert 1, that ended in disaster when a Navy Sea Stallion helicopter crashed into a C-130 transport plane in the Iranian desert, killing or injuring everyone onboard. It was a terrible tragedy, and the entire rescue mission had to be aborted. Dick and Ned could talk of nothing else and began making plans and coming up with strategies for how they would have planned and executed the mission.

Dick was working long, hard hours that summer. Not only was he performing his duties as the maintenance platoon commander for 2/9 CAV, but he and his team of attack pilots had also been put in charge of all the modernization and testing of the Cobra. The Cobra had been flown hard in Vietnam and was outdated. Until the Apache came out of production a few years later, the Cobra had to be updated, reconfigured, and modernized. It was a huge undertaking and involved dangerous test flights, above and beyond Dick's normal, day-to-day test flights in the OH-58 and the UH-1 aircraft for the CAV squadron. Dick was doing some pretty amazing things with his helicopters, and some senior officers at the Pentagon took notice. After the Desert 1 mission failed, the Army Special Operations Command started working on a new plan to get the hostages out of Iran, using Army assets. Because Dick was at the forefront of test-flying attack helicopters, he began getting some unusual requests from the Pentagon concerning modifications on his OH-58 helicopters.

"Hey, Vick, what if Ned and I get selected to go do something like a rescue mission? What if they need a test pilot?" His what-ifs and ideas were endless.

"Seriously, Dick, or are you just dreaming?"

"Vicki, I'm serious. Plans are being made, and I've gotten some interesting phone calls."

By early fall, Dick and Ned's dream of going on a special mission was becoming a reality. During that time of uncertainty, I told myself repeatedly that if Dick did go away, I was in a pretty good place in my life. I had to trust that he knew what he was getting himself into. The hardest part for me and for Ned's wife, Carole, was not being able to talk to anyone about what our husbands might do.

"We need to plan as if I am going somewhere," Dick told me. "I think it will be around the end of October, and I might be gone for two to four months."

I went to Dick's office one day and he had an Army lawyer (JAG officer) there so we could sign a power-of-attorney form. I knew in that moment that he wasn't just going TDY (temporary duty), he was deploying. That night, after the kids were in bed, we talked about other uncomfortable things.

"Vicki, I want to make sure that you know where everything is, where all the important papers are, in case of an emergency," he said.

"I can't believe we're even talking about this stuff. Most young couples don't have to confront these issues until later in their marriage. We've been married only five years!"

"Look, Vick, I know this is hard. But it's good to talk about these things and have a game plan. If we never have to use it, then we're ahead of the game. I just need to know that you'll know what to do, just in case."

"Okay, but I can't even think about something happening to you."

"Don't worry, I'm always careful. Nothing is going to happen to me."

And then, out of the blue, we were blindsided. One evening after dinner, the phone rang, which was not unusual, since Dick's duty officer called every night to let him know when the last helicopter had landed and everyone was down safe. But that particular night, I knew something was wrong when I heard Dick say, "What's the tail number? How bad is it?" He hung up and ran to the bedroom. In just seconds he was coming back down the hall, tripping as he struggled to get into his flight suit, on his way to the front door. I had never seen him so frantic.

"What is it, Dick? What happened?"

"A Cobra went down. I think it's Shaun."

"Oh my God! What do you mean, a Cobra went down?"

"I've got to go. I'll call you." And he was out the door.

I stood there staring at the front door. *Did he say Shaun?* CPT Shaun Murray was one of the pilots in our unit and was a frequent guest at our house. He had just been over for dinner the night before.

I put the kids to bed and tried to fall asleep, but I couldn't shut my mind off to the fear rising up in me. How could there have been a crash? It was a beautiful fall evening. Maybe they'd just meant it was a hard landing.

★ ★ ★

The ringing phone startled me awake. It was Dick, but I was having trouble hearing him, his voice was so soft and low. "Vicki, it was Shaun."

"Is he okay?"

The silence on the other end of the phone gave me that sinking feeling in the pit of my stomach, and suddenly I was very much awake.

"Shaun and his copilot didn't make it. . . . They're dead."

"Dead?"

"Yes."

I couldn't believe what he was telling me. I started crying. "I'm so sorry, Dick."

"I was first to the crash site, but there was a fire. We tried, but we couldn't get them out. They were already gone."

"Oh, Dick."

"I gotta go. I'll call you later."

I lay there for hours, trying to process what had happened, so many thoughts swirling in my head. Most of the time I didn't dwell on the dangers of what Dick did when he went to work each day. I thought I had learned so much and was a seasoned Army wife, but I wasn't. Had I been living in denial? How could I not have known this could happen? Maybe I had known, maybe it was there, deep in the recesses of my mind, but I had chosen to keep it there so I could live my life. But on that particular night, my fears were front and center.

I woke up the next morning and felt like I'd had a very bad dream. I went through all the motions of our normal daily routine with the boys. Dick called and gave me a few more details. He sounded absolutely miserable. I wanted so much to hug him, but I knew he had a long day ahead of him.

That evening I found Dick sitting in our den, staring into space. His face was ashen, and he just looked lost. He turned to me and said, "It was awful, Vick. I can't get the images out of my head. I don't want to eat; I don't want to do anything." I had never seen him like that, and it scared me. I just hugged him—I had waited all day to do that.

Dick racked his brain for answers; he questioned everything leading up to the accident and vowed to learn from what had happened to Shaun. For the rest of his flying career, he coached and mentored not only his pilots, but eventually his own sons, about the importance of emergency procedures and discipline in the cockpit, and also about "crew mix."

That accident changed each of us. It was subtle, but Dick and I felt it. It was there in our conversations, it was with Dick on every test flight, and it was with me every night Dick was out flying. We had crossed a threshold of innocence, and there was no turning back or denying the fact that it was a tough and unforgiving business that Dick was in. And all I could think about was what if something happened to him and I was left alone to raise Clint and Tyler.

Our unit became even closer after the accident. We all met at the Officers' Club the following week for "happy hour." To some, that may sound weird, but the club was our gathering place—a place where we all felt comfortable, where we shared laughter and good times. I think we all needed some normalcy, and the pilots needed a chance to grieve in their own way. Those strong, macho, virile aviators—combat veterans, brand-new pilots, men who lived on the edge, who lived for the rush of adrenaline that flying a helicopter gave them—embraced their fears every day and yet did not know how to express their feelings when something upset their sense of order. So, in the end, they simply offered up a toast to their fallen comrades, wrapped their arms around one another, and vowed never to make the same mistake.

We had barely finished grieving for Shaun when Dick got the call he had been waiting for. He and Ned were to report to Fort Rucker the following Monday. They were on "the deal" (as they called it), and they could barely contain their excitement.

The night before he left, with the boys in bed, we closed our bedroom door to the outside world and made love one last time; then, in the quiet darkness, we talked about some last-minute details.

"Dick, be honest with me, as much as you can. I just need to know some things; otherwise I'll go crazy. I promise I won't tell a soul!"

In a paranoid whisper, he told me, "I'm going to rebuild some Vietnam-era helicopters and turn them into gunship-type attack helicopters. This is so classified, you cannot breathe a word of it to anyone, not even our parents. And we can never talk about it on the phone, so when I call, don't ask me anything. Just say that I'm rebuilding helicopters at Fort Rucker. That's all you need to tell anyone who asks."

"Okay, I promise."

He told me he would call as often as possible. We decided we had better come up with a code in case he needed to tell me something on the phone. We wanted to keep it simple so I wouldn't get confused or forget what it was. We tossed around a lot of ideas, some of which were just plain silly. We ended up laughing so hard that for a brief moment, we forgot the seriousness of the situation. Dick and I always had the ability to laugh at life and ourselves, even in the scariest of times.

We decided to use Dick's motorcycle as the code. If he was going to do an actual mission, he would say, "Get my motorcycle out of the garage." Why we picked that, I still don't know, but we thought we were so clever and figured no one would ever know what we were talking about. In fact, those same code words have been with us all these years, and we continued to use them repeatedly throughout Dick's career.

Saying good-bye was more difficult because of what we had just been through with Shaun's accident. All that was on my mind as Dick was leaving, but I never wanted him to see me crying as he walked out the door—that wouldn't have been fair to him—so I pretended that he was just going off to work. I hugged and kissed him and said, "Please be careful, Dick. Do what you need to do and come home safe."

"Vick, you know me. I'm always careful. I'll call you as soon as I get to Rucker."

The house was so quiet when he first left. Dick is like a force of nature and fills a room with his energy, so I just felt empty. But I didn't have the luxury of sitting around crying that day; it was Halloween, and the boys and I had things to do.

Clint was three and a half, and Tyler was eighteen months, so they weren't really old enough to comprehend that Daddy was gone. Dick worked such long hours that on the weekdays, they didn't really notice his absence. I knew that the most important thing was to keep all three of us on our same schedule and routine; mealtime, naptime, bedtime, preschool, and church were essential to our well-being. I tried not to think too far ahead, or I would get overwhelmed; I just told myself, *One day at a time.* I was so thankful for Sarah next door and my new friendship with Ned's wife, Carole.

I called our parents and told them that Dick had left. We had prepared them as much as we could but had to be careful how much we said on the phone. I knew they still had a lot of questions that I couldn't answer, and I knew they were worried about Dick, so I tried to reassure them. I told them they would just have to trust us and that we would explain things when the time was right.

Dick called whenever he could, usually about every couple of days. It really helped because just hearing his voice let me know that he was okay and allowed me to feel as if he wasn't too far away. He was really excited about what he was doing. Rebuilding and test-flying helicopters was exactly what he loved doing.

"I can come home for Thanksgiving, for about forty-eight hours."

My spirits lifted immediately. "Oh, good—I can make it till then!"

★ ★ ★

It was wonderful to have him home. After a nice big turkey dinner, in the privacy of our bedroom, Dick told me a little bit more about the mission. He was talking in that paranoid whisper again, and I found myself looking around to see if anyone else was in our bedroom.

"The helicopters are built. We call them 'little birds'; they're pretty cool. But we'll be moving to another location for the next phase of the training, a secure place out West. I won't be able to call as often, but don't worry about me."

"Is it going to be dangerous?"

"There's always some danger involved, but you know I never take unnecessary risks and safety comes first."

"I'm still going to worry, no matter what you say."

"I don't think I can get any time off for Christmas. We have such a tight schedule and so much to get done. I think you should take the boys and fly up to Vermont for the holidays. It would be good for you to be with family."

He was leaving the next day, and I didn't want to spend what little time we had crying, so I put on my "not so sad, almost happy" face. We went over our code words again, just to make sure. Then he left and I was on my own again, so I got busy making plans for the trip to Vermont.

At first when I arrived, I was worn out and told my mom that I felt scared and out of control, that there were moments when I was convinced that something awful was going to happen to Dick. And then we got a nice surprise: Dick showed up in Burlington two days before Christmas! He looked different, even since Thanksgiving—he had long hair and a mustache—and he was distracted and subdued, not the Dick

Cody I knew, but the boys didn't notice and it meant the world to all of us that he came home.

We didn't get much alone time that visit, as we were sleeping in my old bedroom in my parents' house, with Clint and Tyler across the hall in my brother's old bedroom, so we had to make do.

"Dick, you look exhausted," I said one night when we were finally by ourselves. "Is everything going okay?"

"It's really challenging work. We fly day and night, practicing and fine-tuning our game plan. This is the toughest flying and tactics I've ever done. Sometimes it's hair raising, even by my standards and Ned's, too."

"But how will I know if you finish practicing and then leave the country?"

"I have to be really careful. We're working for and with some pretty clandestine people. I will tell you that we're down to the wire on this turning into a real-world mission. It really depends on whether President Carter can get the hostages released before President-Elect Reagan takes office. I will continue to call you every couple of days. If my calls stop, then you know I've gone to a secure location."

It was hard to suppress my feelings when we said good-bye that time, as it was probably the most scared I had ever been. Once Dick left, I counted the days till the boys and I would return to Savannah. I felt closer to Dick when I was in my surroundings. As wonderful as it was to go home, it was also a reminder of just how different our life was from that of our civilian family members.

One night in early January, Dick called and nonchalantly said, "I think it's time for you to get my motorcycle out of the garage."

Just as nonchalantly, I replied, "Okay. Hey, Dick, be careful. I love you."

"I love you, too, Vick."

I hung up the phone and felt totally alone. I was glad it was nighttime so I could crawl into bed with my fear and anxiety.

For the next ten days, I had no word from Dick. I waited and watched CNN, praying that the hostages would be released before President Reagan took office. I felt like I was going to burst with pent-up emotion. Then—praise the Lord!—Dick called late one evening and in a very subdued voice told me that the hostages were being released and to watch the news the next day. I had never felt such relief. I wanted to shout at the top of my lungs, for all to hear, that Dick was safe and coming home! However, I detected some disappointment in his voice. While he was thrilled the hostages were being released and he was returning to his family, he was obviously disappointed that they wouldn't get to do the mission that they had trained and worked so hard for.

The next morning, news of the hostage release was all anyone could talk about. I cried happy tears for all the families who had been waiting, and for me, too. It had been only three months, but they were the most stressful three months I had known.

PS: This was the time in my life when the real worrying began, but I could not give in to my fears, and I certainly did not want Clint and Tyler to know how scared I was. They were too young. I had to learn to compartmentalize my fears, a trait that would serve me well years later, when both boys started flying helicopters and deploying.

Thoughts on Faith and Trust

Faith is defined as "belief not based on logical proof or material evidence." Trust is defined as "total confidence in the integrity, ability, and good character of another. One in whom confidence is placed." The two words often go hand in hand and, for me, are words to live by.

Growing up, I did not have what I would call a strong sense of faith. Unlike Dick's family, who went to Mass almost daily, my family rarely went to church. I believed in God and was thankful that I had such a blessed life, but because my childhood was happy and free of any trauma, there was never a time when I felt the importance of faith. When I became Catholic, I loved going to Mass with Dick, and for the first time in my life, I felt the comfort of prayer.

When I think back on my life as an Army wife, I'm not certain exactly when my faith in God deepened, but I'm pretty sure it was during those nights when Dick was test-flying and experimenting with night-vision goggles strapped to his helmet, or maybe it was when he went off on that mission with Ned and there was no clear exit strategy if they went into Iran, or when he first got to Saudi Arabia in the summer of 1990 and he and a few other units were the only deterrent if Saddam Hussein's Republican Guard decided to cross the border of Saudi Arabia. I do know that by the time Clint and Tyler began deploying to combat zones, I had a clear and deep faith in God.

When the boys deployed, I had never felt so out of control and so afraid. It was worse than my fears for Dick. The night before Clint deployed to Afghanistan, as Dick and I struggled to cope with our son deploying, we called our good friend Father Baker, a Catholic priest from Hopkinsville, Kentucky, and asked him to come to the house. It was late, and we hated to impose on our friendship, but we felt helpless, and that was a new and scary feeling for us. Father Baker brought Clint a Saint Christopher medal, and after we chatted, we prayed. It gave us the comfort that we needed.

During the boys' numerous deployments, I've had to rely on my faith more and more. When you realize you have done everything you can to keep your children safe, as you continue to pray for their safety, it reaches a point where you have to give it up and hope that God is watching over them.

As I've grown over the years as an Army wife and matured as a woman, so has my trust—in Dick, in myself, in the Army, and in everything that we have done as a couple and in raising our sons.

Any good marriage has to be built on trust in order to survive, but it is even more important to a military couple, since we face a lot of separations and uncertainty. With Dick gone so much of the time, whether to dangerous places or just on temporary duty, I would have driven myself crazy if I'd had to worry about what he was up to all those times. I have never once doubted Dick's faithfulness to me, and I have never given him a reason to question mine.

I had to trust Dick countless times when it came to our way of life; I had to trust that the next place or the next job was going to be good for our family. How many times did he say, "Trust me, Vick"? And I always did.

I have also learned to trust not only Dick's abilities as a pilot but now Clint and Tyler's as well. Otherwise, how could I live with the inherent dangers of what they each do? And when I myself was learning to fly, it was probably the first time in my life that I had trust in my own abilities, as I had never done anything that my life depended on like that.

Every time Dick was in a command position, I watched how trust was the key element in his leadership. The trust that he established with the leaders under him, which in turn trickled down through the ranks of every soldier, was the reason he and his units were always so successful. It was the reason they were able to accomplish such great feats. When he was commanding the 101st Airborne Division, shortly after September 11, 2001, we began to prepare the soldiers and their families for possible combat deployments. In the previous year, we had built a great team based on trust—trust between Dick, his leaders, and the soldiers, and trust between the spouses and me. That trust was based on a mutual respect that fostered esprit de corps and camaraderie and made everyone feel like they were part of the team. Amid all the uncertainty ahead of us, it was that trust that enabled each of us to prepare for the next "rendezvous with destiny." And it was trust that gave Dick and me peace of mind when our son deployed with those very people.

It was not enough that Dick and I trusted each other, though; we also had to foster trust between ourselves and our parents and extended family. Many times, our parents did not understand our Army life: why Dick was always gone, why we missed a lot of family events back home, why we moved to the far reaches of the world and made it difficult for them to see their grandsons and us. We couldn't always tell them every detail or why, especially when Dick was involved in something clandestine; they just had to trust us. For the most part, they did, and as they learned more about our very unique lifestyle, that trust turned into a love and appreciation for Army life. Our parents got to share enough moments with our family that we made memories to last a lifetime.

Where would I have been without faith all these years? So many times when I thought I couldn't deal with something, when reasoning and logic didn't work, when there was no one, not even Dick to help me, when I was so scared, I put myself in God's hands. Once I did that, I was able to face any challenge and not only live my life but also really enjoy it, even in the darkest of times. I'm thankful that I can do that.

One last thing about trust: I realize I've been trusting Dick Cody since that first night when he took my hand and led me down that dark path to the beach.

8

A Fork in the Road

Dick had some loose ends to tie up as his operation and mission disbanded, so he didn't get home until the beginning of February. We eased back into normal life in Savannah, but he seemed quieter than usual and a little subdued.

One afternoon while the boys were napping, Dick said he had something he wanted to talk about. I still vividly remember sitting at our kitchen table, admiring the cute brown-and-white bamboo wallpaper that I had chosen, while Dick shifted nervously in his chair.

Then he began, "I've been offered a job in the special-operations community. The Army is forming up a permanent unit like the task force I was just part of." He went on to explain that the Army realized the need for a special-operations aviation unit that would be a quick reaction force supporting Delta and Special Forces units for clandestine-type operations, like the hostage rescue mission. The new unit, to be called Task Force 160th, would be built from aviation units from the 101st Airborne Division and based at Fort Campbell, Kentucky. Dick, Ned, and the other pilots from "the deal" had been asked to be a part of the new unit, along with the "little bird" helicopters that Dick had helped build.

I couldn't get past the part about his being in a unit that did dangerous things all the time *and* the fact that we would have to move to a place called Fort Campbell, Kentucky. He was still talking when I interrupted him.

"Do you have any idea how much I've worried about you for the past three months, how I had to live with the fear that you might not make it back alive and I might be left alone to raise the boys? Didn't you tell me how dangerous the flying and training was, that a couple of times you and Ned almost crashed, and that if you guys had really done the mission, there wasn't a clear exit strategy to get out of Iran? Forgive me for being a party pooper, but I'm thinking that was enough excitement to last a lifetime!"

"I know all that, Vick. But this is an opportunity to be part of a new and groundbreaking chapter in Army aviation history. It's what I love doing."

"I know you're disappointed you didn't get to carry out the mission that you and the guys worked so hard on. I can't imagine what you're feeling, but, Dick, you already lead an exciting life flying helicopters. And you have a wife and two beautiful boys who love you. We need you. It's time you start being a husband and father to us."

The ensuing silence made me wonder if I had said too much. I had never wanted to stand in the way of Dick's career, but this was one of the rare occasions when I took a stand. Something told me we were at a fork in the road. I knew that we wouldn't always have a choice, but we did this time.

Finally, he said what I was hoping to hear. "I guess you're right. Ned and some of the other guys are going. I thought I wanted to go, too."

The fact that he didn't put up much of a fight told me that he knew it was an unnecessary and dangerous risk at that point; I think he just needed me to help him along with the decision.

With that settled, I said, "Dick, put away your long face. The kids are napping, and we've got some catching up to do!"

★ ★ ★

Dick returned to his old job in 2/9 CAV. He was glad to be home with the boys and me, but I also knew that he was feeling the letdown after months of living on the edge, working and flying in extreme conditions, planning a mission that was exciting and exhilarating but that never got to play out.

Spring, the most beautiful season in Savannah, was just around the corner, and it was as if Dick had never been gone. But that summer brought some changes. Ned left to go into the special-operations aviation community, and he and Carole got divorced. It was difficult for Dick and for me because we had grown so close to both of them.

Then my best friend Sarah moved, and as I watched her drive away, I thought I would never find another friend like her. I was experiencing one of the most difficult aspects of Army life: making wonderful friends and then having to say good-bye to them after a few years. I was miserable and lonely those first few weeks. Sarah had been my everyday friend, my go-to, the person whom I shared everything with and spent the most time with.

Fortunately, those sad circumstances were offset by one of the most significant events for our family to date: we bought our first airplane. Ever since Dick had gotten his private pilot's license back at Fort Eustis, he had dreamed of buying one, and after he got back from his special mission, he seemed more intent than ever on finding one. Many a Sunday after church, we drove out to the Savannah airport to look at private planes. He finally found his dream plane: a four-seater Cessna 172 that was in excellent condition. After much discussion and going over all our finances, we decided to go for it. It was a bold decision for us and a new chapter in our lives. Our plane would take us on adventures all over our country and play an important role in charting a course for all four of us.

In December 1981, Dick took command of E Company, 24th Combat Aviation Battalion. In one of the huge maintenance hangars at Hunter Army Airfield, he finally realized another one of his dreams: commanding a company. Company command is the first real leadership position for Army officers and offers the most direct influence and impact on soldiers and their well-being. It requires leadership at the most basic level, as well as handling millions of dollars' worth of aviation equipment and aircraft. Not only was it a huge responsibility for Dick, but it was also the first opportunity for me to be part of his job and command.

The boys and I spent time hanging around Dick's company and in the hangar. Clint and Tyler loved being around Dick, his soldiers, and all the helicopters; it was like their playground. I loved watching Dick with his soldiers and the way they responded to him. He was a born leader. He was also breaking all kinds of records in the aviation maintenance business. He even developed his own formula for aircraft maintenance.

We faced some challenges and sadness during that time, including another Cobra crash that killed one of our soldiers, and a lot of hard work, but it was so rewarding that we both felt like we were right where we were supposed to be.

During those long, hot summers, the boys and I spent every day at the pool and went to the beach frequently. On our way back from Tybee Island, we would stop for fresh peaches and tomatoes at roadside farm stands and buy fresh shrimp right off the boats. By the time we crossed the bridge into Thunderbolt and headed down Victory Drive into Savannah, the boys would be fast asleep in their car seats, exhausted from the sun and the ocean. Whenever I looked in the rearview mirror at their sweet little tan faces, their sun-bleached hair stiff with salt and sand, I was so grateful for those times with my kids.

We also flew our plane up and down the Georgia and South Carolina coasts, landing at little airfields on Hilton Head Island and St. Simon's Island, and even flew all the way up the East Coast to Vermont. During those trips, Dick taught me some terminology and the basics of flying, map reading, and making radio calls. At first it was scary flying in a small plane, but once I got used to it, I had complete faith and trust in Dick's piloting skills.

Then Dick came out on the promotion list for major and was selected to attend the Command and General Staff College at Fort Leavenworth, Kansas, and just like that, it was time to move again.

Our four years in Savannah were about much more than Southern charm, hospitality, and a beautiful city. They were also about the memories Dick and I made with each other and our young kids, about the bonds and camaraderie we shared with our fellow Army friends, and about the realization that, in spite of the challenges and tragedies we faced, in spite of Dick's long workdays and the time he was away from us, we had weathered some of life's storms and come out of them just fine. We were thriving and happy as a family and as a couple.

PS: When Ned and Carole got divorced, I can't say for sure that his taking a job in the special-operations community was the cause, but I don't think it helped their marriage. And within months of the Task Force 160th forming up, a good friend of ours was killed in a training accident, flying a "little bird." I didn't want to be divorced, and I didn't want to be a widow. Both of these events were proof to me that we had chosen the right fork in the road.

9

The Year We All Went to School

As hard as it was leaving Savannah, we were looking forward to what had been described to us as a "great year of fun and family time" at Fort Leavenworth, Kansas. It was the next step in Dick's career and would be like going to college for a year. The Command and General Staff College prepares captains and majors for the next levels of command and staff assignments at the battalion and brigade level. The classes are designed to broaden their knowledge on how the Army runs and on the strategic, operational, and tactical "art of war."

We flew our plane to Kansas, and the two-day flight gave us some much-needed quality and quiet time. When we landed at Sherman Army Airfield, one of the few Army airfields that allows private planes, it was 106 degrees, hotter even than any day we had had in Savannah.

I was especially curious about our quarters because of a conversation I'd had with Dick a few weeks before we left Savannah. He had driven our car out and called me from Fort Leavenworth to tell me he had seen our quarters.

"Vick, just promise me you'll stay with me no matter how bad the house is, okay?"

We pulled into a little neighborhood, two cul-de-sacs with a common courtyard in the middle. The houses all looked the same: small; Cape Cod–style; peeling paint that had probably been white at some point. Because there were more students than houses, the lowest-ranking officers were offered money to live in them for the year, and then the houses would be torn down. We had lived in Army quarters before, so I knew what austere was, but these houses gave new meaning to the word. Picture a tiny, two-bedroom, one-bathroom, linoleum-floored, un-air-conditioned box of a house, with no basement, no porch, no frills of any kind. I had to keep reminding myself that the important thing was that we were all together.

While I was feeling overwhelmed and unpacking boxes, Dick came bursting in, as excited as a kid, and said, "Hey, Vicki, Tommy Greco is in my class." Dick had known Tom since they were eighteen years old and cadets at West Point, and it turned out that he, his wife Gail, and their two kids were moving in just a few houses away. I hadn't seen Tom since he and Dick were cadets, and I was excited to meet his wife and children.

Those first few days, huge moving vans came and went all day long, taking up every square inch of our cul-de-sac. There were lots of young kids, so the boys rode their Big Wheels all around the courtyard with their new friends. I couldn't wait to finish unpacking so I could get outside and meet our new neighbors. Gradually, we began to emerge from our houses and all of the boxes. We gathered in our courtyard, meeting new friends and seeing old ones. At first we all commiserated about the heat and our crappy quarters. Before long, we had a couple of picnic tables and some lawn chairs, and then coolers full of beer and soda appeared. I made my homemade salsa, others brought chips and dips, and suddenly it was a party. That first gathering on our lawn set the tone for the rest of the year. We continued to meet in our courtyard throughout the summer, and before we knew it, we were no longer complaining about our houses because we were having so much fun. Tom and Gail Greco became our closest friends. The guys picked up their friendship where they had left it eleven years earlier, and Gail and I and our kids all bonded quickly.

The Saturday before school started, there was a post-wide activity sign-up at the main academic building for all kinds of clubs, organizations, activities, and sports for both kids and adults. I had just finished signing Clint up for soccer when Dick came over to me and told me that the Fort Leavenworth Flying Club had a booth and that I should come check it out with him.

I followed him over to a sign that read FLYING LESSONS: LEARN TO FLY IN THE CESSNA FLIGHT PROGRAM. He introduced me to Mike, one of the head flight instructors. They both looked at me as Dick said, "What do you think, Vick? This would be the perfect chance for you to learn to fly. The airfield is right here on post, I'll have an easy schedule, so I can help with the boys, and you've got the time this year to do it. Do you want to sign up?"

My mind was racing. *Oh boy—wait just a minute. I know we discussed this many times, especially on the plane ride out to Kansas. I was very brave when we talked about it, but actually doing it is a whole other thing. How can I learn to fly? I've never done anything like that in my life. I'm not daring or brave at all, I'm not mechanical, and I was never an A student. And what about the expense? No, I don't think I'm cut out for flying an airplane. I'm beginning to sweat. I need some time to ponder, to think, and then procrastinate for a while. Yes, that's what I'll do—*

"Vicki!" Dick interrupted my thoughts. "Mike is waiting for an answer. We need to make a decision. The ground-school class begins next week."

I could stay in my safe little world of being an Army wife and mother, or I could step way outside my comfort zone and see if I could become a private pilot. I decided to give it a try. Once I made the decision, I was equally excited and nervous.

The following week, Dick started his classes at the Army's Command and General Staff College, Clint started first grade, Tyler started preschool, and I began flight training. It was a lot of firsts for our family. For the past six years, I had been at home with kids, and I was used to devoting every minute of every day to their needs, and Dick's, too. But now that they were all in school, it was a time of letting go for me. At first, I wasn't sure what to do with my little bit of freedom, but once I started Cessna Ground School, I felt a sense of purpose and a sense of *me*. Looking at the books, maps, and gadgets in my flight bag, I couldn't wait to begin. I was as excited as Dick had been when he started flight school.

I began my training in the two-seater Cessna 152, like all the other student pilots. The plan was, once I mastered that, I would transition to our larger and more complex Cessna 172. For my orientation flight, I followed along as my instructor, Mike, performed the preflight inspection. He was so calm as he explained everything and then talked me through takeoff, landing, and some basic turns and maneuvers. I began to feel queasy, but he reassured me that once my hands were on the controls, I would feel fine. We made plans to fly the following week. I couldn't wait to get home and tell Dick all about my first flight.

It was wonderful having Dick around so much, the four of us eating dinner together every night and just knowing that he was in a classroom all day and not doing dangerous stunts in a helicopter. I had peace of mind for the first time in four years. There was almost no stress for us that year at Fort Leavenworth; our days and nights were carefree, and our weekends were completely ours. My biggest challenge was shifting gears from being a mom to being a student pilot and finding time to study. I tried to do it during the day when the boys were in school, but I had so many new girlfriends, it was more fun to go out to lunch or just hang out with them. Many a night, I was up studying after Dick and the boys had gone to bed.

Meanwhile, Dick was learning about leadership. As he had already spent so much time in units with soldiers, he had a wealth of knowledge, experience, and leadership skills that were reinforced in his classroom studies that year. Most of the work came easily to him, and he didn't have to spend a lot of time studying at the library. He enjoyed his classes but liked having time for sports even more. He and Tom were always playing something: tennis, softball, racquetball, and, of course, basketball.

Clint was learning to read and write, Tyler was learning numbers and colors, and I was getting to know the area from up in the air. The United States Federal Penitentiary sits right next to Fort Leavenworth. The United States Army Disciplinary Barracks is on the post, right next to Sherman Army Airfield, and the Missouri River is at the end of the runway. Those landmarks became ingrained in my memory forever. I learned every nook and cranny, every railroad track, road, highway, farm, and field, that surrounded Fort Leavenworth and the town of Leavenworth, Kansas. They were the checkpoints on my flight log and my way home if I ever got lost.

The weather was great that fall, so Mike and I were able to fly two or three days a week. He was right: once I had the controls, my stomach settled down. I was progressing quickly and continued to amaze myself. It was hard work, but I loved the precision and discipline of flying. We practiced takeoffs and landings, called touch-and-gos. We did so many, I dreamed about them at night. Flying, like so many other things, is learned by repetition so that everything becomes second nature to you.

On the weekends, we took the boys and explored the Leavenworth area, apple-picking in a local orchard and taking trips to Kansas City, about a forty-minute drive away. With the Grecos, we discovered the fun nightlife in KC, trying out different restaurants and going to movies.

By the end of October, Mike said it was time for me to transition to our 172, and then I would solo in that. I had already passed my flight physical with flying colors, so the next requirement for getting my pilot's license was to take the FAA private pilots' written exam. I hadn't taken any kind of exam in years, so I was stressed about it.

Dick and Tom both got promoted to major the first week in December. Gail and I remarked to each other that we sure didn't feel like major's wives; they always seemed so *old* to us. I was busy studying for my FAA exam and anxious to get it over with. Most of the time, I just went along, not thinking that what I was doing was anything extraordinary, maybe because Dick was already a pilot and the boys were too young to fully understand what I was doing. My girlfriends were pretty impressed, but it wasn't like we sat around talking about it.

I was a bundle of nerves the day I drove down to Kansas City International Airport for the exam. I had chosen my outfit carefully: wool slacks, a crisp white blouse, a sweater vest, and one of the silk bow ties that were so popular back in the mid-1980s. I figured if I flunked the test, at least I would look nice doing it.

I found the big, daunting FAA building, walked up to the information desk, and asked the man where to go for the FAA written exam.

"You must be here for the flight attendants' exam," he said. I guess my outfit had "flight attendant" written all over it.

"No, actually, I'm here for the private pilots' exam."

He looked at me with surprise, then came out from behind his desk and said, "In that case, miss, let me escort you to where you need to go."

As we walked down the hall, he turned to me and said, "So, you're going to be a pilot?"

"Yes, that's what I'm working on."

"Wow, that's really something. Good luck to you. I hope you make it."

That little boost of confidence from a perfect stranger was just what I needed. In that moment, I realized that what I was doing was indeed special and something not everyone can do. I walked into the test room and took a seat with about a dozen men. I pulled out my stash of freshly sharpened number 2 pencils and my "whiz wheel," and for the next few hours I worked my way through the test. When I walked out of there that day, I felt good and was pretty confident that I had passed. A week later, the results came in the mail. I had passed with an 87 percent! I was so proud, as were Dick and Mike.

With my test out of the way, I was able to focus on the upcoming holidays and our ski trip to Colorado. We left Christmas Day for a great week of skiing and fun with the Grecos and two other families in our neighborhood.

Then, one day in early January after I'd gone flying with Mike, he casually asked me to bring a white T-shirt the next time we flew. I knew the tradition: after a student's first solo flight, the instructor rips the shirt off the student and signs it. Obviously in my case, Mike was not going to be ripping my shirt off, especially in January, but I brought in a T-shirt so he would have it when the time came.

A few days later, I met him out at the airfield for a routine flight. It had snowed about six inches the night before, so when I left the house, I told Dick I doubted I would solo that day. The runway had been plowed, but there was still snow and some ice on it. We took off and flew the traffic pattern, and then Mike gave me my instructions.

"Vicki, you are more than ready to solo. I want you to take off, fly the pattern, and come in for a full-stop landing. If you feel good, I'll signal you to do three more touch-and-gos."

I thought, *Has anybody considered that maybe I'm not ready? Plus, I like having you in the seat next to me*, but Mike got out of the plane and left me alone.

I taxied to the holding line just short of the runway, did my engine run-up, and made my radio call.

"Sherman Tower, Cessna 12369 is holding short of runway 34."

"Roger, 369, you are cleared for the active and cleared for takeoff."

I taxied into position on the center line. With every bit of courage I could muster, I pushed in the throttle.

"369 is rolling, remaining closed traffic."

"Roger that—call on base to final."

I was rolling down the runway that I had taken off from so many times before with Mike. After a smooth takeoff, I was alone in the traffic pattern and it was completely silent. I was doing it—I was flying by myself.

Within minutes, I was on downwind and it was time to do my pre-landing check. I adjusted my power setting, put in flaps, and turned right base. I broke the silence when I made my radio call.

"Sherman Tower, 369 is turning final for full stop, 34."

"Roger that, 369—you are clear for landing."

As with my takeoff, I was all business and concentration as I began my final approach. I was so proud when I made a textbook landing. *Wait till I tell Dick about that!* I thought.

I taxied over to where Mike was waiting. He gave me a thumbs-up and signaled for me to back up. I did three more touch-and-gos, feeling more confident with each one. When I was finished, I taxied over to the gas pump and parking area. Mike hugged me when I climbed out of the cockpit. I was so excited that my whole body was shaking.

I couldn't wait to share my big news with everyone. Dick was in class, so I called my parents, who had been living vicariously and wanted to know every detail of every milestone that I accomplished. They were so happy that day when I called with my news. And when Dick got home, we celebrated with champagne. He beamed as he said, "You really did it, Vick! I knew you could."

That night, we took the boys to Dairy Queen for a celebratory dinner. There weren't a lot of places to eat in Leavenworth, Kansas, especially midweek, but we were so excited, it didn't really matter where we went.

★ ★ ★

After that, whenever the weather was good, I was out flying. Once I soloed, I had to log ten to twenty hours of solo time. I went out and flew around the local area, and I worked on all the maneuvers Mike had taught me. I had to force myself to practice stalls. It was one thing to do them with Mike sitting next to me and quite another to do them by myself. It took all my courage. I continued to fly with Mike every so often because I still had a lot to learn before I took my final check ride for my license.

It was getting close to the end of the school year; there were a lot of activities with the boys and their schools, they were both playing

T-ball, Dick was gone for a couple of weeks on a class trip, and we were waiting for his orders to see where we would be moving. Amid all the distractions, I didn't know how I could get all my flight requirements done. One day, while flying solo, I scared myself trying to land in a tricky wind. I managed to land safely after a few go-rounds, but I was shaking with fear. For days afterward, every time I drove by the airfield, waves of nausea came over me. I didn't want to get back in the cockpit, and I began to doubt myself.

When Dick came back from his trip, he gave me a little pep talk.

"Every pilot at some point scares himself. The important thing is to learn from it. You've come so far; you just need to move forward."

"But it was scary!"

"For God's sake, Vicki, just do it!"

I knew he was right. It was time to finish what I had started.

I was validated when, one day while I was out practicing with Mike, he said, "You are probably the best student I've ever taught."

I couldn't believe it. I had never been the best at anything.

I got another morale boost right before my solo cross-country trips, when I needed it most. One afternoon, I came in from flying solo, taxied over to the gas pumps, and hopped out of the plane. I got the stepladder, climbed up onto the wing, and refueled the plane. I was concentrating on not spilling any fuel but sensed that someone was watching me. I looked over the wing, and out in the field, next to the parking ramp, was a group of prisoners from the disciplinary barracks, working in the field. We had all gotten used to seeing prisoners that year, on work release at the commissary and in the fields on post. But what caught me off guard was that they had all stopped what they were doing and, leaning on their rakes and hoes, were staring at me, kind of awestruck. I didn't know what to do, so I smiled and kind of nodded. A few of them tipped their hats, and a few gave me a nod, and then they went back to their work. They had watched me land and taxi but were probably surprised to see that I was a woman. It hit me once again that I was doing something unique.

In mid-May, I flew three separate solo cross-country trips—a requirement for getting my license. Each trip consisted of three legs, each leg a distance of one hundred miles or more, and I had to land and refuel at each place that Mike had chosen. My trips took me all over Kansas, Nebraska, and Missouri, using all of my navigation skills, and to a variety of airfields and airports. I landed on a barely paved runway at a tiny little airfield in Falls City, Nebraska, where a farmer refueled my plane. I landed at a beautiful corporate jetport in Jefferson City, Missouri, where I planned my next flight in the pilots' lounge, alongside some hotshot corporate pilots in their crisp uniforms. The thought of flying far away from my safety net was intimidating at first, to say the least, but once I took off and was on my way, it was absolutely exhilarating. I learned a lot about myself in those quiet hours all alone in that cockpit. I learned to trust myself and my skills, and I realized that I had more courage than I ever knew I had. It was unlike anything I had ever done in my life. It was just me up there in the sky; nothing else in the world mattered.

All of my trips went without a hitch. I made every checkpoint, nailed every landing, and never got lost. On the last leg of my last trip, I was flying in from the west, toward Kansas City, on my way back to Sherman Army Airfield. It was every pilot's dream of a day—totally peaceful, not a cloud in the sky—and I felt a huge sense of accomplishment as I made my way home, navigating through the Kansas City airspace.

As always, Dick and the boys were there to greet me when I landed at the airfield. Dick worried every time I went out on a solo trip. He would literally pace up and down by the hangars or, if he was in class, would call the airfield every half hour. I appreciated his concern but also secretly delighted in knowing that for once, the tables were turned and he was getting a taste of what I had felt like so often when he was up in the air.

★ ★ ★

Mike and I finished the last of my requirements so I could take my final check ride. I studied every chance I got. While sitting in the sun with my girlfriends, I studied my index cards of emergency procedures and they took turns quizzing me. I was reminded of those times at Fort Rucker when I'd helped Dick learn the same rules.

I barely slept the night before my check ride. I prayed for blue skies and no wind, but I woke up to threatening clouds, a low ceiling, drizzle, and gusty winds. My flight examiner was an Army colonel, and my mouth was so dry that I could barely answer his questions during the two-hour oral exam. But once we went out to fly and I took off, calm came over me. I told myself I had done all of this before and I could do it one more time for the examiner. But after a short while, the weather deteriorated and we were forced to go back to the airfield. Later that afternoon, as the sun began to poke through the clouds and the winds diminished, we took off again. I flew the best I could and finished all the requirements. After about an hour, Col. McBride turned to me and said, "I'll take the controls now and fly us back to the airfield. Congratulations, Vicki, you've passed. You're a pilot!"

All I could think was, *Holy shit, you did it!* It was a defining moment in my life, right up there with marrying Dick and giving birth to Clint and Tyler. When I landed, Dick was there. As I walked toward him, I gave him a big thumbs-up. He was grinning from ear to ear when I hugged him. "Wow, Vick, you're a pilot now, just like me!"

That night, we went out with our friends and while we celebrated my accomplishment, we also celebrated the end of the school year. What a great year it had been, with lots of family time, friends, and good memories. We hated for it to end, but it was time to go back to the *real* Army and new duty assignments. Dick and Tom both had orders for the 101st Airborne Division at Fort Campbell, Kentucky, and we were excited that we would all be together again.

PS: This was a year of huge growth and self-discovery for me. I accomplished something few people can do. Learning to fly gave me a whole new appreciation and respect for Dick and his fellow aviators. It also gave Dick a new perspective on my world, being the one at home, waiting and worrying. He had more time with his sons than he had ever had, and they were old enough to appreciate that.

10

A Rendezvous with Destiny

The boys and I spent much of that summer in Vermont while Dick attended a mandatory refresher course at Fort Rucker. It had been a whole year since we had seen our families, and I always felt like Vermont was our port in a storm.

But as wonderful as it was to go home with the boys, there were also challenges, and after a few weeks, the novelty wore off, especially for the boys. We were living out of suitcases and didn't have our own things. The boys didn't have their toys or bikes or their friends, and I was hard pressed to keep them amused. We all decided that as the boys got older, it was better for us to plan shorter visits, rather than trying to live with family for weeks at a time. Dick and I had to remind ourselves that Vermont was *our* childhood home, not Clint and Tyler's.

After that trip, as we made our way south through Pennsylvania and into Kentucky, familiar feelings of anticipation and apprehension surfaced, and by the time we exited the Pennyrile Parkway and drove south on Route 41A, we couldn't wait to see the large Army post called Fort Campbell. As we drove past the gates (ten in all), pawnshops, liquor stores, check-cashing joints, bars, strip clubs, convenience stores, military clothing and surplus stores, and tattoo parlors, I remarked to Dick, "I've never seen anything like this." It wasn't just the size of the post that shocked me; it was the *seediness* outside the gates. It was a stretch of blacktop with no trees, grass, or vegetation of any kind—just wall-to-wall businesses that catered to soldiers. I don't know what I had expected, but it wasn't that.

"We gave up Belgium for this?" I was referring to the original orders

Dick had received for an assignment in Belgium. He had gotten the orders changed to the 101st Airborne Division.

Dick began with his usual response: "Trust me, Vick, this is going to be great! We're in Screaming Eagle country, home of the world-famous 101st Airborne Division, the greatest division in the Army!" Then, turning to Clint and Tyler, he asked, "Boys, who's the greatest pilot?"

In unison, they said, "You are, Dad!"

He was acting so "hoo-ah." I didn't get what the big deal was with the 101st Airborne Division and the Screaming Eagles.

As we drove through the main gate and a military policeman (MP) saluted Dick and yelled, "Air assault, sir!"—the standard greeting among all 101st Airborne soldiers—neither Dick nor I could have predicted what was in store for the four of us. If someone had told us then that off and on over the next eighteen years we would be stationed at Fort Campbell four times—that our boys would spend more of their childhoods there than anywhere else, or that Dick would command a company, a battalion that he would take to combat, a regiment, and finally the division—I would have said they were crazy, because that day in August 1984, when we first drove through the main gate of Fort Campbell, Kentucky, all I could think was, *Get me the hell out of here!*

The third largest post in the Army, Fort Campbell sits on the Kentucky–Tennessee border and has two area codes and two zip codes. It's its own city within the post, with a daytime population of approximately thirty-five thousand people, which includes about twenty-five thousand soldiers, four thousand dependents, and close to four thousand civilians who help run the post. With its own hospital and some of the best schools in the Department of Defense Education Activity (DoDEA), Fort Campbell is a very desirable post to live on.

For the next three years, Dick and I and our two young sons would experience Army life, the sights and sounds of a large Army post, in all its glory. We awoke every morning to the sounds of reveille and soldiers running PT (physical training) throughout the post. Every evening at precisely 1700 hours, all activity, even traffic, stopped while retreat played and the flag was lowered. At 2100 hours every night, we heard taps. And the helicopters flying overhead day and night, rattling the windows and the dishes in my china cabinet, were sounds that became so much a part of our lives that we didn't give it a second thought. The boys were old enough to enjoy the benefits of living on an Army post: the great schools and sports programs, and being with other Army "brats" just like them. Equally important, they were surrounded by soldiers, NCOs, and pilots who would impact them. Army life would become *their* way of life.

Our house was nothing great—again, very basic: a three-bedroom, two-bathroom brick duplex, with a carport in front—but it was definitely a step up from the house at Fort Leavenworth, and we made friends immediately in our neighborhood. The Grecos lived nearby, and Gail and I were together most days. Our days revolved around the kids' school schedules and sports practices. When we could get babysitters, Tom, Gail, Dick, and I went out for date night and together navigated the fast-paced 101st Airborne Division.

Dick jumped out of bed every morning, slipped into his flight suit, and burst out of the house, headed to Campbell Army Airfield. He was so excited to be back in an aviation unit, specifically an attack helicopter unit. As a new field-grade officer (major and above) and a graduate of the Command and General Staff College, he was expected to be a staff officer, which he didn't exactly relish. He wanted to fly helicopters, not a desk. He was hoping his new job as the battalion executive officer (XO) in the 229th Attack Helicopter Battalion (AHB) would allow him time to fly and that, just maybe, he would get to command another company. His wish came true when, later that year, he took command of B Company, 229th Attack Helicopter Battalion, nicknamed Blue Max.

★ ★ ★

The mid-'80s were a time of relative peace in the United States. We were not at war with anyone; there were no peace rallies or protests as in the previous decade, and no big issues impacting Army life. Ronald Reagan was a popular president and was reelected to a second term in 1984. The hit TV show *Miami Vice* inspired a whole new fashion trend for men: linen pants, jackets with T-shirts, and no socks. I bought Dick a linen blazer and tasseled loafers, and I thought he looked very cool.

If things were relatively quiet and peaceful in the United States during those years, overseas, especially in the Middle East, was a whole other story. In 1983, a suicide bomber blew up the Marine Barracks in Beirut, Lebanon, killing 241 American servicemen, mostly Marines. It was the first time I had heard the terms *terrorist* and *suicide bomber*. Some say that act was the beginning of the war on terrorism that would influence and affect US foreign policy for decades.

I started to pay attention to what was going on overseas because, in the summer of 1985, Dick and his company left for a six-week exercise in Egypt. Bright Star was a joint military exercise between the Egyptian army and the US Army's 18th Airborne Corps, which included the 101st Airborne Division. Tensions from years of war were already running high in the Middle East, and then, ten days before Dick's company left, a TWA jet was hijacked in Egypt.

I was more nervous than usual when we, the families of Blue Max, gathered at Campbell Army Airfield to say good-bye to Dick and B Company. I didn't think the charter plane was in danger of a hijacking; I was just worried overall because they were going to a part of the world that was in constant chaos, not to mention the fact that my and the other wives' husbands would be flying their helicopters in a very tough and unforgiving environment, the Egyptian desert. As unsettled as I felt, I didn't show it as the boys and I hugged Dick good-bye. We had six weeks looming ahead of us, and I was responsible for all the families in our unit, so I put a smile on my face.

Two weeks into the exercise, Dick called. I knew something was wrong because I had not expected to hear from him.

"One of my Cobras went down in the desert. It's a Class A, Vicki."

I was silent. In that split second, I remembered Shaun's accident in Savannah, when Dick had also used the term *Class A*, which meant catastrophic damage and/or loss of life. I opened my mouth to speak, when he said, "We lost one of our pilots, and an Egyptian officer is injured."

"Oh, Dick, I'm so sorry." At times like that, I just didn't know what else to say. "Can you tell me who it is?"

"I will give you the name, but under no circumstances can you tell anyone until after the official notification is made. And that is going to be difficult because once this hits the news, everyone will be calling you for information. You're going to have to be strong, Vick."

"I know, Dick. How are your guys holding up? Are you okay?"

"They're in shock right now. We all are. I'll call you when I can, but with the investigation and the ongoing training exercise, it's going to be hectic."

I could hear sadness and fatigue in his voice. He was anything but his usual upbeat, energetic self. It was difficult any time tragedy struck, but even harder when Dick was far from home. It meant he and his guys had to put aside their grief and continue their training, and that I had to handle everything on my own—not just for my family, but for the families of our unit.

My phone rang all afternoon, and it was agonizing not to be able to tell the other spouses what I knew. It wasn't until that evening that the Brigade XO called to tell me the notification had been made and I could begin the process of telling the spouses in our unit. The wife of our fallen pilot had gone home to her family for the deployment, which made it difficult to reach out to her. Since I couldn't control any of that, I focused on the people in our company who were counting on me for support, and my own two boys. I spent the next few days on the phone, reassuring, calming, consoling, and attempting to quiet the rumor mill. I was in a tough position and had to reiterate to everyone that, as awful as it was, our guys had to finish out their mission in Egypt. Although I missed Dick more than ever, in the end I got my strength and support from the other spouses and was amazed at how resilient we all were.

★ ★ ★

By the time Dick and his guys returned home, it had been four weeks since the accident. I was so relieved when they landed safely at Campbell Army Airfield that I cried when Dick got off the plane. Their return reopened the wound from the accident, and we went through a short period of grief all over again, as a couple and as a unit.

"Do you realize how much I worry about you, especially when you are so far away? And every time we go through an accident, I think it could have been you," I told Dick.

"I know, Vick. What can I say? I can't tell you these things aren't going to happen. All I can do is to be safe and try to keep my guys safe. Sometimes I can't, and that kills me."

Just a few months later, a plane crash on December 12, 1985, shook our entire Army post and the surrounding communities. A plane carrying 248 soldiers from the 101st Airborne Division, returning from a six-month peacekeeping mission on the Sinai Peninsula, crashed after refueling in Gander, Newfoundland. All the soldiers and crew were killed—fellow soldiers, people we knew, friends and neighbors.

Our post transitioned from the excitement of welcome-home ceremonies and the approaching holidays to a horrific scene of news media, images of burning wreckage on TV, and grieving families. The Gander crash was the biggest air disaster in the history of the military and the largest loss of life in a single event in the Army.

Dick and his unit were in Georgia on a training exercise when it happened, and by the time he called, I thought I was all cried out. "Dick, you wouldn't believe what it's like here. This is unlike anything we've ever experienced," I said.

Then Dick told me the name of a friend who had been on the downed plane, and I felt like it was all too much to take. Grief from all the accidents he and I had been through in recent years came crashing down on me that day. I hated to cry to Dick when he was gone, because I didn't want him worrying about me, but this time I couldn't stop myself.

I called Gail and my good friend Connie, and they were as stunned as I was. Connie's husband, Terry, was in the 502nd Infantry Brigade, the unit that had lost the most soldiers. She told me that he was preparing to go to Gander to help identify their bodies.

I tried to prepare myself for Clint and Tyler's return from school, as I had no way of knowing what, if anything, they knew. When they came in, Clint began talking immediately. "Mom, lots of people were crying, and John's dad was supposed to come home today, but then someone said the plane crashed."

Tyler, just six years old, chimed in, "Yeah, and there were kids in my class that had to go home and they were crying, too."

I chose my words carefully and tried to be calm as I explained, "Okay, there was a plane crash. It was a big plane that had soldiers on it that were coming back from the Sinai. The soldiers died, and it's very sad for their families and for all of us at Fort Campbell."

I was walking a fine line. I knew Clint was thinking that the same thing could happen to his dad. I thought, *How in the world can I explain this to them without scaring them too much?* I couldn't just tell an eight-year-old and a six-year-old that there are no guarantees in life. Clint was old enough to understand a little bit about what his dad did for a living, but I had to be careful and not make promises.

"Sometimes bad things happen and we don't know why."

"What if something bad happens to Dad? When is he coming home?"

"I don't think anything bad is going to happen to your dad. He's very strong, and he's the best pilot I know. He called today, and he'll be home next week."

That seemed to put the subject to rest for the time being. I knew in the coming days I would have more discussions with the boys as we learned additional details. Like a tornado that cuts a swath through a community, so, too, did the Gander crash. It was indiscriminate in the lives it claimed. It was unexpected, and it was scary, and as we listened to speculation about a possible terrorist attack or foul play of some sort, we were all unsettled.

On December 20, the entire community—Army families alongside citizens from Clarksville, Hopkinsville, and Oak Grove; ordinary people, dignitaries, and some of the most senior Army leadership from the Pentagon—gathered at the division parade field for a memorial tribute to our fallen Screaming Eagles. I went with Tom and Gail and was so glad to be with close friends, since Dick couldn't be there with me. It was twenty degrees and spitting snow that day, and even with all our layers of clothing, hats, and gloves, we were still shivering. Wreaths of sympathy and condolence from all over the world lined the perimeter of the parade field, where approximately seventeen thousand soldiers from the 101st Airborne Division, bundled up in their winter field jackets, stood in formation to honor their fallen comrades, all the while struggling with their own grief.

There were speeches that day, but I don't remember much of what was said. I do remember the calm voice of the division commander, Major General Burton D. Patrick. Loved and revered by soldiers and officers alike, he was a great and caring leader and was just what we needed at that time.

What struck me most that day, and what I did not expect to feel on that particular occasion, was the most profound sense of pride when

I looked at the formation of soldiers and the huge Screaming Eagle banner, a two-story-high replica of the division patch, in the background. Old Abe, as the eagle is called, always hung there on the parade field, but that was the first time I really looked at it. I was beginning to understand what "soldiering" was all about and what unit pride was. It happened when I least expected it, not on a beautiful summer day, at a happy event, like a change-of-command ceremony or a parade, but instead during one of the most somber events I had ever been to. As we huddled together, we were united in grief but also united in pride for our soldiers and all that they stood for. I had never felt so much a part of the Army family as I did at that moment. I couldn't take my eyes off that huge Screaming Eagle patch. I now knew why Dick wanted to be in the 101st Airborne. That day, I fell in love with the division and with Fort Campbell.

Still, the crash cast a gloomy cloud over all of us. The boys and I were so glad when Dick returned from Georgia. Luckily, my parents had made plans to come to Fort Campbell that year for Christmas. If there was ever a time when I needed family and a sense of normalcy, it was then. I picked my parents up at the Nashville airport, and as we made the one-hour drive to Fort Campbell, I was emotional as I tried to fill them in on everything that had happened in the past twelve days. Also, because this was their first trip to Fort Campbell, I felt the need to prepare them for the huge Army post that we called home. As we made our way down 41A, my parents were amazed at the sight before them. On both sides of the highway were American flags flying at half staff and signs and wreaths in front of each and every business, even the famous strip club the Cat West, expressing sympathy, love, and support for our soldiers and their families. I was no longer embarrassed at the seediness outside our gates; rather, I was proud of it.

Life went on, and we began to heal as a community. But just like the other times after a traumatic event, these incidents brought Dick and me closer as a couple while forcing us to face the fragility of life. I worried about the boys and how much they were processing, afraid that they would grow up with a skewed sense of what was normal, that they would think fathers die or, worse yet, that *their* father could die flying his helicopter. But our sons were pretty resilient. And Dick was such an upbeat and positive person, always moving forward, never dwelling on the past or on sadness, that he made it easier for me to put my fears aside. Somehow, despite all the sadness and challenges going on around us, he and I were able to maintain a balance.

Life in the 101st Airborne Division was hectic and at times overwhelming, but it was a great place to be an Army wife. There was a sense of belonging and order there. For someone like me, with a high need for inclusion, I thrived in that environment. I had so many peers and we learned from each other. I learned from the commanders' wives who were role models for all of the younger spouses, until suddenly, I found *myself* in the role of mentor. Because I was a major's wife, the young lieutenants' and captains' wives considered *me* a senior wife and looked to me for guidance and advice.

Even today, I look back on those years with such fondness, particularly when I remember summer afternoons at the Officers' Club swimming pool. While watching our kids, with our chairs lined up like a beach chair brigade, my friends and I discussed everything from recipes to decorating and entertaining to good books to read to our husband's jobs, speculated on who was moving where and when, and covered just about anything else having to do with Army life. At any given time, any or all of our husbands were gone, but we kept each other company. How lucky we were to have one another.

PS: I truly believe that I came of age as an Army wife there at Fort Campbell. I began to really understand and embrace Dick's profession more than I ever had. The boys came of age, too, as "Army brats." Hanging around the barracks and the aircraft hangars with their dad, they looked up to the soldiers and pilots whom Dick led. Many of these young boys with whom they went to school, played sports, and played soldier in our backyard at Fort Campbell, Kentucky, would one day serve together in the Army.

Thoughts on Moving

At this point in the story, you're beginning to see a pattern—a pattern of moving. In thirty-three years of marriage, Dick and I moved eighteen times. Even though some of those moves were back to a place we had already lived, they still brought up all of the emotional and physical baggage that goes along with relocation. To this day, I have recurring dreams—I call them moving nightmares—about a moving van pulling up in front of our house when I'm not ready; I haven't even packed a suitcase.

The physical act of moving became a routine: cleaning drapes, rugs, and bedding; taking everything off the walls and filling in holes left by picture hooks; removing wallpaper borders; recaulking tubs and sinks; emptying closets, the carport, and the shed; mowing the lawn; and packing suitcases with enough clothing to last anywhere from two to eight weeks. We made daily trips to the thrift shop, Goodwill, and the huge Dumpsters on post. By the time the packers and movers arrived, we were exhausted, but then it took another three days to pack and load all of our possessions. Every time the movers closed and bolted the doors of the huge van containing most of our material possessions and drove off into the sunset, I felt my life pulling away from the curb, too.

Moving tested us and tried our patience in many ways. Dick and I invariably had a big argument at some point during the moving process. I came to expect it and tried to prepare myself for it, but it would sneak up on us and catch us when we were most vulnerable—usually when exhaustion set in. Something big or small would ignite a spark, and in an instant we would be embroiled in a "big one." We fought about anything from who was doing the most work, to how something that wasn't supposed to have been packed had gotten packed, to how someone had lost the check for the cleaning team or had hit the utility box while backing out of the driveway, knocking out power to our street. One time we got a flat tire before we even left the driveway, and one time, the day before we had to drive to our new home, Tyler got strep throat, which involved a trip to the emergency room. All of those things contributed to our already-high stress levels, and there were times when I wanted to walk away from it all, including Dick Cody.

Luckily, our outbursts never lasted long. Once the stress of the decision making and hard labor was over, the moving van gone, the yard neat, the cleaning team on its way, and the suitcases in the trunk of the car, our lives were simplified and we started feeling excited about what lay ahead. It was the four of us again, and we were never closer than when we were headed for that next duty assignment, that next adventure.

For the physical act of moving, we made countless lists, consulted maps, and arranged for all possible contingencies. There was a method to the madness, and with each move we became more savvy. The more organized we were, the better the move went.

That was not the case with the emotional upheaval that a move caused, as there was no checklist, no road map, to help us navigate that. Saying good-bye to a place we had come to know and love, and saying good-bye to friends who had become family, was always difficult, sometimes more so than others. We did that over and over, on average every two to three years, and no matter how exciting the next place was going to be and no matter how I prepared myself, I hated the good-byes. As the boys grew up and had to leave their friends, I hurt for them, too.

After our first tour at Fort Campbell, we had orders for an accompanied tour in Korea. Our best friends, the Grecos, were moving to Panama. Gail and I had become as close as sisters, and we didn't know when or if our paths would cross again. The day we left, Gail and I were in her bedroom, lying facedown on her bed, crying like a couple of little kids, when Dick's loud voice came booming down the hall: "Okay, girls, that's enough! Time to go, Vick."

He and Tom had said good-bye that morning. They probably shook hands and said something really profound, like, "Catch you later; see you on the high ground." I wished I could be like that, but I wasn't. So I carried some of that baggage around with the rest of our suitcases, although I usually rebounded soon after we got to the new place. After a period of adjustment, I made new friends and we all enjoyed these new experiences.

Our overseas move to Korea, however, was a logistical challenge that tested even my best organizational skills. While it was an accompanied tour, I was pretty much on my own with Clint and Tyler, ten and eight (respectively) at the time, not just for the long flight over but for much of the year we lived there. Dick was the aide to a three-star general, and the two of them lived on another Army post about an hour away from us. The boys and I lived on Yongsan, a post right in the middle of Seoul. Dick came home to us on the weekends, which was a big adjustment at first but definitely better than the unaccompanied short tour that we had already endured. It proved to be a great year, full of rich experiences that I wouldn't trade for anything. Most of all, I was proud of myself not only for surviving some lonely days and evenings without Dick, but for doing so in a foreign country, without all the comforts of the United States. I didn't let Dick's absence get in the way of the fun the boys and I could have. I learned how to navigate and get around in a huge foreign city, and I made sure our sons got to do all the things they would normally have done. I was pleased with how good they were and how they matured that year.

When we left Korea, part of me hated for the year to be over. There were things that I would miss about Korea: my friends; our houseboy, Mr. Chy; and all of the interesting Korean people that I had gotten to know. I would miss shopping in the back alleys and side streets of Seoul, bartering to get a deal, and I would miss not getting to see the Olympics, but this girl was ready to go back to the land of shopping malls and department stores, fast-food restaurants, *fresh* potato chips, American TV and movies, and driving my car wherever I wanted. I had missed that sense of freedom and wide-open spaces that I did not feel while living on a peninsula surrounded by water on three sides and North Korea on the fourth. Call me frivolous, but I had missed my country!

Army life even afforded me character-building opportunities like moving into quarters by myself. When we left Korea, Dick had to attend a course at Fort Rucker, so the boys and I made the move to Fort Campbell by ourselves. I handled two overseas shipments and our storage shipment and learned how to hook up our washer and dryer, which was not easy and not a pretty sight—me wedged behind the machines, squatting down with plumber's crack, sweat pouring off me, cuss words flying out of my mouth, all my anger directed at Dick for not being there.

When we moved back to a place where we had previously lived, it was an added bonus. We lived at Fort Campbell four times in all and Fort Hood, Texas, twice. Both were places that we loved, and sometimes when we returned, some of our friends were still there.

After each move, once the last box was unpacked, the house in order, and the boys squared away, I had to take stock of myself and chart my course for the new tour of duty. Each time we moved, my world (and the boys') was turned upside down, and then it was up to me to put all the pieces back together and create a sense of order. As often as we moved, I still always went through a transition period when I was full of self-doubt and questioned the life we had chosen. I wondered if I could make a home for us and if we would be happy.

There were times when I worried about how all of the moving was impacting Clint and Tyler. But as they got older, I realized it kept our boys closer to us longer than usual. Because they were always the new kids, they didn't have a crowd or group that they had belonged to for any length of time. During the high school years, most kids start experimenting with or dabbling in various "things" because they have the comfort of close friends with whom they've grown up. Clint and Tyler were lucky to have each other, make a few friends, make the tennis team, and find their way in a new community. They didn't have a lot of time to get into trouble.

Our many moves took on a different dynamic when Tyler relocated the first time without his big brother, since they had always had each other when they started at a new school. And then, when both boys were in college, it got even more complicated. One of the most challenging moves logistically was the one from Fort Hood, Texas, to Washington, DC, in the summer of 1999. Clint had a job in Killeen, and Tyler was leaving for Advanced Camp at Fort Lewis, Washington. Both boys would be going to Texas A&M by the end of the summer, so there was no need for them to move to DC initially. My best friend Nancy offered to let Clint live with them for the remainder of the summer. Once Tyler left for Fort Lewis, I joined Dick, who had already moved to DC. Just as Dick and I did, the boys learned to roll with the punches.

11

Summer 1990

Everything Dick had accomplished in his career was leading up to and preparing him for battalion command. In 1988, while we were stationed in Korea, he was selected for promotion to lieutenant colonel and to command the first Apache battalion in the 101st Airborne Division. After one year in Korea, we went right back to the 101st Airborne Division and Fort Campbell. Dick took command of 1-101st Aviation Battalion, the Expect No Mercy battalion, in the summer of 1989. It was the perfect scenario for all four of us: Dick would get to command soldiers again, and all of us were going back to a place we loved. We even had friends who still lived there. The best part of all was that the Grecos were coming back to Fort Campbell after their tour in Panama. Tom had been selected for promotion and command of an infantry battalion.

In February 1990, Dick's battalion left for a four-month training exercise at Fort Hunter- Liggett, California. Their mission was to test the Apache helicopter by flying against the most advanced radar and air defense systems in the world—and in extreme desert conditions. The exercise would test not only the helicopter's abilities but also those of every pilot, crew chief, and mechanic; it would test Dick's crew mixes and all of his skills as a leader. The California desert was unforgiving, and the flying schedule was relentless—day after day, with no breaks. It was similar to combat conditions.

The deployment to California was a test for me, too, as a mother but also as a commander's wife. It had been a while since Dick had been gone for that length of time, and we had a lot of new, young pilots and families who had never been separated or deployed. I worried about all the what-ifs that could happen in four months' time. As we had seen in the past, life throws curveballs when you least expect them.

About halfway through the exercise, "it" happened: a midair collision between two of Dick's Apaches. Miraculously, all four pilots survived; three of them walked away with minor injuries, but one was critically injured with head trauma and burns. It was a devastating blow to Dick, his pilots, and all the soldiers in the unit. For me and the wives back home, it was yet another wake-up call about the dangers of what our husbands were doing.

As difficult as the accidents were for me when Dick was gone, I could only imagine what it was like for him and his soldiers. As with the time in Egypt, I was amazed at the resiliency it took for them to be able to finish their training exercise and the courage it took them to get back in their cockpits. Dick believed in leading by example, so he was the first one to take off and fly after the accident.

While their fellow pilot Chuck lay in a coma, it was time for the unit to return home. The hardest thing Dick ever had to do was leave one of his pilots behind. Except for the accident, his entire battalion performed magnificently under the most extreme flying conditions. They learned to defeat the most sophisticated radar and air defense systems in the world. They proved that the Apache was worthy of all its notoriety and expense. But, more important, Dick had flown with each of his pilots during the training exercise and felt confident about the capabilities of every one of them. That experience confirmed his crew mixes: the teams that flew together in California would fly together from then on.

On August 2, 1990, Iraq invaded Kuwait. It was also Dick's fortieth birthday. The day began like his birthdays always did: with a 6:00 a.m. phone call from his mother singing "Happy Birthday." Seven kids, countless grandchildren, and a very full and busy life, yet the amazing Jan Cody never missed a birthday.

However, that morning, the conversation turned serious and I could tell from Dick's end that something was wrong. He told his mom he would call her later.

He was out of bed and headed down the hall for the TV room, with me right on his heels.

"What is it, Dick? What happened?"

He was muttering to himself, and then he said, "Iraq just invaded Kuwait."

It was breaking news on every channel. Before I could ask another question, the phone rang. Dick needed to go to the Emergency Operations Center (EOC). I followed him back to the bedroom while he got ready.

"We've been following the intelligence reports, and there were indications that something was about to happen in that region. The United States cannot let Iraq take over Kuwait and their oil fields."

Within minutes, Dick had shaved and showered and was heading out the front door. I followed him to his car and asked, "Do you think you can get home at a reasonable hour tonight?" I hated to be selfish at such a critical time, with a world crisis looming, but it was his fortieth birthday and, unbeknownst to him, I had invited all of his officers over for a surprise birthday party that night.

"I'll do the best I can, but we might be preparing for war by the end of the day."

I realized how little I knew about the country of Kuwait and the trouble with Iraq. Dick hadn't mentioned anything going on in that region of the world, but he had remarked to me just a few weeks before that it was unusual that his unit had been on extended QRF (Quick Reaction Force) past their normal thirty-day cycle. The 101st Airborne Division always had a QRF ready to deploy at a moment's notice, and Dick's Apache battalion had been on call much of the summer. Still, his comment about "war" caught me off guard.

"Jeez, you don't have to be so dramatic!" And then, as he pulled out of the driveway, I called out, "Happy birthday!"

I was surprised that the boys were still asleep, as well as my sister, Chris, and her daughter, Ashley, who were down for their annual summer visit, amid all the activity and phone calls. I went into the house and got everyone up. We had a lot of work to do for the party that night (about eighty people were coming), not to mention the phone calls that were sure to start pouring in. We ate breakfast in front of the TV; then I delegated chores to everyone and we got so busy that we had no more time for watching the news.

By afternoon, the keg had been delivered and the big wooden sign that I had rented was in the front yard, with GUESS WHO'S 40? spelled out in Christmas lights. I was making some appetizers while Chris cleaned the patio and the backyard. It was close to one hundred degrees that day, and Clint, Tyler, and Ashley were out back, videotaping themselves on the Slip'N Slide, with the usual amount of bickering, pushing, and shoving. It seemed like a typical summer afternoon; whatever was going on in the world would have to wait until after Dick's party.

Dick called at one point to say that his company commanders wanted to take him to the Officers' Club after work for a birthday beer.

"Fine, but don't stay too late. I'm making you a nice birthday dinner."

Some of the bachelors started to show up in the late afternoon. Some insisted on helping me, and some of them were working on gag gifts for Dick. Everyone knew something was up, because Dick had been in meetings all day, and they seemed anxious to be together. By 6:00 p.m., the sign out front was lit up, the bamboo torches in the backyard were blazing, and people had started arriving . . . everyone except Dick. At about seven thirty, with the party in full swing, I called Tom Greco and asked him to go over to the Officers' Club and bring Dick home. They showed up shortly after that, and Dick was totally surprised, but only because he had been so busy all day that he hadn't given much thought to a possible surprise party.

Someone handed him a beer, and the party really got going. Dick's celebration was our first chance to gather as a group since his unit's return from Fort Hunter-Liggett. Because of everything that had happened—the great job they had done as a battalion, juxtaposed with the accident—everyone seemed very happy to be together. The day's news events created an undercurrent of drama, as each of us wondered just what Dick had found out and how it would affect the unit. We didn't know then that it would be the last time we would be together as a group for a very long time.

There was something special about that night—something in the laughter, in the way they gave Dick silly gifts, in the way they looked at him, hanging on his every word, in the way they put their arms around one another—that makes me remember vividly how touching it was, even after all these years. An outsider never would have guessed what was going on behind the scenes and what lay ahead. There was fun and lots of laughter; we were a team, we were a family, and we could all feel the closeness.

When the party was over and most of the guests had left, Chris and I were cleaning up and I noticed Dick and a group of his pilots sitting out back, in lawn chairs, having a last beer and a cigar. They were in quiet conversation. I loved watching him with his guys, how they gathered around him and how he was like a father to them. I couldn't wait to get Dick alone and find out what had happened over the course of the day, but I knew to let him have that time.

Once everyone was in bed and the house was quiet, I finally had Dick all to myself. He told me a little bit about his day and what he thought was going to happen.

"I'm pretty sure the 18th Airborne Corps will deploy a quick-response force that involves my Apache battalion to Saudi Arabia. The oil fields in Kuwait and Saudi Arabia are too important to risk losing to Iraq. Even if it's just a show of force, President Bush has made it clear that the United States will not stand by and do nothing. It could even lead to war."

"War? Really, Dick?"

"Vicki, the United States can't let a dictator take over a country like Kuwait. It may not stop there, and if Iraq goes into Saudi Arabia, it will upset the balance in the entire Middle East. There's a lot at stake."

It had been such a long day, and we were both so tired by then, that I put my thoughts of war on the back burner so I could get some sleep, but in the coming days, I felt melancholy. I was worried about the possibility of war, and I also didn't want summer to end. It had been a good one, in spite of everything. We had taken the boys to Florida after Dick returned from Fort Hunter-Liggett, and then the boys had gone to 4-H summer camp, giving Dick and me some alone time. My sister's annual visit was fun as always, but when she and Ashley left, I knew the reality of the deployment would take over my life.

Dick's Apache battalion was the first unit to go on alert. It was a scary time for the boys and me. We were missing our support system, as some of our closest friends had recently moved and Gail and her kids were on vacation out West and wouldn't be home for another two weeks. By then, Dick would be gone.

Dick worked nonstop, going to meetings and getting his unit ready. I was thankful for the distraction of preparing the boys for the start of school; that took my mind off the knot that was forming in my stomach. Dick came home for dinner every evening, and for those brief moments, we could pretend that things were normal.

Dick and I had already made plans for our first family support group meeting. Over the years, we had learned the importance of having good accountability, current information on everyone, and points of contact (POCs) for each of our companies, and connecting as a group. We had built a good, close team, and we were hoping that would carry us through the deployment.

Our post chapel was packed with about two hundred family members; many came with their soldiers. Our brigade chaplain opened up the meeting, and then I addressed the unusually quiet group. I tried my best to sound reassuring: "I'm just as scared as you are, but your soldiers are in good hands, and somehow we will get through this, together. We need to take care of ourselves and each other so that our soldiers can do what they need to do, what they have been training to do."

By the time Dick stood up in front of the crowd, he had their undivided attention. Because of operational security (OPSEC), he couldn't talk about actual dates and times, so he said simply, "You need to trust me that I will keep you informed as best I can. You need to trust the leadership and the competence of each and every soldier in this unit. This unit is the best-trained Apache battalion in the Army. You need to prepare for a six- to twelve-month deployment."

Dick was every bit the fearless leader that night. He finished, "I will take good care of everyone. I promise I will bring everyone home safe."

I thought, *How can he be so sure? I can't believe he said that.*

As we answered people's questions, I could see fear in their eyes and the shock as it registered that the soldiers weren't going on another training mission—they were preparing for a combat deployment. The full weight of responsibility hit me that night in the chapel. Some of the soldiers looked so young; I felt as if Dick and I were the parents of a huge family facing a massive challenge.

Finally, alone in our car, I said, "How in the world are we going to get through this one?"

"We'll be okay, Vick. I promise we'll be okay."

"But how can you be so sure? I'm scared, Dick, not just for us, but for all those families."

"You did great tonight, Vick. You really connected with the families, and what you said was so heartfelt. I was really proud of you."

"As scared as we all are, you made us feel safe. You were so reassuring. But how will you keep your promise? Look what we've been through already, and it wasn't even combat!"

"I will not lose anyone. If we go to combat, there are some things I can't control, but there is also much I *can* control, and I will do everything in my power to keep them all safe."

Something told me that Dick would manage to keep his word.

That night when we talked to the boys, the minute Dick said the deployment could last up to twelve months, they said, in unison, "What about Christmas?"

"Boys, we will do everything that we always do; it will just be without your dad."

They started to cry, which made me cry. Old Stiff-Upper-Lip Dick remained calm and tried to reassure the three of us that it would be okay. After a big group hug, he said, "Let's go get some ice cream."

From that moment on, it was all about making the most of our time together and living in the moment. We tried to keep things as regular as possible for the boys—going to the movies, playing tennis, or just watching TV together. Still, as the entire division prepared to deploy, activity, anxiety, excitement, and chaos prevailed.

Each day we prepared to say good-bye, and then there would be another delay. We were on an emotional roller coaster, and it was hard to act as if things were normal, when the situation was far from it. I was tired of the stress, the distractions, and the fear of what was looming just ahead. I was tired of nightly "mercy sex"—having sex just for the sake of having sex because you think that is your last time together. Most of all, I was tired of the Army creeping into our relationship. I needed to feel like I had some control over what little time I had left with Dick. So one afternoon when he came home from work early, I decided it was time for our last "rendezvous with destiny," as we affectionately called our trysts. I didn't care how many more days and nights we had before he left; I was declaring it our last rendezvous, and I wanted it to be meaningful. The boys were at the pool, and the house was quiet. We closed ourselves off from the outside world, if only for a little while, and it was just what we needed.

We were all sitting at the dinner table when the call came in. Dick said, "Okay. I got it. Make the calls. I'll be right in." The boys and I knew what that meant: the Air Force planes had finally arrived to pick them up.

There were already lots of soldiers and family members milling around the battalion area, piles of kit bags and duffel bags everywhere. We went into Dick's office and chatted with people, but we knew he had things to do. There wasn't much more to say; the good-bye had been going on for days. Dick had his game face on, as did most of his soldiers and officers.

We said good-bye with a kiss and hugs all around. It was anticlimactic after the days of waiting and with so many people around us.

On the drive home, the boys and I were relatively quiet and calm. I was so thankful that Clint and Tyler had each other. Even though they bickered like typical siblings, I noticed that whenever the going got tough, they banded together better than any two friends ever could. Surprisingly, sleep came easily to all three of us that night. A ringing phone at six o'clock the next morning woke me with a start, and for a second I forgot what was going on. It was the airfield commander telling me that Dick and his battalion had taken off at about 4:00 a.m. I was thankful for the call—it gave me closure—but when I hung up, all the pent-up emotion and angst came pouring out of me in big, choking sobs. I cried into my pillow so the boys wouldn't hear me; I didn't want to alarm them. I wanted Dick back.

In those first moments, as reality set in, I wondered how I was going to get through the coming months, and I was scared for Dick and his soldiers, not knowing what they would face when they arrived in Saudi Arabia.

★ ★ ★

Those first days and weeks after he left, I was exhausted both physically and mentally. I was very weepy and cried easily, especially when someone said or did something kind to me. I was standing in line at the commissary when an acquaintance came up to me, put her hand on my arm, and, with genuine concern, said, "Vicki, is there anything I can do for you?" For some reason, that kind gesture opened up the floodgates and I started crying right there in the express line at the commissary. As much as I hated doing it in public, there were times when I just couldn't control the tears.

School started, and that was a blessing. It gave the boys a purpose. They were starting sixth and eighth grade, and, for the first time in a long time, they went to the same school. Because they were growing up so fast, and maybe because Dick was gone, I felt the significance of the moment even more. I had a lump in my throat as I watched them get on the school bus together.

I read about Dick and his helicopters in the local newspaper and in *USA Today* long before I actually heard from him. I felt some relief just knowing that they had arrived safely. It was big news because it was the first "real-world" deployment for the brand-new Apache helicopter, and the world was watching what the United States was going to do in response to Iraq's invasion of Kuwait. I started keeping a scrapbook for Dick. And then one day he showed up on CNN! He was saying something about how many tanks the Apache could take out, but I couldn't get past how handsome he looked and how good he sounded. The boys came home from school that day all excited because their teachers and principal had seen their dad on TV. That was the biggest morale boost for me, the boys, our parents, and all the families in our unit, because it meant that Dick and his guys were safe.

Later, when Dick's letters started arriving, I found out about their abysmal living conditions. They made their home in the parking garage at King Fahd International Airport in Dhahran, Saudi Arabia. It became their base camp for the majority of their time there, along with the rest of the aviation units from the 101st. Dick and his guys had to set up their own camp, and it was two weeks before they got showers and latrines going. In those early days, Dick's was the only Apache battalion in the country to support a 5th Special Forces Group and a Saudi National Guard unit along the Saudi–Kuwait border. That was all there was to protect the border and stop or deter any aggression from Saddam Hussein's Republican Guard. From what I read in the newspaper and saw on TV, I knew how dangerous it was those first weeks and I had to force myself not to dwell on bad hypothetical scenarios.

When all you have are letters, it's amazing how they can lift your spirits. As busy as Dick was, he took the time to write to each of us so the boys got their own letters. Dick always revealed so much more to me in a letter—a softer side to him, no game face, just his heartfelt words.

It took six weeks for the entire division to pack up, load up, and deploy to Saudi Arabia. Once everyone left, it got easier. We wives banded together and found comfort in one another while the boys got busy with school and sports. By late fall, the stress levels and emotions in our family support groups seemed to be settling down and replaced with a sense of acceptance. The boys and I were moving forward, making plans for Thanksgiving and Christmas, and counting down the days and weeks until Dick came home. But for the tens of thousands of soldiers, sailors, airmen, and Marines who had amassed in and around Saudi Arabia, Operation Desert Shield had only just begun.

PS: By this point, I had gotten even better at compartmentalizing my emotions. I had to, because I had so many people counting on me that I couldn't give in to my fears. But I never lost sight of how grateful I was to have Clint and Tyler and my parents, in-laws, siblings, and great friends from all over the Army, because their love and support were what kept me focused on what was important.

12

Operation Desert Shield/
Desert Storm

It took every bit of my energy to take care of Clint, Tyler, and myself, as well as my responsibilities as a commander's wife. I was fortunate to be surrounded by fellow Army wives who were having a similar experience, but my best friend Gail was the one whom I spent the most time with, and we managed to have fun and make the most of the situation. Our weekends were all about our kids, taking them to a movie or to dinner, even if it was just Burger King. Saturdays were filled with soccer or basketball games, and on Sundays we went to church.

I also had endless meetings to attend—division and brigade-level meetings, battalion family support group meetings, company potlucks—and monthly newsletters to write. What I didn't realize then was that we Army wives were charting a new course for future Army families, paving the way for what family support and family readiness should and would be in the coming years. By 1990, as female soldiers began to deploy alongside their male counterparts, the profile of the Army family had changed dramatically from what it had been when we were fighting in Vietnam.

Operation Desert Shield/Desert Storm was the first time we had dual military couples, and there were more single-parent households than at any other time, which created a new set of needs for family care plans. The nice little coffee groups of the past, designed for social purposes, no longer provided for and served the soldiers and their families during a large-scale deployment like Operation Desert Shield/Desert Storm. So while we joked about our lot in life and what we referred to as "death by meetings," those meetings actually served an important purpose, not only by keeping us busy and connected with one another but also by helping us devise a better plan for family support and readiness.

We spent Thanksgiving in Atlanta with our old friends the Lesters. It was the perfect road trip for us, not too far away but just far enough for us to feel like we were taking a little vacation. It was wonderful to be with old friends.

Dick called the Monday after Thanksgiving. "How was your trip?" he asked. "I'm glad you and the boys got to go, but I was worried about you on the road, especially over a holiday weekend."

"We had a great time, Dick, but we missed you. Why were you worried?"

"You have no idea how hard it is to be so far away. If anything ever happened to you or the boys, I couldn't help you or get to you. We all worry about our families."

"Wow, I've been so busy worrying about you, I haven't thought about *you* worrying about *us*."

That phone call came at the perfect time, as Clint and Tyler had not talked to their dad since August, when he had left. He usually called in the middle of the night, and I didn't want to wake them on school nights. They were outside playing, and I called to them that their dad was on the phone. They came rushing in and each took a turn on the phone. Tears streamed down my cheeks as I listened to them talk.

"Dad, we went to a basketball game between the Atlanta Hawks and the Philadelphia Seventy-Sixers!"

"And, Dad, we got to meet some of the players after the game, and we got pictures and autographs! We got to meet Dominique Wilkins and Charles Barkley!"

They talked about school and soccer, and after a few minutes they handed the phone back to me and ran off to play with their friends.

Dick hinted again about something he was working on, something he had been trying to tell me about in his letters.

"Vicki, think about what Ned and I trained for back in 1980-81. Remember that in the coming weeks."

"I don't understand what you're trying to tell me, and I don't dare ask you any questions."

"Just watch the news."

I told him of our plans to fly up to Vermont for Christmas, and he said he would call on Christmas Day. With no e-mail, very few phone opportunities, and ten-day-or-more mail delivery, we had to plan way ahead for our calls.

Unbeknownst to me, Dick was planning the mission of a lifetime, almost the exact mission that he and Ned had been part of in 1980-81, the mission they had never gotten to execute. I was confused, because based on what I remembered about the Iran mission in 1980, it involved rescuing hostages. For the life of me, I couldn't figure out how that applied to what was going on in Kuwait and/or Iraq. There were no hostages that I knew of. While I made plans for the holidays and busied myself with all the usual seasonal tasks, Dick had the difficult job of choosing the flight crews that he would send into battle.

The boys and I were glad to have the trip to Vermont to look forward to. There was nowhere else we wanted to be that Christmas, but it was also a reminder that everyone else lived normal lives and that my husband, Clint and Tyler's dad, was in a combat zone. Dick's phone call on Christmas Day was the highlight for everyone. We passed the phone around Dick's large family, and everyone got to talk to him. I had a long and satisfying cry that evening.

★ ★ ★

When the holidays were over, back at Fort Campbell, we entered a new stage in the deployment. January 15, President Bush's deadline for Iraq to pull out of Kuwait, was looming in the very near distance. Dick called on Saturday, January 12, in the early evening. He talked to each of the boys. They talked about their basketball games, school, and ordinary things. I got back on the phone, and we chatted about the usual mundane things, but I could sense something in Dick's voice, and then he said, "I might not be able to call for a while. I think it's time to take the motorcycle out of the garage."

He pulled out those code words from the past as if we used them every day.

I tried to swallow, but my mouth was dry. "Okay. I figured you might want me to do that, I just wish I knew why."

"Just watch the news."

"Hey, Dick, you don't have to prove yourself to me; I'm already proud enough for a lifetime. Just promise me you'll be careful."

"Don't worry about me, Vick. You know I always am."

And then, because the conversation was getting too serious, I said, "Dick, you better not let anything happen to you, because if you do, I'll kick your ass when you get home!"

We both laughed. There wasn't much else to say after that, even though I knew it was more than a typical good-bye, so I just told him, "Fly safe, Dick. I love you!"

"I love you, too, Vick."

I hung up the phone, and, as scared as I was, I actually felt a strange sense of relief. Things had been building and brewing for so long, I was tired of the suspense. Whatever he had to do, I just wanted him to get it over with. Maybe it was Dick's ever-optimistic voice, maybe it was his confidence, or maybe it was the fact that I knew without a doubt he was doing exactly what he was meant to do, but just talking to him made me feel good, and I slept well that night.

★ ★ ★

January 15, the day we had all been obsessing about, came and went without anything happening. My phone rang constantly, people wondering what I had heard from Dick. It meant a lot to me that we had so many good friends who cared about us, but I felt like I was spending too much time on the phone and not enough with Clint and Tyler, so I tried to keep the calls brief.

I busied myself doing what I always did when I got scared: I cooked elaborate meals, baked cookies, cleaned closets, mopped floors—anything to occupy my mind. It was my way of hunkering down, and our house was the cleanest it had been in months. It's amazing what you can accomplish with some nervous energy.

On the night of January 16, while I was making a chicken-and-broccoli casserole, all hell broke loose as the United States began bombing Baghdad. Gail called me and said, "Put the news on—it's started!"

And just like that, on the six o'clock news, Operation Desert Storm officially began. I told the boys there was no need to worry, because it didn't look like the Army was involved yet—it was the Air Force doing the bombing—but when I tucked them in that night, they each had some concerns that somehow the war might change our lives.

Tyler asked me, "Will we have school tomorrow? And what about basketball practice?"

I reassured both boys that the war would not affect things for us at Fort Campbell, but when I went to bed that night, I had a nagging feeling that Dick was involved in the initial strikes; I just didn't know how.

I would find out later that at approximately 0237 hours on January 17, 1991, eight Apache helicopters from the 101st Airborne Division flew deep into Iraq and destroyed all the early-warning radar sites leading into Baghdad. Task Force Normandy opened an air corridor that allowed the Air Force to fly into Baghdad undetected. Dick and his Apaches fired the first shots of the war.

The next morning, I waited until the boys left for school before I put the news on. As I watched the Pentagon briefing, my ears perked up the minute I heard General Colin Powell mention something about Apache helicopters. I wasn't sure exactly what he said, but then the phone started ringing. First it was Dick's parents, then mine, and then a host of other calls from so many people, and everyone was saying they had heard something about Apaches from the 101st Airborne Division going into Baghdad before the Air Force began the bombing. I told them I had heard the same thing but wasn't sure what it meant.

When the phone rang at noon, I was completely surprised to hear Dick's breathless voice. I had never dreamed he would call me so soon.

"I'm fine, Vicki, and all my pilots are fine. We're back at King Fahd Airport. All is well."

Somehow I just knew that he was grinning from ear to ear.

"I'm so glad to hear your voice! I've been worried because I heard on the news something about Apache helicopters from the 101st being involved in last night's bombing."

"I cannot confirm or deny anything. But I will tell you I am so proud of my pilots. We flew over thirteen hours and 'it' was great!"

"You sound so official!"

"I'll try to call again, but I didn't want you to worry about me."

"Whatever you did, I am so proud of you!"

Then a friend, Lynn Carden, called and said she had just talked to her husband, who told her to call me and tell me, "Dick Cody just made history."

"Vicki, those were his exact words," she said.

When the boys came home from school, I relayed what I knew, basically what had been on the news and in the paper. Since there was only one Apache battalion in the 101st, I was pretty sure it was Dick's that had flown into Iraq; I just didn't know to what extent. A few days later, an article appeared in the Nashville *Tennessean* newspaper that said the same thing I had been hearing—"Apache helicopters from the 101st fired the first shots of the war"—but made no mention of Dick's name or his unit. The following week at our commanders' wives meeting, our brigade commander's wife told the group, "Dick Cody fired the first shots of the war." That was all she said, but it was the first time I had actually heard Dick's name in connection with the mission. I thought my heart would burst with pride, but I would have to wait until Dick got home to hear all the details of Task Force Normandy.

We went from the excitement of the initial stages of the war, thinking that it put us that much closer to the end and our husbands' returning, to the doldrums of a four-week air campaign. We all knew that the 101st Airborne Division would not return until after a ground war, so we found ourselves anxiously anticipating that, just to get it over with. We tried to stay busy, but with no communication with our husbands during that time, we had a hard time not worrying. We wives counted on one another more than ever.

The highlight of February was First Lady Barbara Bush's visit to Fort Campbell. She came to show her support and to rally our families. I was selected to be part of a small group of spouses who got to meet with her privately, before the rally. I had never met a First Lady before, so that in itself was mind-blowing to me. We chatted nervously while we waited in a room at Campbell Army Airfield Base Operations for her arrival. I had no idea what to expect, but when Barbara Bush, wife of the president of the United States, walked into the room, my eyes filled with tears—something that happened frequently that year.

We sat in a circle of chairs, and she was like a grandmother, very sincere, when she asked the group if there was anything she could do for us. Someone immediately asked if she knew when the ground war was going to start. We all laughed, including Barbara. It broke the ice.

She went around the circle, asking each of us to tell who we were and what our spouse did, things of that nature. She was gracious and she listened. She posed with each of us for a photo, and as she put her arm around me, I thought, *In this moment, she seems to genuinely care about each of us, out of all the millions of people in our country.* I will never forget that. I am grinning from ear to ear in that photo. I wrote every detail to Dick, but it took a while for the letter to get to him because the ground war began the very next day.

The actual ground war, just one hundred hours long, was short by any standard, but, amid news coverage of every move the 101st Airborne Division made and talk of the Apache helicopters leading the way for the largest and longest air assault in military history, I had a hard time remaining calm. And there was always the threat of chemical weapons being used against our soldiers. Even after the president declared the war over, Dick's unit was still in Iraq, providing cover for the infantry units.

Those weeks after the end of the war were actually more stressful than any other time. It was mid-March before I heard from Dick. It was a short phone call, and he sounded exhausted, but it meant the world to me.

"We're all fine, Vick. I've been working with Tommy Greco and his battalion, and we're trying to finish things up here. It's still dangerous, but I think the worst is over. My guys have been doing great. If I can keep them safe a little bit longer, I can bring them all home."

"I've been so worried. You have no idea how much news coverage we've seen. We would be better off not knowing everything that goes on."

He went on to say that if all went well, he and his soldiers might be returning in April. That was all I needed to hear.

April 1 was a psychological milestone for Clint, Tyler, and me because it meant we were almost through the deployment. But we were all about to find out that the redeployment phase was every bit as stressful as the deployment. Everyone wanted their soldier home and wanted to know when that would happen. The rumors ran rampant, and everyone turned to me for answers. I felt as if I spent every waking minute on the phone with concerned family members, not just spouses but also parents and grandparents. What I wouldn't have given for e-mail back then! It would have made my life so much easier.

★ ★ ★

There are things that we carry with us throughout our lives—a thought, a conversation, a moment, a person or place, an experience—that, for whatever reason, stay with us. There are things from that year that I carry with me even now, that are so clear to me it seems as if they happened only yesterday: a beautiful Saturday morning in April, the boys and I, Dick's parents, his two brothers and a sister, standing in a crowd of hundreds of family members, all of us on our tiptoes, scanning the horizon for that first glimpse of the plane carrying our loved ones home from combat; flags waving; a band playing; people cheering. I had never felt such excitement and anticipation, and I will never forget the thrill of seeing Dick emerge from the huge plane, watching Clint and Tyler run up to hug him, the butterflies in my stomach, feeling like a sixteen-year-old when he kissed me.

Dick had never looked more handsome to me than he did that day. My love was mixed in with the pride that I felt for him. It was the greatest feeling in the world.

The local news was there to interview Dick about his unit and their mission. I was pacing up and down while the boys were trying to contain their nervous energy. I understood the significance of what Dick had done, but I resented the media for taking him away from us just after we had greeted him. I couldn't wait to get my hands on him. Finally, the interviews were over and we family members got back on the bus to head over to the battalion area. The soldiers had to turn in their weapons before we could be with them, and it was like torture to be separated again.

When we pulled into our driveway, Dick was surprised to see the white Corvette with a big yellow ribbon tied around it and "welcome home" written on its windows. After having spotted it at the family Chevrolet dealership, I had decided he deserved a Corvette when he got home. It was used but in great condition, and he was as excited as a little kid when he saw it.

We waited another week and then loaded up my big Caprice Classic with all of our ski gear and began the two-to-three-day drive to A-Basin and Keystone, Colorado—just the four of us, and nothing but the open road in front of us and the best spring skiing in the world awaiting us. We had much to be thankful for and so much ahead of us. We talked nonstop, sometimes taking turns and at times all four of us vying for center stage. More details about Dick's mission emerged during our cross-country journey, and I was amazed at the historic significance of what he and his guys had done.

Skiing in the Rockies was just what we needed: warm, sunny days, the most brilliant blue skies, and tons of packed powder. Most evenings after sunset, Dick took a cigar and went out for a walk by himself. I sensed he needed some space and alone time, but I didn't mind—I was used to being on my own.

I would like to tell you that it was a smooth transition, that we didn't miss a beat, that it was pure bliss and like something out of a movie, but that is not reality. We definitely went through a honeymoon phase and had the best sex we'd had in years, and because the stress of worrying about Dick was over, I went to bed every night feeling peaceful and content. But, as with all the other times we had been separated, we were a little out of sync.

PS: In spite of everything that happened back then—the fear, the worries, the loneliness, the reunion blues, and so on—I remember the good times that came out of it: how close the boys and I became and what good company they were for me; the fun the three of us had by ourselves and with our fellow Army families. I will never forget the undying support of our parents, siblings, and close friends. Above all, what stays with me most is the love that Dick and I shared. When I read the letters that Dick wrote me, I am struck by the fact that in every single one he told me how much he loved me and how proud he was of me. I keep the letters in a box, tied in bundles with red, white, and blue ribbons, so I can read them whenever I want to. I look at his handwriting, and suddenly I've been transported back in time. I don't believe phone calls and e-mails can do the same thing, and I don't believe many couples today express themselves like that nearly enough.

Thoughts on Reintegration

Separations are a way of life for Army couples and their families. Soldiers go far from home to do what they do, and not just across town or to another city, but oftentimes halfway around the world and to a very dangerous location, for months at a time. It's just one of the realities of Army life that, over time, I learned to deal with. Still, my separations from Dick were like big chunks of time missing in our marriage. Each time we were separated, it made us work that much harder at our relationship, at communicating with each other, and at staying connected. Each time we were pulled apart, it was entirely up to us to put us back together.

The length and the nature of Dick's deployments often determined how difficult or easy the reintegration period was. I learned from each reunion, and just when I thought I had it all figured out or what to expect, something would upset my sense of order. In the end, there was no rhyme or reason to our reunions; each one was unique.

Dick's very first deployment, to Guam, before we were married, was more of a big inconvenience. I didn't worry about something happening to him; I just plain missed him. So when he returned and we were able to get married, all was well.

When Dick returned from his short tour in Korea, we went through a definite period of adjustment. Unlike the times when it was just the two of us, having a baby changed the dynamics. Dick needed to feel like he was a part of the family again, not an outsider, and I had to work on giving up a little control of Clint, as I took my mothering very seriously. Just as I wanted to be in Dick's world, I had to let him into mine and Clint's. It took a few weeks of communicating and verbalizing our feelings to each other to get us back on track.

When Dick left us in Savannah to go off on that special-operations deal, I worried about him almost every day. I lived with a lot of fear and stress during that relatively short period of time, but somehow that reintegration was surprisingly easy. When he returned that time, I was just plain relieved, and the boys were too young for that deployment to have impacted them.

The Gulf War presented us with a whole other set of issues. It was a lengthy, dangerous deployment, and before Dick's unit returned, our battalion was assigned a counselor to help prepare us for the reunion and reintegration. It was all pretty basic information; most of it made sense, based on what I had already experienced with Dick, and I even learned a few new things to keep in mind. Our husbands went through similar briefings in the combat zone. The battalion chaplains talked to all the soldiers and the leadership about what to expect and what to do and not do when they returned home. Dick and his command sergeant major spent the first few weeks after their return trying to identify any soldier who was having a rough time reintegrating or anyone having problems at home. They even set aside some vacant rooms in the barracks in case a soldier needed to cool off.

Clint and Tyler were just so glad to have their dad home that they didn't seem to miss a beat. Maybe because of their ages (twelve and ten) and their ability to comprehend what their dad had done, to them it was over now that he was home safe. They didn't exhibit any weird behavior and didn't test us in any way. They were busy with their friends, school, and sports. They did enjoy their dad's recent fame and even had friends ask them for their dad's autograph.

Those first weeks after Desert Storm were, in many ways, idyllic. When you've worried about your loved one for nine months and lived with stress and fear for much of that time, it's a huge relief to put all that aside. Plus, something about Dick's having been gone for so long and the added danger of the mission made for very intense and exciting sex—we were like young kids again. Our communication was good, and we got caught up on everything during our trip to Colorado. We had little power struggles over day-to-day things—usually when I didn't want to give up control of something because I was used to being in charge—but no significant hurdles.

So I was caught off guard when I realized Dick had broken a

promise to me, which triggered a rage in me that I did not know I possessed. He had promised to quit smoking and chewing tobacco (I didn't mind an occasional cigar) when he returned from the deployment. He always did those things sporadically, but more so during deployments. I thought it was an annoying habit that he could easily stop, but when I dropped by his office one day and through thick smoke saw a lit cigarette in his hand and a wad of chew in his cheek, I went from adoration to pure hatred in a split second. I couldn't say a word, because a journalist was interviewing him, so I quietly backed out of the room and ran to my car. In that moment, I wanted to leave him. All the way home I was thinking, *How dare he! He didn't even try to keep his promise! I've worried so much about him all these months, and then he comes home and continues to do something to jeopardize his health!*

I knew I had to do something with my anger, so when I got home, I packed his duffel bag with some essentials and put it by the front door. He came home as soon as he finished his interview because he had seen the look on my face. I told him to go to the barracks until he was ready to quit smoking. He knew I was serious. By the time the boys got back from school, I calmly told them that their dad was going to spend the night in the barracks because he hadn't quit smoking. Completely on their own, they made NO SMOKING signs on construction paper and taped them on every door in the house. I was so proud of my sons for taking a stand with me.

Later, after I had calmed down, Dick and I talked. I told him everything I had been thinking. I realized I wasn't just angry about his broken promise; it was a buildup of nine months of stress and worrying about him. I felt he had no regard for himself or for the boys and me. He begged and pleaded and promised to quit, so I let him come back home. The issue was resolved for the time being but would persist on and off for years.

That argument had as much to do with Dick's reintegration as it did with his smoking. I came to realize that with each reintegration, we had to have at least one big blowup in order to clear the air and move on. It happened every time; some were worse than others.

Also during that time, we experienced the emotional upheaval of Dick's giving up command of his battalion and moving. We argued about that, too, because he had been selecected for a command in the

special operations community. Again, I felt as if Dick had come home
safe, only to go right back into another dangerous job. He didn't see
things the way I did. It was a bone of contention with no easy com-
promise, and it wasn't until we were all settled in the next place and
I accepted what his job was that we could begin to feel normal again.
All in all, that reintegration took us a couple of months to get through.
After that one, it always seemed easier.

The weird thing about reunions and reintegration is the fact that
two different dynamics are at play at the same time, creating a conflict
of emotions. You're riding high on the actual homecoming, but then, at
any given time, something can trigger emotional outrage and bring you
down. In that instant, you hate the very person you love, the person
you just welcomed home. You think you're going to get divorced over
who gets control of the checkbook or the TV remote, or for not quitting a bad habit, and then you feel guilty for even feeling that way. As
we got older and more mature, we learned just to ride it out, knowing
that it would all pass in time.

Dick did not experience—and we were luckier than most in this
respect—any lasting psychological effects related to actual combat.
Maybe because he was a pilot and so much of what he did was from
up in the air, thus distancing him from the death and destruction on
the ground, he didn't experience what soldiers on the ground do. There
were times during Desert Storm when he did see the effects of his missiles and guns; he told me about flying low over the Highway of Death
at the end of the war and what that looked like. He showed me some
of the footage of Task Force Normandy from the video gun tapes on
his Apache, but to me, it was blurry. Maybe I didn't want to know what
I was looking at. Dick seemed unemotional as he pointed out to me,
"When bullets and missiles are coming at you, you will do whatever it
takes not to get shot down."

By the time Clint and Tyler were flying Apaches in combat, they
said pretty much what Dick had said: "You're firing at a target on
the ground, and you try not to think what that target is." There is no
emotional attachment when they pull the trigger. (The trigger being a
button on the cyclic.)

I know that each of them has seen things, and has had to do whatever it took not only to keep themselves safe but to protect the soldiers

on the ground—because, after all, that's what Apache pilots do in combat. Maybe being in their cockpits has shielded them from some of the trauma. Like their dad, my sons have had buddies die in helicopter crashes and in combat and those images will be with them for life.

We've been luckier than most families who have been through the ups and downs of Army life, and I know that not everyone gets off as easily as we have. When it comes to reintegration and my family, I've adopted an attitude similar to Dick and the boys: I will do whatever it takes to get through it.

13

The Best Year of Our Lives

We left Fort Campbell in the summer of 1991 after tearful good-byes to the unit and the people who had become our family. Fort Campbell felt like home to us, and none of us wanted to leave. Just eight days after giving up command of his Apache battalion, Dick took command of a Special Missions Unit (SMU). We had had lengthy discussions and gone around and around about his taking the job, but there was still no easy answer.

"Vicki, I can't really turn this down. If I do, I might as well get out of the Army. Do you want me to do that?"

"Of course not! I just wanted you to take a nice, safe job like everyone else we know. Why do you always have to have these high-stress, dangerous jobs? Aren't you tired? *I'm* tired!"

"This job is what I do. It's the kinds of missions that I just did in Desert Storm. As the commander, I won't be going on all the missions, but I will have to travel and it is highly classified. I won't be able to tell you everything. And you can't talk about anything."

"That's impossible for me, Dick!"

Still, when he asked me to go with him to look at houses, I went, and when he said, "Trust me, Vick," I did.

That first year of Dick's new command, he was gone 200 of 365 days. I had few friends and lived in a civilian neighborhood where I didn't know my neighbors. I was lonely after living on an Army post surrounded by other Army families; it forced the boys and me to live outside our comfort zone. I had to get used to answering people's questions about Dick's comings and goings and questions, like "If he's in the Army, why doesn't he wear a uniform?" I learned to keep my answers simple. The less said, the better, and the story I stuck with was that he was in "research and development." I found things to do; I got involved in the boys' schools and made a life for us. There were some advantages to Dick being in a Special Missions Unit; when he wasn't traveling, he worked decent hours and was able to attend the boys' sporting events and even helped coach them. The boys were old enough to enjoy the same movies as we did, so we spent Friday nights with them and had a date night every Saturday.

After all the time that we had just spent apart, I was more determined than ever not to let Dick's new job or the US Army come between us, but that took patience, trust, and effort. Because I was not working, I had time to devote to my husband and the boys. I believed my job was to be there for Clint and Tyler during what I thought was a very important time: puberty, middle school, and high school. I was the constant in their lives. I was the constant in Dick's life, too.

That assignment was not my favorite, by any means, but I made it work. When given a choice to be happy or sad, I choose happy every time. I greatly enjoyed Clint and Tyler's company, and Dick and I were both proud of what fine young men they were becoming and of how well they adjusted to new surroundings and public schools. I found my niche in writing, too: I wrote a children's book based on Clint and Tyler's experiences in Army life. I didn't know where it would lead me, but it was something that I felt compelled to do and that occupied me when Dick was gone.

When that tour of duty was over, there were no tears shed and no foot dragging on my part. We were on our way to the US Army War College in Carlisle Barracks, Pennsylvania. It was billed as what would be the "best year of your lives" by everyone who had ever been there. After two back-to-back commands and four years of pretty stressful living, we were all more than ready to let the games begin.

Nestled in the Cumberland Valley of South-Central Pennsylvania, at the edge of the Shenandoah Mountains, just south of Harrisburg and just west of the battlefields of Gettysburg, is the small town of Carlisle. Carlisle Barracks is home to the US Army War College, established in 1901 to prepare selected senior officers for high command and staff positions. The first class had just nine officers. Dick's class, 1994, had 304 students, including officers from all the services, Department of the Army civilians, and international fellows from thirty-six different countries.

For the next year while Dick went to school, the four of us would experience Army life at its best. We would be surrounded by other Army families, reunite with old friends, and make new ones. And, for the first time in a long time, we would have no deployments, no separations, and no stress.

We moved into one of the little white, cottage-type houses in what was nicknamed Smurf Village (because the houses were so small). Imagine my surprise when I found out not only that my old best friend Sarah Pearce was there at Carlisle but also that she, her husband, Bill, and their three kids lived just around the corner from our house! I walked over to see her that first day, and we cried as we hugged, long-lost friends who had seen each other only twice in eleven years. We could not have planned it better. My old friend from flight school, Eleanor Young, whom I hadn't seen in thirteen years, was there as well. Every day, someone else moved into the neighborhood; our old friends from Fort Leavenworth, George and Marilyn Higgins, ended up right down the street. Literally overnight, I went from having practically no friends in our previous assignment to having more of them than I could handle.

There were lots of teens on post, so the boys had instant companions, too. Army brats, like their parents, learn to make friends quickly. It was something we had all missed while living in a civilian neighborhood.

Like everything in the Army, there was a method to the War College, not just to educate and prepare officers but also to build cohesive teams. There were all kinds of planned activities and sports events that facilitated bonds and friendships that would be beneficial later on, when the students were serving together in key command and staff positions.

Campus life was fun for us, simple and easy. We loved the quaint feel of the post and the small town of Carlisle. It was the farthest north we had lived since we'd gotten married, and we enjoyed our close proximity to the big cities of the East Coast and to our families in Vermont. With our plane parked at the Carlisle Airport, we could fly anywhere we wanted and we made lots of trips that summer and fall. When the leaves changed and the weather turned cold, we were reminded of our childhoods. We bought a season pass to the Roundtop ski area, just twenty minutes from Carlisle, and prayed for lots of snow.

The War College offered classes and seminars for the spouses that were designed to prepare us for our husbands' next commands and/or staff positions, and I attended as many of those as I could. Dick's own class schedule was easy compared with the jobs he'd had for the past ten years, and he signed up for every sport and extracurricular activity available.

Shortly after school began, I noticed a role reversal between Dick and the boys. Now that their dad was a student, just like they were, they checked up on him, and I had to chuckle when I heard them questioning Dick about his homework. It was good for them to see their dad in a different light besides officer, commander, and leader.

We all felt carefree, but then that fall, two things happened that were reminders of the realities of Army life—realities that we thought we had left behind but that were actually never far from us. First, a helicopter crash in the California desert claimed the life of a young pilot who had worked for Dick in our early years at Fort Campbell. Dick shared a special bond with Phil, and his death was especially difficult for us.

Then, about a week later, on October 3, the news was full of US military operations in Mogadishu, Somalia. We watched in horror as angry mobs dragged dead US soldiers through the streets. We watched footage of Mike Durant's helicopter going down, his capture, and eventually his rescue. That was when Dick confided in me some of the things in which he had been involved over the previous two years on the "black" side. Dick knew many of the pilots involved and many of the ground troops, and it was agonizing for him to watch all that on TV, from the sidelines.

On the upside, we got plenty of snow that winter and skied every possible Saturday with the boys. Dick figured out a way to not have any classes on Friday afternoons so he and I could go skiing. It was just like old times.

Basketball took up the rest of Dick's and the boys' free time. Dick was either playing or coaching every night of the week. The boys were on the post's all-star traveling team, which Dick coached, and we spent many fun Saturdays traveling to military installations throughout the mid-Atlantic region, from New Jersey to Washington, DC.

Clint was a junior in high school when we began talking about where he wanted to go for college. Since he'd been a small boy, helicopters, airplanes, and everything else his dad did had fascinated him. Both boys had spent so much of their childhood hanging around Dick's hangars at the various airfields and being surrounded by soldiers and pilots, and all the time we had spent as a family taking trips in our plane, had made flying a way of life for all of us. So it was natural to think that one or both boys would choose to go into the military.

"I want to try to get into West Point and have a career in the Army, just like Dad," Clint told us. "Someday I want to fly helicopters."

Dick and I were encouraging and supportive but at the same time tried not to sway Clint in any way. Entering the military had to be his decision and his alone. Secretly, Dick and I were thrilled at the prospect of either or both of our boys wanting to go into the Army, but more than that we just wanted them to choose careers that would give them the same satisfaction that their dad had experienced in his.

★ ★ ★

As the snow melted that winter, excitement hung in the air as everyone began to talk about where they were going next. Our precious time at the War College was coming to a close, and Dick had orders for Fort Hood, Texas.

In a small, private ceremony after graduation, Dick was promoted to the rank of colonel. I thought, *It seems like I just pinned on his oak leaf for lieutenant colonel; things are moving fast.*

My girlfriends and I exchanged lots of tearful good-byes, since we were all going in different directions. As I watched the boys say their good-byes to their friends, it was heartwarming to see teenagers hugging each other and crying. They were old enough to understand one of the hardships of Army life: making wonderful friends, only to leave them. The US Army War College had definitely lived up to its reputation. It really was the best year ever.

PS: Our year at Carlisle gave us a much-needed break. It came at a perfect time for all of us. When we left there, we would all get busy again—Dick would have his new job as a brigade commander, I would resume my duties as a commander's wife, Clint would go off to college in another year, and Tyler would be busy with his last years of high school. But for that year, we ate dinner together every night, we went to church every Sunday, we studied, we played, and, most of all, we had fun as a family. Many civilians may take that for granted, but for Army families, it's something to be cherished.

West Point Homecoming, 1971
courtesy United States Military Academy

"The Popsicle Man" handing out popsicles to the kids in Tent City
Operation New Life, Guam 1975, courtesy Stars and Stripes

Our wedding, August 30, 1975
courtesy Marty LaValley

Me, very pregnant, pinning on Dick's flight wings
Fort Rucker, AL, 1977, courtesy Janice Cody

Clint and Tyler visiting their dad on the flight line,
HAAF, Savannah 1981, courtesy Vicki Cody

Saying good-bye at Campbell Army Airfield as Dick leaves for Egypt
July 1985, courtesy US Army

Dick by his Apache, Operation Desert Shield,
Saudi Arabia, 1990, courtesy Dick Cody

Dick with his Soldiers in Iraq, Operation Desert Storm,
Feb. 1991, courtesy Dick Cody

Dick's "Welcome Home"—Fort Campbell, KY, April 1991
courtesy Vicki Cody

Dick's parents, me, and the boys...and Dick's new corvette
courtesy Vicki Cody

Dick teaching his sons the art of boot shining, the night before
ROTC Advanced Camp, 1998, courtesy Vicki Cody

Pinning on Clint's wings at Fort Rucker, AL 2001, courtesy US Army

Pinning on Tyler's wings at Fort Rucker, AL 2003
courtesy US Army

A very special day; President and Mrs. Bush visit
Fort Campbell, KY, Nov. 2001, Courtesy US Army

Dick awarding Clint his first Air Medal in Afghanistan, 2002
courtesy US Army

Saying good-bye to Clint as he leaves for Iraq
Feb. 2004, courtesy Vicki Cody

Tyler's first deployment to Iraq, Sept.2003, courtesy Vicki Cody

The boys in front of their Apache helicopter
Iraq 2004, courtesy Clint Cody

Brooke and I welcoming Tyler home in Feb, 2004, courtesy Vicki Cody

My mom welcoming her grandsons home from Iraq
Feb. 2004, courtesy Vicki Cody

Clint and Tyler pinning on Dick's 4 stars at the Pentagon
July 2004, courtesy US Army

Dick being sworn in as the Army's 31st Vice Chief of Staff
Courtesy US Army

Speaking to the spouses at Fort Campbell, KY, 2002
courtesy Officers' Wives Club

Me with Soldiers at the National Training Center, Fort Irwin, CA
July 4, 2007, courtesy US Army

Me with President Bush outside the Oval Office (the sharpie pen incident!) April 2007, courtesy White House photo

At the Indianapolis 500 in 2006 with the Judds; Wynonna on my left, Naomi on Dick's right, courtesy Vicki Cody.

Brooke and Austin welcome Tyler home from Iraq in 2006
courtesy Vicki Cody

Kimberly and Connor welcome Clint home from Afghanistan in 2013
Courtesy Lauren Shrader

Dick's last flight in the Apache, Fort Rucker, AL
July 2008, courtesy US Army

Dick and Tyler after their flight, courtesy US Army

Dick's retirement ceremony, Aug. 2008
"Trooping the Line" for the last time

What a moment for both of us! Courtesy US Army

Our family today 2014
Left to right: Kimberly holding one-day-old Dillon,
Clint, me, Dick, Brooke, Tyler
Front: Connor, Zachary, and Austin

14

Welcome to Texas, Y'all!

Dick had prepositioned the plane earlier that spring, so we were two cars, loaded with everything we could squeeze into the trunks, two teenage boys, and Sandy the cat, on the two-day journey to Texas. As we headed west, the heat became more stifling, and once we were on I-35 south of Dallas, there wasn't much to look at for the last three hours of the trip. It was so flat, so brown, so vast—just miles and miles of endless highway ahead of us. And whoever said it would be dry heat was just plain wrong; it was sticky, humid, and scorching. By the time we made our last pit stop, at a Love's truck stop outside Waco, I swear I was talking with a twang.

As we drove down Rancier Drive toward the post, we passed pawnshops, gun shops, 7-Elevens, check-cashing joints, a drive-through margarita bar, tattoo parlors, topless clubs, lingerie shops, and cowboy-boot stores. It looked pretty much the same as route 41A outside Fort Campbell, but with a Western flavor. I knew very little about Killeen and central Texas, but for some reason, I was excited; we all were. I had a feeling that it was going to be a great assignment.

We pulled into the guest house that Fourth of July weekend, along with all the other Army families who were coming or going; the parking lot was full of U-Hauls, boat trailers, and campers. We were lucky to have a room at all at the overbooked guest house, but our one-bedroom, one-bathroom suite got crowded really fast, as the boys argued over the pullout couch and the four of us constantly bumped into each other because it was too hot to do anything outside.

Fort Hood, the second-largest Army post in the United States, with approximately forty-five-thousand soldiers, seemed daunting at first.

Those early days, I didn't see how such a huge post could ever feel like home. There were not one but two divisions, and the III Corps headquarters. The rows of tanks, Bradley fighting vehicles, and heavily armored trucks went on for miles. I could feel a lesson coming on: it was time to learn all about tanks, air cavalry, and armor divisions.

The 1st Cavalry Division, called the First Team, has a long and storied history that dates back to the battle of the Little Bighorn. Dick took command of the aviation brigade in a unique ceremony with all the leadership, including Dick, on horseback, and a cavalry charge at the end. Our parents had flown in from Vermont, and we were all blown away by the event and the rituals of the cavalry. Dick would have to learn a whole other way of training and tactics, but he was always up for a new challenge.

I was surprised at how quickly we all settled in, given the fact that we had never even been to Texas before. It had not been on our wish list, yet it was a welcome and pleasant surprise. We embraced the unexpectedness of a new unit and a new part of the country. The boys adjusted to their new surroundings, which gave me peace of mind. Killeen High School was huge, so I was glad they had each other; they were, too. I noticed even more closeness between them as they became old enough to realize they could count on each other, especially when they started a new school. They both made the tennis team, and in such a big school, one where football clearly ruled, the tennis team gave them a place to belong and a way to make friends.

Dick and I immediately fell into the rhythm of the division and our brigade and made friends, too. Everyone made us feel welcome, especially the division commander, Major General Shinseki, and his wife. At the division off-site conference later that summer, we got to know our fellow brigade commanders and their wives and felt the same camaraderie that we had come to love about Army life.

Dick was in his element, doing his innovative, hands-on, tough-yet-caring type of leadership. He was involved with every aspect of the unit and his soldiers' lives. He put his personal touch on everything, from giving every soldier a handwritten birthday card to turning wrenches in the hangar with his crew chiefs.

I was in my element, too. I loved getting to know everyone in our brigade, coaching and mentoring the battalion commanders' wives and the younger spouses in the unit, and doing what Dick and I loved doing: creating a team and family atmosphere.

During that time, Dick and I learned to balance and juggle even more. The boys weren't little kids anymore, and while we had certain freedoms because they were older, we also had other, new obligations. Clint was a senior in high school, and there were a lot of extra activities that went along with that. Still, I was as determined as ever to participate in all of the boys' school and sports activities; I didn't want to miss a thing. The eighteen years we have with our kids go by all too quickly, and I didn't want any regrets when the boys went off to college. There were times when I had to choose Clint's tennis match over Tyler's, and times when I had to choose my boys over my Army wife duties. Dick managed to attend all the important events and made sure the boys' tennis matches were on his brigade calendar.

Before we knew it, Clint's senior year was coming to an end. When he found out he had not gotten into West Point, Dick and I sat him down so we could come up with a plan B.

"Dad," he said, "I just want to be in a corps of cadets, get commissioned in the Army, and eventually go to flight school. I want to be a pilot, just like you. Tell me how to do that if I can't go to the academy."

An old friend and Dick's former boss, Colonel Seth Hudgins, who worked at West Point, had in fact called us with the news about Clint. He recommended New Mexico Military Institute (NMMI). Dick told Clint about the school, which has an excellent reputation for academics, military tactics, and its corps of cadets, and Clint liked the idea.

Dick and Clint made the quick flight to Roswell, and both of them loved the school. With that settled, we began to make plans for Clint to attend NMMI at the end of the summer. While he wanted to do everything just like his dad, his journey would take a different turn. It was an important life lesson for all of us: we don't always get what we want, and sometimes we have to change course.

I tried to live in the moment and not think ahead to Clint's leaving home, but time was slipping away. He turned eighteen, graduated from high school, and got his first paying job at Patriot Pontiac/Chevrolet in Killeen. Tyler mowed lawns to earn spending money and continued to beg us for a puppy for his sixteenth birthday—specifically, a chocolate Lab that he could name Barkley, after his hero, Charles Barkley.

We finally found the perfect one through a friend, and that was how Barkley came to our family. While he was a lot of work in the beginning, as puppies are, it was a good distraction for me as I mentally prepared myself for Clint's going off to college. And Barkley turned out to be the best dog that ever lived.

★ ★ ★

Taking Clint out to NMMI was truly an emotional event for our family. I remember the three of us in our room at the Roswell Inn the night before we signed him in; I was doing the whole worrying-mom thing, obsessing about everything, afraid that there was something important that I had forgotten to teach him, some detail I had missed. It was like cramming the night before a big exam—the biggest one of my life. While I was doing my obsessing, I could hear Dick giving Clint the mother of all safety briefings. Dick, in his own way, was feeling just like I was, and his anxiety manifested itself in a series of safety briefings about everything imaginable. I wanted so very much to stop time; I wanted to pack up and for the three of us head back to Fort Hood and our nice life. I kept thinking, *Why do I want to leave my kid here, out in the middle of nowhere, and have no contact for the next three weeks while they shave his head, make him do push-ups, probably starve him, deprive him of sleep, and God knows what else?* It was so hard to let go. It wasn't just leaving him at college; it was the beginning of his Army career. Like most parents, Dick and I wondered if we had done everything to prepare our son, not just for college but also for the Army and that big world out there.

We had flown our plane, so, with our headsets on during the peaceful flight home, I allowed myself a good cry and collected my thoughts. It seemed like only yesterday I was holding Baby Clint and waving good-bye to Dick as he left for Korea. Those eighteen years went by way too fast.

I turned to Dick and asked, "Will he be okay? What do you think they'll do to him the first days and weeks?" I had met Dick after his first year at West Point, so I had little frame of reference for what life is like the first weeks in a military school.

"It will be tough the first week or so. But Clint has a big advantage

I didn't have when I went off to West Point. I knew nothing about the Army and the military. I was just a naive kid from small-town Vermont who had good athletic abilities. Clint has grown up around the Army; he's used to seeing the discipline, the structure, the uniforms; he's watched me with my soldiers; and he's lived all over the country and overseas. He's had to make new friends and adjust to new surroundings on a continual basis his whole life. He's going to be just fine."

"You're right—I hadn't thought about all of that. I think we did a good job raising him. He's a great kid with a great sense of humor, he's smart, and he knows exactly what he wants. I'm just nervous for him. I miss him already."

"I know, Vick; me too. He'll be okay—trust me."

★ ★ ★

After three grueling weeks with no contact, Clint was finally able to call. It was monumental.

"I'm not going to lie—there were times in the first days that I doubted my decision to come here, but then, all of a sudden, I started to get it. I like it, in a weird way. And I met a kid from Killeen and we have the same sense of humor. We have fun and make each other laugh," he told us.

"That's so good to hear, Clint. We knew you would be okay. We're so proud of you! We'll be there for your first parade." We hung up the phone with relief. Clint was not only okay but already on his way to realizing his dream. It was all any parent could ask for. We counted the days until we could go visit him.

★ ★ ★

Dick and I enjoyed everything about our time in Texas, from spending time with our peers and fellow brigade commanders and their wives to sightseeing and exploring in Austin and San Antonio. For the next two years, I wore every variation of denim and khaki, Western boots, and Brighton silver jewelry. We two-stepped and line-danced and consumed enough barbecue brisket, beans, potato salad, and sweet tea to last a lifetime. We went to fish fries in Copperas Cove, boat rides on Belton Lake, and the annual Christmas-tree lighting in the little town of Salado. We ate chicken-fried steak in Killeen, Mexican food in Austin, and the best German schnitzel in New Braunfels. We witnessed the beauty of springtime in the hill country, where brilliant wildflowers and bluebonnets painted the fields along the highways. We strolled the River Walk in San Antonio, visited the Alamo, and, while attending the boys' numerous tennis matches, learned the back roads and quaint little towns of central Texas. Texas was so diverse and so much more than just cowboys and football. Just as the saying goes, it really was a whole other world.

We visited Clint as often as possible and loved watching him march in the parades. He seemed happy and more mature and confident with each visit. He told us that his years as an Army brat had prepared him for military school. Some of the things that other kids struggled with were just not an issue for him, and not a lot intimidated him.

And now that Clint was gone, I was able to devote all my free time to Tyler, who, like his older brother, was growing into a fine young man. He did really well in school and tennis and made some good friends. He was polite and had a great attitude, and he was fun to be around. He was confident and strong willed, but he didn't really test us in any way; he didn't do things that many kids his age were doing.

Dick and I also began a new chapter in our marriage as we celebrated our twentieth anniversary. We went to Jamaica on our first vacation without our boys. As we reflected on all our years together, we were struck both by how quickly the time had gone and by the fact that we still had the magic that we had when we first met. We were happier and stronger than ever, and we did not take that for granted.

"Do you realize how blessed we are, Dick?" I asked him. "Back when we got married, I never dreamed I would love Army life the way I do. And our sons . . . how did we get so lucky?"

"I know, Vick. Clint and Tyler are so squared away, and that's all your doing. You did a great job with them."

"They got the best from each of us, but you're the biggest influence on them. They want to be just like you!"

★ ★ ★

Our two years in Texas were coming to an end, and it was time for Dick to give up command of his brigade. I had not expected to fall in love with the state, so the thought of leaving was difficult, although we were heading back to Fort Campbell, which made it somewhat easier. But the dilemma we faced was moving Tyler his senior year. Naturally, he wanted to stay in Killeen and graduate with his class and friends. We hated to move him, but Dick and I stood together on our decision: we would not separate our family. Clint had decided to stay on at NMMI for a second year and then transfer to a four-year university.

We left Texas with heavy hearts, an appreciation for a state and its people, and a slight drawl. It was hard saying good-bye to the people in our brigade. For the first time in years, there had been no helicopter crashes and no real-world deployments. It was such a gratifying experience, and Dick and I were richer for it in many ways.

PS: Texas was every corny cliché I had ever heard, and it lived up to all of them. It was Friday night football like we had never experienced before; it was school pride and Texas pride; it was a place where football players (and cheerleaders, too) were treated like gods; it was a Dairy Queen on every street corner; it was driving all day and never reaching the other side of the state; it was big hair, big jewelry, beauty queens, and prom queens; it was marching bands and drill teams; it was rednecks in big trucks with gun racks; it was a place where kids addressed adults as "sir" and "ma'am," where it was okay to say a prayer before a football game, where people carried their Bible and their gun together, where faith and church were the center of people's lives, where little kids dreamed of being football players or cheerleaders. Everything really was bigger in Texas, or maybe you just feel that way after you've lived there for a while. Our friendships and memories for those two years matched the size of Texas, and I can't help but smile when I think of those times.

15

A Time of Transition

In hindsight, I realize that when we left Fort Hood that summer of 1996, we were entering a time of transition. Dick had been selected to command the infamous 160th Special Operations Aviation Regiment (SOAR). It was the very unit that he and Ned had been part of back in 1980 and had helped form up, and that was built around the "little bird" helicopters that Dick had helped build. The unit that he had secretly followed and wanted to be part of since its inception had finally become a reality for him. But that command, more than any other, past or future, proved to be the most challenging that Dick had faced. I would like to tell you that he was the beloved commander he had always been and that all of his proven leadership skills worked, but that was not exactly how it played out. Maybe it was perceptions; after all, Dick had spent much of his career in the "green" Army and was considered an outsider by many in the regiment. Maybe it was the timing; it was just three years after the 160th SOAR had suffered huge losses in the battle of Mogadishu, Somalia—an operation that Dick had not been part of, which, again, made him an outsider. Maybe it was the fact that Dick was put in the position to bring about much-needed changes, a touchy subject for any unit. It could have been any or all of those reasons. And sometimes the very things we want the most just don't live up to our expectations.

Soon after we moved to Fort Campbell and before Dick took command of the 160th SOAR, he had gone down to Fort Rucker to learn to fly the Blackhawk helicopter. He wasn't due home for another week, so I was surprised one afternoon when I pulled into our driveway and saw him sitting on a cooler on our carport. Two thoughts hit me immediately: 1) something was really wrong, and 2) I had forgotten to give him a house key before he left for Fort Rucker. But then I saw the smug look on his face. He was smiling.

"Dick, what are you doing home? Is everything okay? How long have you been waiting?"

"I've been here about an hour." Then he walked up to me and said, "Guess what? I'm on the promotion list for brigadier general! I decided to drive home and surprise you!"

"Are you kidding me? Really? You're on the list?"

"Can you believe it?"

"Oh my God!"

I gave him a huge hug and whispered in his ear, "I've always wanted to sleep with a general!" (I had been saying that to him about every promotion since he'd become a lieutenant colonel.)

As we walked into the house, we immediately began discussing the implications. But then I looked at my watch and said, "Tyler won't be home for at least an hour; we've got the house to ourselves . . . I'm thinking this definitely calls for a celebration."

"I was thinking the same thing," he said, as we walked down the hall to our bedroom.

And so began our time of transition. Dick was committed to commanding the 160th and deferred his promotion for the time being. But soon he would enter the higher levels of Army leadership. The jump from field-grade officer (major to colonel) to the general officer ranks was a big one. We were excited but humbled all at the same time.

Meanwhile, Clint did very well his second year at NMMI, graduated, and got accepted into the Corps of Cadets at Texas A&M. He would be transferring from a school the size of a high school, with approximately nine hundred students, to a huge university with forty-five thousand students, but he had greatly matured in his two years at NMMI and was ready for the next chapter in his life.

Tyler adjusted to a new school and had a good senior year. During what could have been a difficult transition, he amazed us with his flexibility and great attitude, making friends, playing three varsity sports, and doing well in academics. When he graduated, he decided to go to NMMI and follow in his brother's footsteps.

The summer of 1997, both boys went to the ROTC Basic Camp

together. When Dick and I sat in the bleachers at graduation and watched the Pass in Review, it took me a minute to find my boys in that sea of green camouflage, but then I spotted each of them: Tyler, so tall that he stood out, and Clint, with the same gait as his dad. I leaned in and whispered to Dick, "Just look at our boys, so grown up, so much like you." I had a strong feeling that day that they were living their destiny. And when they returned home, Dick and I noticed an even stronger bond between them and a new respect toward each other.

★ ★ ★

Later that summer, we took Tyler to New Mexico to begin a new chapter in his life. It was easier than leaving Clint, because we knew what to expect, but it was still an emotional event for me. Letting go of my youngest signaled a *real* empty nest.

At the end of August, Clint and I set out on a day-and-a-half road trip to Texas A&M University in College Station, Texas. I welcomed the chance to spend some quality time with my oldest son; we hadn't had many opportunities to be alone in the past couple of years. As the boys grew older and I had less time with them, I learned to take advantage of and savor little stolen moments with each of them.

From his very first day on that huge campus, Clint loved everything about being an Aggie in the Corps of Cadets. And within just days, he told me that he had found his "home." Texas A&M would be his proving ground and eventually Tyler's, too. The week that I spent out there I witnessed a school pride that is so unique to Texas A&M. With every "gig 'em" and "howdy" that I was greeted with, I fell more in love with the school. When Dick came to pick me up, he, too, was impressed. We didn't know if it was the Fightin' Texas Aggie Band (the largest military band in the world) or watching the Corps of Cadets in their World War II uniforms, the seniors in jodhpurs and boots, march through the campus; whatever it was, we both agreed that, in all our years in the Army, we had never felt such pride and esprit de corps. We were proud Aggie parents from head to toe.

Now that both boys were in college, as I went from full-time to part-time mom that fall, I had that feeling that all mothers have of not wanting to let go, not wanting the kids to grow up, wanting to turn back the clock. I just kept thinking, *It's gone by too fast. Clint and Tyler have been so easy and such a joy to raise; I'm not ready for this part of my job to be over.* Initially, I thought I was going to be lonely, but all of my Army wife duties kept me busy and filled in the gaps that my empty nest created.

On December 1, 1997, Dick gave up command of the 160th Special Operations Aviation Regiment. I was so proud of what he had accomplished in those thirteen months in the regiment—he never gave up, never took the path of least resistance—but secretly I was relieved that the job was done and that he would be removed from the day-to-day stress that had become so much a part of his life.

The same day, Dick was promoted to brigadier general in a ceremony in one of the large hangars on the 160th compound, out at the airfield. Clint, Tyler, and I pinned on his new rank before hundreds of family members and friends. As I sat there listening to speeches, my mind wandered and took me back in time. I thought about all of Dick's promotions up to that point and could remember what I wore to each one. I thought about my evolution as an Army wife, from second lieutenant's girlfriend to brigadier general's wife, and I reflected, *What a journey this has been. Clint and Tyler are on either side of me in their respective military school uniforms, and Dick is out in front of us, wearing a star! Who would've thought?*

Dick and I understood the significance of that particular promotion; he had passed through the eye of a very small needle. It was very humbling for both of us. In his speech that day, he told the audience that I deserved stars as much as he did and presented me with a pair of diamond earrings in front of everyone. I was very touched by his thoughtfulness, and we felt blessed to be surrounded by so many of our loved ones.

PS: Dick's success in the 160th SOAR was not measured in accolades, awards, popularity, or even pats on the back. It was measured in how well the unit and the soldiers did long after he left. I love this man who faces challenges head-on and, in doing so, inspires everyone around him.

16

The First Star

Dick's first job as a new brigadier general was in the 4th Infantry Division, as the assistant division commander maneuver (ADCM). So it was back to Fort Hood that April 1998. I felt like a yo-yo after all the back-to-back moves between Fort Hood and Fort Campbell, but we were overjoyed to move back to a place we loved, where we would be closer to our sons' school; plus, it was a great job for Dick.

I wasn't exactly sure what my role was, but I had learned to observe, listen, and wait, and was confident that it would present itself to me. As I watched and learned from our division commander's wife and the other generals' wives on post, I realized I was even more of a mentor and advocate to the younger spouses. Also, at that level, we each served on various boards of organizations, on and off post, that catered to the needs of our military community.

When the boys came home for their summer break, Clint began flying lessons. He loved flying and was a natural, and it was fun to talk about all of it with him, since I understood everything he was learning.

At the end of the summer, both boys packed their bags for ROTC Advanced Camp at Fort Lewis, Washington. The night before they left, I came upon the three of them—Dick, Clint, and Tyler—hunched over the kitchen sink, tins of black Kiwi shoe polish on the counter, Dick instructing the boys in the fine art of boot shining. The smell of the polish took me back in time to memories of Dick shining his boots in our little apartment in Hawaii. As a brand-new Army wife, I had been fascinated with his twice-weekly ritual: newspapers spread out on our coffee table, his tools laid out before him, the tin of Kiwi, an old undershirt, a book of matches. Now, I thought, *All those years watching him shine his boots . . . Now here he is, teaching his sons.* It was a passing of the torch, a coming-of-age for our kids. I ran to get my camera so I could capture the moment.

I was glad the boys would be together at Fort Lewis, as I knew they would look after each other. Things were going well until, partway through, Tyler came home unexpectedly. Among other things, he was having problems with his feet—hammer toes—and if he wanted to go into the Army, we would have to address those issues. He was devastated; we were concerned. We gave him a few days to decompress, and then we sat him down and talked to him about his future.

Dick began, "Tyler, I know you're disappointed you didn't finish the camp, but maybe it's for the best. I think the first thing we need to do is see a doctor about your feet. But before we move forward, your mom and I want to know if this is what you really want to do. We don't care if you want to do something other than go into the Army."

"It's *all* I want to do," he said. "I want to be in the Army, and someday I hope to be a pilot."

"You have to be sure," I said. "It can't be because you think we want you to or because your brother chose that. It has to be your decision."

Dick said, "If you have the surgery and your feet are okay, then you will have to work that much harder to go back to the Advanced Camp next summer. Are you willing to do what it takes?"

"Absolutely, Dad."

We believed we had given Tyler every opportunity to change course, but he seemed to know what he wanted and was determined to do it. He had surgery on both his feet and spent the rest of the summer recuperating. Clint finished Advanced Camp, and we flew out for his graduation. It was bittersweet because Tyler should have been there, too.

About that time, a new best friend came into my life. Nancy Taylor moved in two doors down from us. Her husband, Joe, was Dick's counterpart on the division staff, as the new ADC for support. I liked Nancy from the day I met her. She reminded me of some of my other favorite girlfriends—strong, capable women with a great sense of humor. She and I were finding our way at a new level in our husbands' careers, in roles with new expectations and responsibilities, and we navigated that maze of activities, functions, meetings, briefings, ceremonies, and social events together. We laughed a lot, finding humor in the most inane, mundane, routine, and ridiculous things.

Dick and I enjoyed our close proximity to Texas A&M, less than two hours away, and visited Clint often. We made it to all the home football games and parades that fall. Clint's being a senior in the Corps of Cadets made it that much more special, as we knew we wouldn't always have that opportunity, and who knew where we would all be the following year?

Life was moving along so smoothly that I had no complaints. Even amid Dick's busy schedule and lots of traveling, we made time for each other and enjoyed our visits to see the boys at their schools. Tyler was doing great in his second year at NMMI. Our parents were all in good health. There were no upheavals, no deployments, and nothing looming on the horizon. It was one of those times in life where there was nothing to keep me awake at night. We were on a nice little plateau.

That spring, Dick took leave and we went out to Keystone, Colorado, for some spring skiing. We had a little money set aside and decided it was time to buy a condo or townhouse in the Keystone ski area, the place we had been going to off and on for the past twenty years. We had so much fun that week, skiing at A-Basin and looking at properties. Riding up on the chairlift, looking at the mountains and the gorgeous blue sky, we reminisced, talked about our hopes and dreams, and made plans.

Then, just three days after we returned from Colorado, my antennae went up the minute I saw Dick come charging into the house with a fresh high-and-tight haircut and carrying his clean uniforms from the laundry. He could barely contain his excitement.

"Guess what, Vick? I'm going to Germany to be an 'advisor' to a task force that is being formed up by General Wesley Clark, the NATO commander."

"Why would you be going to Germany? You're in the 4th Infantry Division."

"They asked for me because of my expertise in aviation, specifically the maintenance and tactics of Apaches."

I immediately thought back to the previous week in Colorado, when Dick had been exchanging e-mails with General Shinseki, who was then a four-star general and the vice chief of staff of the Army. Dick had told me that the general had asked his advice on the deployment, tactics, and maintenance of Apache helicopters in connection with the recent unrest in Kosovo.

"So, when are you leaving?"

"Tomorrow morning."

"Tomorrow morning?" So much for that nice little plateau we'd been on.

Dick assured me that it was no big deal—he was just going TDY (temporary duty) to Germany. He said he would probably be gone a few days, maybe a week or two. We didn't get to finish our conversation because the phone rang and Lieutenant General Leon LaPorte, the III Corps Commander there at Fort Hood, wanted to talk to Dick. Before I could get another question in, Dick was out the door.

I had plans to go to a meeting that night with Nancy, so I went ahead with my plans. We met on the corner and walked over to our neighbor's house, and I talked the whole way. I had lived with Dick long enough to know that feeling when something was on the horizon. I relayed that to Nancy as I told her what had just happened. We sat in the meeting, rolling our eyes with boredom because most of the information was a repeat of what we had listened to at our division meeting just days prior. Suddenly, I got that sinking feeling in the pit of my stomach. I turned to Nancy and whispered, "I think I need to go home. What if Dick is really going away for a while and I'm sitting here? I should be at home with him."

Nancy, ever my comrade in arms, whispered, "We're out of here!"

When I got home, I nearly tripped over the kit bags lined up by the back door. I found Dick lying on our bed, asleep, still in his uniform and boots, with an open book on his chest. I stood there staring at him for a moment. He looked so peaceful. It was one of those moments that I wanted to savor. I lay down beside him and noticed the book he had been reading was titled *Fighting in the Balkans*. Nothing like cramming the night before a big exam!

I snuggled up next to him. "Dick, are you all packed? Do you need anything?"

In a soft voice, he said, "I'm all set." He paused, then continued, "I've never been stationed in Europe. What if I can't do what they need me to do?"

"You always know what to do. You're the best when it comes to

Apaches. Do what you always do." And I thought, *I love this man—so strong and capable, yet so vulnerable.*

Morning came all too quickly, and I woke up full of nerves. I kept telling myself it was just a TDY trip, like so many others Dick had made, but my heart was pounding.

I found Dick outside, in the shed, rummaging through boxes and making a mess. "I'm looking for my flight helmet."

"What do you need that for? I thought you were going there as an advisor."

"You know I never go anywhere without my helmet. Besides, they might need another pilot." (The Apache helmet is custom fit to each pilot, so you don't just *borrow* someone else's.)

"But you're not on flight status anymore." (Since he had made brigadier general, he was supposed to close out his flight records; generals don't fly themselves.)

"Oh, yes, I am, as of yesterday!"

He finally pulled the helmet out of a box, put it on, and triumphantly declared that it still fit. (*Unlike some of your old flight suits*, I might have added, but I didn't.) He turned to me, and I saw that he had his game face on. He was already gone.

About that time, Eric, the aide, pulled into the driveway and literally jumped out of the jeep. They loaded those bags faster than you could say the word *deployment*. Following Dick and Eric around the car, I was still in my robe and slippers, coffee cup in one hand and my calendar book in the other, questioning Dick about some upcoming social events, trying to get a sense of how long he might be gone.

"Vick, I think you better cancel anything we have for the next few weeks."

A quick hug and kiss in front of the aide and the driver, and then they were gone. I must have looked comical that morning, standing there in the driveway. *What the hell just happened?* I thought.

When I called the boys, each was concerned about what their dad was doing. Clint said he couldn't wait till he was a pilot and got to do fun things like his dad; Tyler offered to come home and keep me company. I reassured them that I would be fine.

Dick called two days later and, in his breathless, excited voice, told me he had good news and bad news.

"Guess what, Vick? They've got a job for me here in 5th Corps. I'm going to be the deputy commanding general [DCG] of Task Force Hawk!"

I had learned over the years that anything that involved the words *task force* was exciting for Dick but usually meant worry for me. "Gee, Dick, I don't know what to say. I guess I'm excited for you, but what about me here at Fort Hood?"

"I'm attached to 5th Corps while we get the task force ready to go. The bad news is, I think I'm going to be here a while . . . Actually, I'll deploy from here. But guess what? I'm working with Ray Odierno! Isn't that great, Vick?"

I thought, *Did he just say "deploy"?*

"Well, that's just wonderful, Dick." I tried to keep the sarcasm out of my voice, but it was there. "Do you have any idea how long you'll be gone?"

"Realistically, I'm thinking a couple of months to do what needs to be done."

I can't say that I was surprised, but at the same time I felt entirely vulnerable. When I got off the phone, I went straight over to Nancy's house. I had to unload on someone. I felt better just talking about it with my closest friend.

When I took Barkley for his walk that day, I gave myself a pep talk. *What's the big deal here? I love Fort Hood, I have wonderful neighbors and lots of activities to keep me busy, the boys are well and safe in their respective schools, and I have the support of our parents and families. I can get through a couple of months. I've done it before, and I'll do it again.*

Amid all the functions, ceremonies, meetings, and other duties in the division and III Corps, I stayed busy and the time passed. I visited Clint at Texas A&M for Parents' Weekend and watched his parade and awards ceremony. I hated that Dick wasn't there to see Clint's unit receive the award for best battalion in the corps, but I had a fun weekend with Clint, his buddies, and their parents.

Dick called often and was clearly enjoying what he was doing in Germany. He explained more about the mission; Task Force Hawk was constructed and deployed by General Wesley Clark to provide additional air support to NATO's Operation Allied Force against the former Yugoslavian government during the 1999 unrest in Kosovo.

In May, Dick moved to Tirana, Albania, to set up the command post and get the airfield ready for the arrival of the Apache battalion and everything else that was deploying into the country. They would use the Tirana airfield as their base to conduct operations in Kosovo. It was a big deal that the Apaches were on their way, so I watched the news and scanned the newspaper for any word about Task Force Hawk. One night I saw Dick being interviewed on *Nightline*. Seeing him on TV gave me peace of mind, but there had already been a helicopter accident in the task force, and although no one had been killed, there was so much unrest in the area surrounding Kosovo and Albania that I couldn't help but worry about him.

★ ★ ★

Before I knew it, it was time for Tyler's graduation from NMMI. Clint couldn't go with me because he had his last parade in the corps. I hated to miss it, but I couldn't be in two places at once. When I started my road trip to New Mexico, I hadn't heard from Dick in a few days, and while my heart was heavy, I welcomed the eight hours of quiet and solitude. It was an easy drive—no traffic, no congestion, no big cities, just wide-open spaces. I left my worries behind me, and the farther west I got, the better I felt.

I sat in my seat at graduation and looked around at all the families and felt very much alone. It seemed like everyone had family except me. I had to force myself to live in the moment. It was a gorgeous day; the sun warmed my face and I *allowed* myself to feel happy and at peace. I counted my blessings and watched our youngest son graduate and thought how quickly the two years had passed. I wished Dick was there with me, but I realized it didn't take away from the moment. I was thankful that *I* was there. Afterward, there was the usual flurry of activity, picture taking, and good-byes. We loaded up the car with two years' worth of stuff, and as we left NMMI and Roswell, New Mexico, I felt a twinge of sadness, born of closing another chapter. But as we drove through New Mexico, Tyler behind the wheel, the sunroof open, the radio blaring, and the two of us singing along to Ricky Martin's "Livin' La Vida Loca," I looked at him, just shy of his twentieth birthday and so grown-up, and thought, *I am so thankful for the simple pleasures in my life: a road trip with my son and the chance to have some time with him before he goes off again.*

Once both boys were home for the summer, the house was full of life again. Clint got his summer job back again at the Pontiac dealership and resumed his flying lessons. Tyler was at loose ends because he would go to ROTC Advanced Camp in July, so there wasn't really time for him to get a job. He mowed lawns and thought up ways for him and Clint to get into trouble, usually involving paintball wars and fireworks.

The boys were bored and needed their dad. I missed him, too. Dick's boss called to tell me that Dick was on the promotion list for major general. It was exciting news, but I didn't even have Dick to share it with. Not knowing when he would return and where we would be moving next, I felt like our lives were on hold. There was another accident in Albania—an Apache crashed, and both pilots were killed—and Dick was beside himself. All of that just added to my unease.

Finally, in mid-June, he called and said, "We're closing up shop in Albania and making plans to disband the task force. The mission is over, and we should be heading back to Germany soon. I might be home in a few weeks."

"Thank God, Dick. It's been a long three months. Oh, I almost forgot—congratulations on being on the promotion list for two-star general! I'm so proud of you! Where do you think we'll go?"

"Pretty crazy, huh? I'll be stopping in Washington, DC, on my way home to brief General Shinseki, so he'll probably give me an idea where I'm going next."

"Well, hurry home. I miss you, and the boys do, too."

About a week later, Dick arrived at the Killeen airport. I was so nervous as Tyler drove me there, you would've thought Dick had been gone for a year. Clint came from work, and the three of us welcomed their dad home with relief.

On the way back to our house, Tyler said, "Do you guys want me to disappear for awhile, maybe go get an ice cream?" We all laughed. We were reminded of the time when Dick came back from Desert Storm and his parents, who had come to welcome him home, took our sons out for ice cream to give us some "alone time." We obviously didn't fool the boys back then, and it cracked us up.

Dick had big news from his meeting with General Shinseki: the general wanted him to work on the Army staff at the Pentagon. We were moving to Washington, DC.

The week before the movers came, Dick was helping with some chores around the house and in the yard while Nancy and I refurbished my wicker patio furniture. Wearing masks and gloves, we were busy spray-painting when Dick came outside and announced, "The shit just hit the fan in Washington!"

That certainly got our attention. Dick had written an honest After Action Review (AAR), a standard requirement after any operation or mission on lessons learned, and sent it to General Shinseki. Intended for General Shinseki only, it had somehow been leaked to the press and had created quite a stir in the Pentagon and on Capitol Hill.

Dick's stunned look scared me. "I have to go to Washington and testify before the House Armed Services Committee."

"What does this mean? I don't get it, Dick. Are you in trouble?" I was aware that Task Force Hawk had become a controversial operation, and while I knew that Dick had done everything that was asked of him and had done his job well, I couldn't understand why *he* was being summoned to DC.

He brought me out of my reverie when he said, "Vicki, I've got to get up there this weekend. I testify on Tuesday, but on Monday, I've got my murder board."

"For God's sake, what's a murder board?"

"It's just what they call the practice before the testimony. I'd better get packing; I'm leaving on Saturday."

"That's the day after tomorrow! What about the movers next week?"

"I'll get someone to help you."

Over the next two days, with my head still spinning, I helped Dick get ready to leave. He packed his Corvette with his uniforms, including dress uniforms for testifying; important folders and files; and his golf clubs. Don't think that went unnoticed by me. I thought, *What the hell is he going up there for, to play golf or save his career?* But I knew the golf clubs were in the same category as the flight helmet—never leave home without them.

I was close to tears. "Dick, you just got back from Albania. I'm overwhelmed; we have so much on our plate right now."

"I know, Vick. This isn't how I planned this, either. For all I know, this testimony could be career-ending for me."

"Are you kidding me? That's not fair—you haven't done anything wrong! You gave an honest assessment of the mission. They can't fire you for that, can they?"

"I hope not, but budget cuts, money, and fixing a worn-out aviation fleet are very touchy subjects on Capitol Hill and in the Pentagon. I stand by what I wrote in the AAR, and I'm going to be honest with the committee. That's all I can do."

Dick called the night before his testimony to tell me that it was going to be televised, but our TVs had already been packed, so I wouldn't be able to watch it. He read me his opening statement, and I told him it was perfect. I wished him luck and told him to call me the minute it was over.

Dick did a great job testifying, and in the end he was able to get enough money to update, reset, and overhaul most of the Army's aviation fleet. It was a huge deal, for which he was lauded in the halls of the Pentagon. Whew!

PS: During that time, the complainer in me wanted to stomp my foot and just say no to the new plan that was thrust upon me at the last minute. I wanted to complain that Dick had just returned from a deployment, I wanted some time with him, and I didn't feel like moving alone. But to whom was I going to complain? It wasn't Dick's fault. If I had learned one thing over the years and our many moves, it was that the US Army was pretty much in charge. I sucked it up and took it like the true Army wife that I had become, and decided that I should be a little more concerned about Dick and what he was facing in DC than about my need for the perfect moving plan. My, how I had grown.

17

Washington, DC, 1999–2000

We were on the brink of a new century. Who could have foreseen what was ahead for our country, how all of our lives would change in those first years of the new decade? Who could have predicted how all of that would impact the Army and my family?

It was also the beginning of a new chapter, a milestone in Dick's career. He was getting promoted to major general and, for the first time in his career, he would work in the Pentagon. For twenty-seven years, he had managed to avoid working in "the building," and, except for attending the required schools at Fort Leavenworth and Carlisle Barracks, he had spent his entire career in tactical units with soldiers. He was proud of that fact; to him, it was a badge of honor. Sitting behind a desk in the Pentagon was not his idea of fun; plus, it meant no flying. The reality was that there were only so many jobs for Dick at his rank. And much like when he was younger and worked at the battalion and brigade staff levels, it was time for him to work at the highest level: the Army staff. So while he may have acted as if he were dragging his feet, he was ready for the next step in his career progression. And for both of us, having spent most of our time living in small Army towns in out-of-the-way places, the prospect of living in our nation's capitol, with its history, monuments, museums, and so much culture, was more than appealing.

If Dick's promotion to brigadier general was the ultimate family celebration, his promotion to major general was the opposite. In the bowels of the Pentagon, where Dick's new office was located, a group of coworkers and friends crowded into a small room while General Jack Keane read the promotion orders and I pinned on his new rank. It was lunchtime, so the ceremony was brief. After cake and coffee, Dick took me to lunch to celebrate. Neither one of us knew our way around DC, so we went to the only place he knew how to get to that was close to the Pentagon. While we drove down I-395 in the Corvette, I looked at the gleaming silver stars on his shoulder epaulets and realized what an extraordinary moment it was. The fact that we were going to an ordinary place like TGI Friday's just made us laugh.

While we ate our cheeseburgers and fries, I couldn't help remarking to him, "Can you believe this, Dick? You're a two-star general!"

"I know, Vick—pretty crazy, huh?"

Dick and I were surprised at his rise in rank. I think we always knew he would make the rank of colonel—most of our friends did—but when he got his first star, we thought that was as good as it gets. However, when he got his second star less than two years later, that was amazing to us. Neither one of us ever took any promotion for granted. The "eye of the needle" definitely got smaller the higher up Dick went, especially in the general officers' rank. The year Dick was selected for brigadier general (one-star), only forty-four were selected out of approximately nine hundred eligible colonels. Then, when he was selected to the rank of major general (two-star), only twenty-five were selected out of approximately one hundred eligible one-star generals. We had seen many of his peers who were good leaders with great files not make it to the next rank. You can try to predict, you can do everything that is expected of you and do it well, but the bottom line is, not everyone makes it. Because it was unexpected, we appreciated it all the more.

We moved into our quarters at Fort Myer, a quiet little post situated right next to Arlington National Cemetery and home to some of the top brass in the military—some of the service chiefs, the chairman of the joint chiefs, and plenty of one-, two-, and three-star generals. Steeped in history, it was also home to the famous 3rd US Infantry Regiment (the Old Guard). The post sits on a hill overlooking the cemetery and, beyond that, the Potomac River and Washington, DC. Our house, a big, red brick duplex with lots of character and a wraparound screened-in porch, was one hundred years old and unlike any set of quarters we had ever lived in. To us, it was a mansion, and I loved it the minute we walked through the door.

I had told both boys that we were living on a pretty famous post with even more generals than at Fort Hood, and that I didn't want any childish shenanigans going on—no paintball wars, fireworks, or pyrotechnics of any kind. I told them they would have to behave themselves and act their age. I could tell they didn't believe me and could just picture them rolling their eyes as they said, "Yeah, Mom, whatever."

Dick was on the Army staff in the G-3, the Operations Center. After one week in his new job, he explained to me, "The G-3 is the heartbeat of the Army, and if I have to work in the Pentagon, it's one of the more exciting places to be. But, Vick, the hardest part is not learning my new job; it's navigating my way through the rings and halls of the Pentagon. It's so huge that I get lost daily!"

"But what does it feel like to be a two-star general in the Pentagon? You must feel pretty special."

"Just when I think I'm *somebody*, I look around at all the one-, two-, three-, and four-star generals, and it's very humbling. The joke is, two-star generals are a dime a dozen here."

★ ★ ★

That summer, Tyler graduated from the Advanced Camp at Fort Lewis, Washington, and Dick swore him in as a second lieutenant at the commissioning ceremony. When Tyler arrived at Fort Myer to spend a couple of weeks with us before leaving for Texas A&M, he understood his very first day just what an important Army post it was. He sauntered out onto our back porch, shirtless and in his boxer shorts, and noticed a big parade and ceremony going on at Summerall Field, which our house overlooked. When he saw the military police and their dogs, he headed back inside. The TV was on, and he saw President Clinton speaking at a large military ceremony, but what caught his attention was the scroll along the bottom of the screen saying, "Change of Command for the Chairman of the Joint Chiefs of Staff, Summerall Field, Fort Myer, Virginia." He looked closer and saw, in the background behind President Clinton, the back of a big brick house. *Holy crap*, he thought, *that's our house on TV!*

"Mom, I had no idea there was a ceremony with the president and all the top military brass practically in our backyard! I didn't believe you when you told me we were living on such a historic Army post!"

At the end of the summer, Tyler and I flew out to College Station, Texas. He was following in his brother's footsteps, having been accepted into the Corps of Cadets at Texas A&M. It was the first time in four years that the boys would be attending the same school. I left College Station with a light heart, thinking how glad I was that they were together again.

★ ★ ★

We had plenty of visitors that year in Washington, DC. My parents came often and loved seeing all the sights in the picturesque city, and our big house came in so handy, oftentimes I felt as I were running a bed-and-breakfast.

As the Pentagon was a hub for military personnel, we were always running into people we knew from other places, people moving in or out, people attending a course or a school. Dick frequently called to say he was bringing someone home for dinner or to spend the night. One of the things I loved about Army life was reconnecting with friends from previous assignments. I made new friends in my neighborhood and enjoyed a simple life at Fort Myer. After the hectic pace of our husbands being in command positions and the associated responsibilities, it was a welcome break.

Dick worked long hours, but I was so content that it didn't bother me. He hardly traveled, and even if he went in to his office on the weekends, we had more time together than we had had in years. We explored DC and enjoyed numerous movie theaters, restaurants, museums, and plays at the Kennedy Center. Georgetown was just minutes from Fort Myer, and we loved the old restaurants and bars, particularly in Old Town Alexandria, just a fifteen-minute drive down the George Washington Parkway. We were invited to embassy receptions full of interesting people from other countries, and festivities at the homes of the high-ranking generals at Fort Myer; I loved seeing their beautiful houses. There were just enough official commitments to be fun and interesting.

We also made two trips to Texas A&M that fall. The first time we saw Tyler march onto Kyle Field with the Corps of Cadets, it was every bit as awe-inspiring as our initial glimpse of Clint doing the same. The boys were happy and enjoying every minute of being Aggies.

As the millennial new year approached, there were fears that all
the computers and communications systems would crash at midnight
on December 31, because computers were not configured for the year
2000. That could have been a disaster, militarily and strategically, since
the Pentagon is the nerve center of the entire US military. Dick worked
around the clock to make sure that the Army's operations center would
be up and running no matter what happened. As excited as everyone
was for Y2K, we were all a little apprehensive and didn't know what to
expect at midnight on December 31.

The boys came home for their Christmas break, and the house was
filled to capacity with my parents, Chris and Ashley, Chris's fiancé Tom,
and two friends from Texas A&M. What I remember the most about
those holidays was the laughter that filled the house. When we weren't
sightseeing, we were making funny videos and cracking up until our
sides ached. At midnight on New Year's Eve, bundled up in our winter
coats, with glasses of champagne, horns, and poppers, standing arm
in arm on the hill overlooking Washington, DC, we watched the spectacular fireworks across the Potomac. Dick was at the Pentagon, but
just after midnight, when all was quiet and the communication systems
hadn't crashed, he was able to come home. He joined us on the hill, and
we watched more fireworks with the monuments in the distance and
rang in a new decade.

While the boys were home, a young woman named Brooke with a
soft Texas drawl called regularly for Tyler. Also an Aggie, she had met
him at A&M right before he left for the Christmas break. He told me
that she was different from any other girl. "Mom, I think she's the one,"
he confided.

I was surprised that he seemed to know so soon, but, then again, I
knew the first time I met Dick, so we were anxious to meet her.

The boys went back to school. It was Clint's last semester, and he
would get commissioned into the Army after graduation. He was anxiously waiting to hear whether he'd gotten into the aviation branch and
flight school.

And if life wasn't already good, it got even better when Joe and
Nancy Taylor moved to the DC area. I thought, *My prayers have been
answered!*

When the boys went off to college and I saw them with their civilian friends, I realized yet again just how different Army life was. Tyler told me how he tried to explain his childhood to Brooke's family, generations of East Texans who had always lived in Mount Pleasant, when Tyler had lived in eleven different places in his twenty years. I decided to make scrapbooks that would tell their stories and capture their unique lives as Army brats. I worked on Clint's scrapbook that winter so I could give it to him for his graduation. It was an outlet for my creative juices, and it fulfilled my need to put things in order. I couldn't wait to give it to him.

Our parents joined us in College Station for Clint's graduation. It was hard to believe he was finished with college, getting commissioned, and heading off to flight school. Another proud moment for all us was watching Dick swear Clint in as a second lieutenant. Clint and Tyler were officially second-generation Army officers.

That same weekend, Dick got some big news. When he got off the phone with General Shinseki, he turned to me with a huge grin and said, "I've been selected to command the 101st Airborne Division! We're going back to Screaming Eagle country!"

One of the most important phone calls of his career, and it happened right there in our room at the La Quinta Inn in College Station, Texas. We had much so celebrate that weekend: Clint's graduation and future career in the Army, and Dick's future assignment in the 101st Airborne Division.

We went back to DC ready to pack up for a really big adventure for the two of us. I had loved every minute of the ten months we'd lived there, but we were on our way to division command and our final rendezvous with destiny.

PS: Who would've thought in 1983, when Dick took command of his first aviation company, in Savannah, that it would someday lead to his being the first aviation branch Army aviator to command the famed 101st Airborne Division—a division that infantry generals usually commanded? While it seemed unbelievable, it felt like the most natural thing, as if everything had been leading us to that point in time.

Thoughts on Just Being Me

I t's pretty much a full-time job just being me. Unlike Dick, who, as he went up in rank and position, had an entourage that grew in relation to the number of stars he acquired, I was always an army of one. By the time he was a four-star general, Dick had enlisted aides, officer aides, speech writers, public affairs people (PAO), drivers, personal security (PSD), a communications soldier (COMMO), and an entire staff working for him. I had me. During those years, we had one or two enlisted aides who worked at our quarters during the day. They kept the house clean, took care of Dick's uniforms, and helped me with all our official entertaining. They were invaluable to me because of the amount of entertaining and the scope of it, but I didn't enjoy having people in my space, in my kitchen, on my turf. That was always a struggle for me. I guess it was a good thing I didn't have a big entourage, because I probably would not have liked it.

I've always thought that in order to really get to know yourself, you need to have some alone time. After all, how can you know what you are made of, how can you really get to know yourself and listen to your inner voice, if you have people around you all the time? Being an Army wife affords you the opportunity to be on your own from the day you get married. I went from being a daughter living at home to a sorority house full of young women to being an Army wife. As soon as I married Dick, I spent more time by myself than I ever had, and in a place far from home. At first, staying by myself, especially at night, was a bit intimidating. In Hawaii, when Dick went to the Big Island for training, a family with whom he had become close while he was a bachelor insisted I stay with them. I was more than glad to accept their offer, but after a few of those weekly visits, I realized I wanted to stay at our apartment, alone. It was nice to know that I had somewhere to go if I wanted to, but I was ready to be by myself. That first year of marriage taught me that it was okay to feel that way, and that was a milestone for me. To me, it was empowering to know that I could handle things in Dick's absence, and it gave me a chance to get to know myself a little better.

Once, during a lengthy deployment and a lot of alone time, I remarked to my sister, "I've had time to take a good look at myself, and I'm not sure I like all that I see." She just laughed, but it was the truth. It's important to know your flaws and idiosyncrasies, as well as your good points. I've had people tell me that I possess great self-awareness, and I always say that's because Dick has left me to my own devices too often. Indeed, I do a better job at "policing" myself than anyone else, and I can give myself a good talking-to when I need to. All of that self-analysis is easier to do when no one is around.

Over the years, as I came to grips with my separations from Dick, I tried to use the time to my advantage. Whether I was taking a class or teaching one, learning a craft or taking Barkley to dog obedience school, I learned to embrace those solitary moments. Army life gave me opportunities like moving overseas with two kids, learning my way around a large foreign city, moving into and out of Army quarters by myself, taking long road trips with the kids or by myself. All of those experiences made me stronger and emboldened me to feel like I can do pretty much anything. There's not much that intimidates me at this point, and that is a good feeling.

Besides the separations, I also had to learn how to deal with the fact that my life could change in an instant because of what Dick did for a living. After each accident, each loss of a friend, as I watched young widows face their fate, I thought a lot about how I could prepare myself, just in case it happened to Dick. I never had a morbid obsession with those kinds of thoughts; rather, I was just learning to accept the nature of Dick's business. I knew that being strong mentally, physically, and spiritually would help me face whatever life was going to throw at me. Once we had kids, it was even more important, because who would take care of them, if not I?

Both of my parents were good role models who instilled in my siblings and me compassion, kindness, respect for others, proper manners, and enjoyment of life's blessings. From my dad, I inherited a sense of adventure and a love for the open road. We were not wealthy, so we didn't go to Europe or exotic locations like the Caribbean, but every summer we hit the highway for a vacation. My dad, armed with maps and brochures and our Pontiac Bonneville loaded to capacity, took us to spots up and down the East Coast and into the Midwest: World's Fairs, Florida, Cape Cod, Niagara Falls, Lake Placid, and annual Yankees ballgames in New York City. My love of map reading began on those journeys, and I learned from a pro. My dad knew the entire United States—you could call him day or night for directions. If he didn't know something, I would hear him rustling the road maps that he kept by his chair. If my dad were alive today, he would scoff at the use of GPS devices for navigation, and I couldn't agree more. There's nothing like the challenge of finding your way from a map or, better yet, from memory.

My mother served as my role model for being a good wife and a stay-at-home mom. She showed my sister and brother and me that nothing was more satisfying and more important than raising good kids. It was from her that I learned the importance of taking care of myself and nourishing my mind and body—things like eating properly (three meals a day), having a regular sleep schedule, looking presentable, and having hobbies and interests that gave me pleasure. It was a combination of those lessons that my parents passed on to me when I was growing up that helped prepare me for my role as an Army wife.

Dick brought out the athlete in me. Since he played every sport known to humankind, it made it easier for me to stay active and to try different sports with him. I always belonged to a gym, a fitness center, or an aerobics studio. I didn't work out because I wanted the perfect body; I worked out or went to classes because it made me feel good. It was important that I have some "me" time, if only for an hour or two a few times a week.

I've talked about skiing throughout this book; from our early days of dating to our ski trips with our sons to the years when he was a general and we needed to get away from everything, it was the sport that was best for our souls and that rejuvenated us when we needed it most.

My hobbies—knitting, sewing, reading, cooking, and so on—were also gratifying, and I loved learning new crafts, like woodworking, painting, and calligraphy. I also taught knitting classes. Hobbies not only gave me pleasure but were constructive things to do while the boys were in school, and they kept me sane while Dick was gone.

Eventually, I started writing. Dick bought me my first computer/ word processor, and the words just poured out of me. I wrote what I thought would be a children's book about Army life. I loved writing about Army life; it was like therapy for me and a way to express myself. I didn't know where it would lead me, but I knew there was a reason for what I was feeling and writing. It was just what I needed during those lonely times when Dick was off doing his "Rambo" thing. Maybe those first writing exercises were meant to be a learning experience that would lead me down *this* path and inspire me to one day write *this* story.

Another critical aspect of my well-being is my sense of humor. My ability to laugh at myself, at Dick, at life—even in scary, dark times— has gotten me through some of life's biggest challenges, and I'm thankful for it. I try hard always to find a silver lining in difficult situations.

I don't know what I would have done without my friendships with my fellow Army wives. While I had a very close relationship with my mom and my sister and considered them my closest allies, they lived far from me, so it was my Army girlfriends whom I counted on day to day and especially when our husbands were gone. They were the only ones who truly understood this crazy way of life.

When I look back over the years and all the different volunteer work and advisory positions that I held with organizations—the Red Cross, the thrift shop, the boys' various schools, booster clubs, Officers' Wives' Clubs, women's conferences, a homeless shelter, the USO—I realize how much all of those experiences enriched my life in countless ways. I learned to facilitate, foster teamwork, mediate, manage, supervise, plan events, fund-raise, speak before groups, and make decisions—and, most important, I learned about life and people. While the courses and classes that the Army offered taught me about the Army, it was my volunteer work with people that taught me the most about life. And all of those experiences prepared me for the role I would play when Dick rose to the highest rank in the Army.

Being a mom was, and still is, the best role I have played and my greatest accomplishment. When the boys went off to college, some of my friends and relatives thought I would have a really tough time. Because I had built my world around raising our boys and was very close to both of them, I guess people assumed that I would have trouble adjusting. But I proved them wrong. I suppose the first twenty years of my marriage, I *was* defined by my role as Dick's wife and Clint and Tyler's mom—and that was absolutely what I wanted. I would not change one thing about those years. But I never lost sight of who I was, as a woman and as a person. When the boys left home, I just had to shift gears and find my inner self again. (I think it was always there—I was just busy being a mom.) I knew that my role as an Army wife, sharing my experiences and mentoring young spouses, would carry me through the next phase of my life.

As Clint and Tyler prepared to go into the military, they called on their dad more and more for advice and counsel. There was a definite shift in my caregiving, a natural evolution—but when an opportunity presented itself, whether it was a road trip, sleeping on air mattresses in an empty apartment while waiting for household goods, or a quiet midnight snack before a deployment to Afghanistan, I seized the moment and relished it. To watch our two sons grow into fine men, husbands, fathers, and great Army officers has been my greatest source of joy.

I have always loved the French phrase *raison d'*être, which means "reason to be." I love being Clint and Tyler's mom, and I loved being Dick Cody's Army wife, walking beside him on his journey. That was *my* raison d'être.

18

A Final Rendezvous with Destiny

As the soldier at the gate snapped to attention and yelled, "Air
assault, sir!" I thought back to that first time, sixteen years earlier,
when we drove through the gates of Fort Campbell, Kentucky. A flood
of memories washed over me as I recalled our three different tours
(seven years) there, in different units and different neighborhoods,
raising our boys and making some of the best memories and friends we
will ever know. I realized, *We're not that young couple anymore. We're*
older, more worldly, more seasoned, and those two young boys are now
lieutenants in the Army. Barkley, our dog, is the only passenger in the
back seat. Maybe we look a little different, but we are still the same Dick
and Vicki Cody that we were back in 1984—excited for the new assign-
ment, committed to the Army, and, most importantly, still committed to
each other.

A few days later, sitting in the stands, surrounded by family and
friends, looking out at approximately fifteen thousand soldiers on the
huge parade field, a field that held so many memories, with the sun
shining and Old Abe in the background, I was completely in awe of
Dick, more so than I had been at any other promotion or event in his
career. There were only ten divisions in the active-duty Army, and he
had been selected to command one of them. I looked at him standing
at attention and thought, *He can do anything.*

Dick and I settled into our new roles. We went to twenty-five change-
of-command ceremonies that summer, at the battalion and brigade
levels. Not only did those events help us get to know the command
teams in the division, but they also helped educate me on the various
units and what their missions were. And we knew from experience how

much it meant to the people and the units that we were there. I loved getting to know the officers, NCOs, soldiers, and their families. Dick was not only the division commander but also the post commander, which was much like being the mayor of a midsize city. We had a lot of civic duties both on and off the post, and our calendars were filled to capacity. That was the first time Dick had an enlisted aide who worked for him and was in our house during the day. The aide was a big help to both of us, given our busy schedules, but it was an adjustment for me.

Meanwhile, Clint signed in to flight school at Fort Rucker and began his career in Army aviation. When I helped Clint settle into the condo he was sharing with some buddies, I thought how different it felt to be back at Fort Rucker in that capacity, as the mother of a student pilot. I couldn't help thinking, *Twenty-four years ago, Dick and I arrived here and I got pregnant with Clint. Now he's here, following his dream, just like his dad did.*

★ ★ ★

When I got back from Fort Rucker, a phone call from my dad in early September pulled the rug right out from under me.

"Vicki, I've been to the doctor. They did some tests." He paused, then continued, "I have lung cancer."

I felt as if someone had knocked the wind out of me. I struggled to get the words out: "How can you have lung cancer? I don't get it."

Dad's voice was shaking as we continued to talk. While he was telling me about the tests, his symptoms, and all that, I wanted to run somewhere. I was not prepared at all; none of us was.

My dad had just turned seventy, and while he had had a stent put in an artery earlier in the year, he was active, ate healthfully, and looked great. He hadn't smoked or drunk alcohol in almost forty years, so lung cancer was not on anyone's radar. I had lived a very sheltered life up to that point; neither Dick nor I had lost anyone in our immediate family to serious illness besides our grandparents. No one in my family had ever had cancer.

Dad's cancer was inoperable, and he would begin chemotherapy immediately. After the initial shock and the tears, we were optimistic— my dad was going to be the one who beat lung cancer.

When I asked if I should come home, both my parents said, "Not just yet. Let's wait and see."

Everything else was so good, I had been just cruising along life's highway. Clint was doing well in flight school. Tyler was happy and thriving at Texas A&M. Dick and I were delighted to be back in the 101st and Fort Campbell. But the word *cancer* changed everything and made it hard to enjoy my life's blessings. There was always that nagging feeling, that pit in my stomach, that all was not well. My dad was sick, and none of us knew what it meant. I talked to my parents, my sister, and my brother regularly, and gradually we started to come to grips with the diagnosis. The plan was that Dad would finish the first round of chemo just before Thanksgiving, and then he and Mom would come down and spend the holiday with us. Dad needed something to look forward to. We all did.

That fall, Dick and I hosted a division off-site conference at Lake Barkley, Kentucky, for the brigade and battalion commanders, command sergeant majors, the division staff, all the chaplains, and their spouses. We brought in some great facilitators and guest speakers, all designed to help us set goals as we talked about expectations for the next two years. The conference was a big success, a time of bonding, team building, and sharing, and we became a very close-knit command group. We were laying a good foundation, one that would later hold us up when fate stepped in and challenged every single one of us.

At Fort Rucker, Clint felt not only the pressures of being a student pilot, but also the pressure of being Dick Cody's son. By the time our boys were starting their careers in the Army, Dick was pretty well known. Clint tried his best to be anonymous, but it was especially hard to do at Fort Rucker, where everyone knew the Cody name. Try as he might, Clint couldn't do anything without being noticed. He told me he felt as if he had to do everything just a little bit better than everyone else. One time early in his flight training, he got a pink slip on a check ride, nothing hugely important but a test nonetheless. He said by the time he landed, everyone on the flight line was saying, "Did you hear? General Cody's kid busted a check ride!" That was the first and last time he didn't get a stellar grade on anything.

We were looking forward to Thanksgiving. Dick's parents were coming for the week, and Clint would drive up from Fort Rucker the day before. Tyler was going to spend the holiday with Brooke's family in Mount Pleasant, Texas. My parents were driving down after Dad's last chemo treatment, and I couldn't wait to see them. But at the last minute, my dad was not able to make the trip. I knew then that it was time for me to go home.

I spent that last week of November with my parents, just hanging around, not doing much of anything besides being there. I shifted gears from the hectic pace of our busy life in the 101st, tried not to think about all the things that needed to be done back at Fort Campbell, and just focused on being with my family.

After seeing my dad in November, I knew that we were on borrowed time and that suddenly, all the things that were waiting for me back at Fort Campbell were not important. When I got back to Fort Campbell, with the help of our aide and my friends, I got everything done—decorating, baking, cooking, and shopping—just in time for the busy social season and our holiday open house for hundreds of people. The boys came home from their respective schools, and then we drove up to Vermont. I had a feeling that it would be our last Christmas with my dad.

That winter my parents went to Florida, as they did every winter, even though the doctor advised against it. But Dad was determined, so we all agreed to help make it happen for them. Chris drove them down, and then I would drive them back in the spring. They had made some really good friends there, and Dad would continue his treatments in Venice, Florida.

Things didn't go as planned. Two days into their stay, my mom fell and broke her wrist and cracked her pelvis. It was something none of us had ever considered; we had been more worried about my dad's health. I flew down there the next day.

I walked into Mom's hospital room in Venice, Florida, and my knees started to buckle. I had tried to prepare myself on the flight down, but I was shocked when I saw the two of them. My mind flashed back six months earlier to their fiftieth-anniversary celebration, where they were the picture of health, a very attractive couple, totally independent, always on the go, traveling, fun-loving, enjoying retirement and life. All I could think was, *How did we go from* that *to this: Mom lying in the hospital bed with a huge apparatus on her shattered wrist and Dad sitting by her bed, barely able to stand up to hug me because he's so weak from the chemo? These are not the mom and dad I was with just ten days ago.* They had changed seemingly overnight, and I was not used to seeing both of them so down and out. I realized at that moment that I was in charge; I had become the parent.

From then on, I tried to take each day as it came and just live in the moment. Blessings came in the form of little, everyday things. I got to spend time alone with my dad, and sometimes, if he felt good, we went out to lunch. One afternoon, we just sat on the beach together. I created and cooked healthy meals for him in their tiny apartment kitchen, and he was so appreciative. I had time to reflect and collect my thoughts when he was napping. I got to see a different side of my mom—an inner strength that emerged—and I was amazed at how well she dealt with the situation. She didn't complain or give in to her fears; she just focused on getting herself well because she knew what was ahead. Dad and I visited Mom daily, and in the evenings we played cards in the hospital lounge and laughed so hard and loudly that the nurses gave us our own room so we wouldn't disturb the other patients. We never lost our sense of humor. I also got to know the wonderful friends that Mom and Dad had made in Florida—people who would do anything for my family.

And in the midst of all of that, I reconnected with my childhood friend Becky. Over the years, we had stayed in touch through Christmas cards and an occasional phone call, but I had not seen her in twenty years. I knew her parents had retired in Venice and that she, her husband, and their kids lived in Sarasota. I called her and unloaded all my troubles on her. We spent an afternoon together and we talked daily while I was in Venice. She may never know just what it meant to me, what a comfort it was, just being with someone from my past who knew me and my family so well. It lifted me up when I needed it most. I'm not sure our paths would have crossed again if not for my dad's cancer and my going to Venice, Florida, that winter. Becky and I have stayed in contact ever since, and I count her as one of the blessings that came out of that dark time.

Another, similar blessing was a visit from my aunt Nancy and my cousins Toby and Terry, who just happened to be in Naples, Florida, during that time and came up to see Dad and spend a couple of days with us. We had not seen much of each other in the past ten years, as all of us were raising our kids and living in different parts of the country, but that reunion started a tradition that continues today: the six of us get together once a year for what we call Girls' Week. We gain strength from one another and share nonstop laughter. Again, I can't help but think that my dad's illness brought us back into one another's lives.

And so it was a winter of upheaval and uncertainty, juggling, balancing, and prioritizing. It was a time of extreme emotions—a time of grieving one minute and counting blessings the next, a time for reflecting, a time for wishing and hoping, and a time for despair. When I was in Florida, I missed my life back at Fort Campbell, and when I was at Fort Campbell, I wanted to be with my parents. I had never felt so pulled in different directions. I made three trips to Florida that winter. Between my brother, sister, and me, we managed to be there for Mom and Dad as best we could. When one of us couldn't be there, Mom and Dad's good friends helped out.

The last trip, at the end of February, all three of we kids were there together. One afternoon, Dad gathered us together and told each of us how proud he was of us, what great kids we were, and how much he loved us. We were lucky to have that time with him and lucky that he shared his love for us. How many people go through life and never know that kind of love?

In March, we made the move to get Mom and Dad back up to Vermont. They flew, and Chris and I drove their car. A freak blizzard hit the East Coast, and Chris and I drove right into it. It was pretty exciting, even given all that was going on in our lives. We were forced to hole up at a Comfort Inn in Hazelton, Pennsylvania, for two days. As we hunkered down for the next thirty-six hours, watching old movies and Jim Cantore on the Weather Channel, the snow piled up outside. Now, I think that blizzard was a strange blessing that forced my sister and me to totally shut down. It had been pretty intense and emotional getting our parents out of Florida, and I believe we needed those days alone in our hotel room in the middle of nowhere to recharge our batteries.

Vermont had gotten twenty-four inches of snow, so we were relieved when we pulled into our parents' driveway and our journey was over. Dad seemed to be doing okay. He would be getting hospice care at the house. At that point, I had been away from my life for almost two weeks, so I headed home to Fort Campbell. Dad drove me to the airport in the early morning, and I told him I would be back in mid-April, just after Easter.

"Dad, how will I know if I need to come home sooner than April? You've got to let me know if things start to go south." I didn't know how else to say it.

"I promise I'll let you know if anything changes."

I cried most of the flight back to Nashville and felt such a conflict of emotions: hating to leave, feeling guilty for wanting to go back to my life. I didn't know how long it would be, but I couldn't just stay there and wait for *it* to happen. It could be weeks or maybe a month. Unlike my sister and brother, who could see Dad anytime they wanted, for any length of time, and still have their lives, I had to leave my whole life to fly up to Vermont. Going back and forth worked, but it was like I had two different lives. That was one of the tough things about Army life, in fact. There is no way we can be in two places at once; we make sacrifices, and one of them is not getting to spend enough time with our parents and siblings. When there is an illness or a death in the family, it becomes even more apparent. At the end of the day, I know without a doubt that my life as an Army wife did not diminish or adversely affect my relationship with my parents and siblings. I didn't have the quantity of time that they all had, but I had quality time, and I had some moments and made some memories with my parents that my siblings never could.

During those difficult months, I never felt any pressure from Dick or anyone at Fort Campbell; it was *I* who struggled with how often to go home and for how long. My fellow Army wives understood what I was going through; many had already experienced the same thing. During our monthly meetings, I shared myself and all that was going on in my life with them. I knew it was an important life lesson and also an opportunity for me to set an example to the spouses: my family was my first priority. So many young wives told me during that time that they appreciated the example Dick and I set for them. I, in turn, gained strength from their support and understanding.

In my heart, I knew my dad didn't have much time left, so I got organized and tied up loose ends. I went to meetings, functions, and all the usual events that served as temporary distractions.

And then my dad called me one day and in a quiet voice said, "Vicki, I don't think I'm going to make it to Easter."

"I'll call the airline, and I'll be there tomorrow. And, Dad, I'm so glad you called me." My biggest fear during that time was that he might pass in the middle of the night, with no warning. I was proud of him for being brave and facing the inevitable and still making sure that I had time to get there, but I wiped away tears as I packed my bag and my black suit. I hated what life was doing to my family and me, and I hated that I had to bring my black suit. I wanted more time.

I got to spend my dad's last three days with him. Dick arrived in time, too. I will always be thankful that we were all there together. As painful as it was, it was a part of life that we needed to experience together, as a family. Dad died on April 11, 2001. Through our grief and tears, my family and I found strength in one another. We told ourselves we were lucky that we had those seven months to prepare for Dad's death and that we still had our mom and each other. But it didn't stop the tears from flowing and the hurt in our hearts. Life would not be the same without my dad.

That spring and summer, I made frequent trips to Vermont to spend time with my mom, sister, and brother. Mom had spent her entire adult life with Dad, from high school through fifty years of marriage. She had never really been alone. It was heartbreaking to watch her and to know that she had to make the rest of the journey by herself. Once again, she surprised us all, and by midsummer she was doing well, considering. It was time for me to go back to my other life, and my mom agreed; I had missed being with Dick and all of my duties as the wife of the commanding general. And Dick and I finally took the anniversary trip to Hawaii that we had postponed because of my dad's illness.

★ ★ ★

It was a busy summer at Fort Campbell, involving all the usual changes of command and everything that goes with the season's typical turnover. Dick decided to get rated in the new Longbow Apache, since that was the newest attack helicopter that his pilots were flying. I have no idea where he found the time to get rated in another helicopter, on top of all his duties as the division commander, but he spent weeks studying and flying with an instructor pilot and got his rating. I admired his zeal and stamina.

Dick was such a caring, hands-on leader, even at the division level. He would ride his bicycle through the housing areas in the evenings just to check on the neighborhoods and to get a feel for what was going on. He checked on his barracks, the motor pools, the aviation hangars where he himself had spent much of his career, the athletic fields, the hospital . . . He had more energy than anyone I have ever known. Together we visited the schools, often taking time to read to the children; we went to high school sports events; we spent time at the summer day camp for handicapped and special-needs children that was one of a kind in the Army; we checked on our teen center and our cooperative nursery. We did those things not because we *had* to but because those kids were the kids of our soldiers and they were part of our Army family. We tried to be involved and take part in as much family life at Fort Campbell as possible. We had just two years to make a difference in the lives of our soldiers and their families, and we took that very seriously.

Dick's creative approach to leadership continued to amaze me. Long weekends, especially during the summer months, were notorious for witnessing accidents and deaths on such a large Army post. The division had gone a record three hundred days without losing a soldier. So that year, before Memorial Day weekend, Dick called a division formation on the parade field. He stood in the center of the formation of over ten thousand soldiers and began by having them hold hands, and then he gave them the ultimate safety briefing about drinking and driving, drugs, sex—exactly what you would talk to your own kids about.

"You take care of each other every single day at work when you are in uniform," he began. "You take care of each other at the firing range, on the flight line, in the aircraft, during deployments, and in combat. You need to take that same care of each other when you are out of uniform and off duty. Are you willing to lose the person on either side of you to some senseless accident?" he asked. He went on to talk about choices and decisions. He closed by giving them all a four-day pass and told them to have a great weekend, but a safe one. It was one of those speeches that the soldiers remembered and talked about for a long time. And the 101st Airborne Division did not lose one soldier that holiday.

★ ★ ★

Clint's graduation from the primary phase of flight school was on August 8, 2001. The night before, at the formal dance, as we watched him get his wings off the board in the Officers' Club in the same time-honored tradition, I thought: *I remember so clearly the night when Dick took his wings off that board. I was nine months pregnant with Clint.* Who would have thought, when I pinned those wings on Dick back in 1977, that twenty-four years later I would do the same for First Lieutenant Clint Cody?

Dick gave a great speech at the graduation ceremony. Something he said gave me pause: "When you leave the gates of Fort Rucker, be prepared for anything. You never know where you will end up, when you will be called into combat; just be ready and always fly safe." There was a lot more to his speech, but for some reason, that comment stood out in my mind. At the time, I thought it was an odd thing to say, given the fact that we were not at war. I certainly did not think my son or any of his classmates would be going to war. I was taking pictures and living in the sweet moment of it all. What an exciting day, and a bittersweet one, too, because I couldn't help think about my dad, who would have been so proud to see Clint get his wings. I told myself he was watching from above. Dick's comments would prove to be very prophetic a few weeks later, when we were attacked by terrorists and the course of all those young aviators' lives was forever changed.

PS: Life doesn't always follow the game plan that we carefully plot and try so hard to control. We can't predict or alter the future. My dad's passing proved to me once again the importance of family, of spending time with our loved ones and showing that love to one another. It also taught me that there are "angels" out there who come to us when we need them. There are blessings everywhere, all around us—just open your eyes, your ears, and your heart and let them come into your life.

19
September 11, 2001

September 11, 2001, was a perfect early-fall day—the kind of day that makes you wish it were still summer, and every pilot's dream flying weather. Watching *Good Morning America* that Tuesday morning, as I had been doing almost every day of my married life, I saw no hint of the doom that was about to befall our country. At 8:30 a.m., Eastern time, the weather report emphasized one of those rare occurrences: miles and miles of clear skies throughout much of the United States. Hurricane Erin, the longest living hurricane that season, had been taunting us for over a week, first as a tropical wave, then as a depression; then she had weakened and dissipated, only to reorganize, intensify, and turn into a hurricane on September 9, moving northwest. But she stayed east of Bermuda, and by September 11, she no longer posed a threat to the United States.

How different it might have been if Hurricane Erin had in fact blown over Bermuda and struck even a glancing blow to the southeast coast, bringing just enough weather to delay flights and shut down some airports; just *maybe*, the terrorists would not have been able to execute their plan. Did they watch the Weather Channel or call Flight Service ahead of time for a weather briefing? Did they know they were going to have such a beautiful day to destroy so many lives, to wreak havoc on our country and our way of life? I often wonder if they were that smart or just plain lucky that day.

I was getting myself ready for the day's events and was away from the TV when Dick's mom called. Like everyone in America, from that moment on, I was simultaneously on the phone and glued to my television. I was talking to my mom when the second plane hit the second tower. Approximately twenty minutes later, the Pentagon got hit, and that was when I felt my world really change. I didn't know anyone who worked at the World Trade Center, and I didn't know anyone serving in the NYPD or the FDNY, but I did know plenty of people who worked in the Pentagon. I called Dick, but his secretary told me he was on the phone and would call me back.

Tyler called from Texas A&M, very concerned. "Mom, please tell me Dad isn't at the Pentagon today."

Dick was still traveling to the Pentagon a few times a month for briefings and meetings, so I understood Tyler's apprehension. I assured him that his dad was safe and sound at Fort Campbell. We talked for a few more minutes, but everything was happening so fast that all we could do was speculate; no one had answers yet. I told him we would call him when his dad got home from work. Nothing seemed right or normal in those first minutes and hours. All I knew was that I missed my boys more than ever and hated being so far from them. Clint was still at Fort Rucker and just weeks into his Apache transition course, so I knew I couldn't call him. I would have to wait until he got out of class to talk to him.

I made phone calls, checking on people we knew in DC. I was worried about Nancy's husband, Joe, who still worked in the Pentagon, and I was relieved to hear that he was fine; his office was on the side opposite the one that got hit.

I had never felt so unsettled as I waited for Dick to call me back. When he finally did, I was hoping that he would have some answers. After we both talked about the shock and horror of it all, he said, "I'm sure this is an act of terrorism. I've locked down the post. That's it—no one is coming onto my post. Traffic is backed up for miles, and it's a mess out there, so don't even try to go anywhere."

"What do you think is going to happen here?" I asked him.

"Vicki, until we sort this out, I have to go on the assumption that any military installation could be a potential target for terrorists. I've got fifty thousand people and the largest fleet of Army aviation to protect."

I had heard that all air traffic, every commercial flight in the United States, had been ordered to land. No plane would be flying into or out of the country, and all of the planes already in the air had to land somewhere.

Dick went on to explain, "I've been on the phone with the FAA and NORAD and told them I just can't take a chance with commercial flights landing here. I got permission to set up Avenger missiles around Campbell Army Airfield, and I've given the order 'no commercial planes are to land here.' There could be more hijacked planes out there. I've got Apache helicopters circling over the post, and the military police are sending guards to the house. You need to stay put for now."

"Wow, you did all of this already?" I hadn't thought that far ahead. I was still thinking in terms of major US cities' being targets.

I knew Dick had a million things to do, so I made him promise to call later with any updates. I hung up the phone and went out onto our front porch, needing to feel the air and listen to the sounds of life. Just beyond a grove of trees, the main gate was a few hundred yards away, but it was eerily quiet for that time of day. I heard Apache helicopters circling overhead, and as I stood there, looking toward the sky, I felt something I had never experienced in my lifetime: I was afraid for our country, and for all of us at Fort Campbell. Suddenly, all of our day-to-day routines—the boring, mundane details of everyday life—became insignificant. My priorities changed in a heartbeat.

I, like everyone else that day, felt the whole gamut of emotions: shock, outrage, anger, fear, and utter sadness at all the loss of life that occurred and the uncertainty that we faced as a country. The phone lines at Fort Campbell became tied up, but every so often someone got through to me. When Clint finally reached me, I was so glad, because talking on the phone with my kids was one of the only things that assuaged the overwhelming loneliness I had been feeling all day.

When Dick got home that evening, we had a chance to decompress a little and we watched the news together. As we saw the acts of patriotism and heroism emerging from such devastation, we felt a glimmer of hope that we were going to be okay. I couldn't remember ever having felt such pride in my country.

If the terrorist attacks were a turning point for all of us in the United States and our way of life, they were also a turning point for the Army. We went from a peacetime military to one preparing for combat operations almost immediately.

On September 12, I was in Dick's office when Clint called. The boys called me daily, but once they were in the Army, more and more they called just to talk to their dad, as Clint wanted to do that day.

Dick's tone was serious. He was pensive as he hung up the phone. "He wants to come to the 101st, Vicki." Dick then relayed what Clint had said: "If you're going to combat, I want to go with you and the 101st."

I looked at Dick. He seemed to be struggling with something. Clint had turned to him for advice not as a father, but as the commander of the 101st Airborne Division. Dick and I both knew then that we were at yet another crossroads.

"What did you say to him?"

"I told him if that's what he wants, he should call his assignments officer at Aviation Branch and put in his request. The 101st always needs Apache pilots, especially if we deploy. I'm sure they'll approve it. I didn't ask *him*, Vick; he asked *me*."

Clint and Tyler were just beginning their careers, and I had never given any thought to their deploying to combat. I said, "I know, Dick. I just hadn't thought about that piece of it. I'm still processing what happened to our country. I guess if there is a chance the division is going to deploy, then I would rather Clint be in the 101st with you."

While we all dealt with the emotional aftermath of the attacks, Dick and I went into preparation mode. Dick visited every school on post to reassure the teachers, the administrators, and, most importantly, the students. Less than two weeks after the terrorist attacks, he and I held a meeting for all the leadership at Fort Campbell, both military and civilian. Dick believed that either all or part of the division would deploy at some point, and that when that happened they would be called upon, whether as part of a deployment or in support of the deployment, and he wanted everyone—active-duty military, civilians, and family members—to be prepared.

Dick and I already had plane tickets for a trip to College Station to visit Tyler and go to a football game, but Dick did not want to leave his soldiers and the division and was already working on contingency plans for possible deployments. I hesitated for only a moment before I told him I would go by myself. I wasn't going to miss out on seeing Tyler and doing something that had become a fall tradition for us. The terrorists had taken enough from all of us—they weren't getting that, too. Nancy had plans to fly out there from Washington, DC on the same weekend, since her daughter, Abbie, was also a student at Texas A&M.

When I boarded the plane in Nashville that September day, I felt vulnerable and nervous, which I had never been before when boarding a commercial flight. As I settled into my seat, I gave myself a little pep talk about the unlikely chance of a terrorist attack occurring on my flight from Nashville to Houston and then to College Station. I made some bargains with God that day, too, just to be sure.

I was so glad to see Tyler and wrap my arms around him, even more so because of everything that had happened since I had last seen him. That Saturday, Tyler, Brooke, Nancy, Abbie, and I stood in the stands at Kyle Field and, along with eighty thousand other Aggie fans, enjoyed a typical Saturday ritual. For many of us, it was the first time we had gathered in such a huge crowd since the attacks. There was a different feel to the game that particular Saturday—a sense, a feeling, that went above and beyond the usual, intense Aggie pride. Maybe it was just an overwhelming sense of patriotism, but whatever it was, it felt good.

That weekend at Texas A&M soothed my soul; I spent time with my son, reunited with a close friend, got my fill of some good Mexican food, and witnessed, yet again, the wonderful Aggie spirit. When I said good-bye to Tyler at the College Station airport, I felt almost normal again.

Life back at Fort Campbell was very different, though. Getting on and off the post was still an issue because of all the new security measures. We had guards around our house, initially MPs and then soldiers in Humvees. At first I was glad for the added safety measures, but then I felt isolated. Eventually, I got used to it and it became the norm for me. There were a lot of new norms for all of we Americans to get used to.

Once again, fate stepped in and a very special person came into our lives, someone I doubt we would have met if not for the events of September 11. In late September, Dick received a phone call from Ms. Wynonna Judd, country-music star and half of the legendary singing duo the Judds. Born in Kentucky and living just down the road in Nashville, Wynonna asked what she could do for the soldiers of Fort Campbell, Kentucky. Dick was taken aback but over the course of the conversation realized what a sincere and genuine person she was. As he later said to me, "She's the real deal, Vick." She and Dick talked about her coming to Fort Campbell and doing some concerts for the soldiers to show her support.

We got a lot of VIP visitors at Fort Campbell—senators, congress-men, high-ranking military leaders, and a celebrity or two—so Dick and I had become accustomed to hosting VIPs. When he asked me to go with him that day to escort Ms. Judd, I didn't hesitate. Tyler was home on break and went along with us, too. I knew very little about Wynonna and her famous mother, and I wasn't sure what to expect, but Dick, Tyler, and I were excited to meet her. When she emerged from her big tour bus with her signature sunglasses and bright red hair, she certainly looked like a celebrity—there was a definite star quality to her—but within minutes I could tell she was a normal and ordinary person who just happened to be a famous singer. I liked her immediately.

As we took her on a tour of the post and to the Air Assault School and watched her with soldiers, she endeared herself to Dick and me. Over the course of the afternoon, she told us she had never been to an Army post and knew little about those serving in the military. She was like a sponge soaking up everything that day, from Army "stuff" to personal information about Dick and me.

She performed two concerts for the soldiers during that visit. When we sat in the front row and watched her perform, we were blown away by her voice. She sang like an angel. There was something about her—maybe it was her heart, maybe it was her spirit—that made her seem like a ray of sunshine during a very dark time. The connection between us and the mutual fascination of that first encounter marked the begin-ning of a close and enduring friendship with her and her family.

★ ★ ★

By mid-October, life at Fort Campbell returned to a somewhat normal routine, but with a sense of urgency in all the training and the leader-ship meetings Dick and I facilitated. The Air Force had begun air strikes in Afghanistan in early October, and elements of the 160th SOAR and 5th Special Forces Group quietly left Fort Campbell for Afghanistan. Dick and I tried to anticipate what was in store for the 101st, but we, our entire country and military, were in a holding pattern, just waiting to find out what the next move would be.

The World Series was postponed because of September 11, and it began on October 27, the latest starting time ever. It was nicknamed the November Series because the last three games were played in November. The New York Yankees had won the American League pennant and played the Arizona Diamondbacks for the world championship. After the first two games in Arizona, the Yankees brought baseball and hope back to New York City. President Bush threw out the first pitch of game three, to nonstop chants of "U-S-A, U-S-A," in a packed Yankee Stadium. At a time when we were all searching for meaning, looking for something good to come out of what had happened, needing an outlet for our patriotism, just wanting some semblance of normalcy, the Yankees provided us with that during those evening games in the late fall. The devastation in Manhattan contrasted sharply with the jubilation at Yankee Stadium in the Bronx, but it seemed fitting that the Yankees got to be in the World Series that year. Dick would rush home from a long day at his office to watch the games and stayed up until all hours just to see his team play, just to feel the comfort of baseball. It was a seven-game series, and even though Arizona won, it represented much more than a sporting event—it provided relief from all the sadness and uncertainty; it gave us all a reason to stand up and cheer for New York; it gave us something ordinary to talk about.

That November, we got the mother of all VIP visits. Imagine my surprise when Dick called to tell me that President and Mrs. Bush were coming to visit Fort Campbell the day before Thanksgiving. It was President Bush's first visit to Fort Campbell, and it came at a perfect time. While the pain of the terrorist attacks was still fresh in our hearts and talk of war and deployments was on our minds, President Bush's visit to our post was a rallying cry for all of us, especially our soldiers.

The day they arrived was picture-perfect. Dick and I stood on the tarmac at Campbell Army Airfield, watching Air Force One taxi toward us. We kept squeezing each other's hand because we couldn't believe what we were about to do. President and Mrs. Bush emerged from the plane with their very large entourage, and shaking hands and greeting each of them felt like an out-of-body experience. We then followed them in the motorcade, with secret service surrounding us, to one of the soldiers' dining facilities for a Thanksgiving meal. In our van, I turned to Dick and said, "Can you *believe* we're doing this?"

At the dining facility, about one hundred soldiers who represented our division were waiting to have lunch with President and Mrs. Bush. Dick and the president sat at a table, Laura and I at another. The rest of the official party, including Condoleezza Rice, was interspersed among the other tables of soldiers. Dick and I were like proud parents as we watched the soldiers, so sharp and poised, talking with all the VIPs. Laura and I chatted easily with each other and with the soldiers at our table. I was trying to relish every moment, every word. I could barely eat my delicious turkey dinner, which killed me because I was hungry and I love to eat, but it's not every day that you get to sit with the First Lady!

After lunch, the president went around the entire room and posed for pictures with all of the soldiers, who were thrilled to have that opportunity.

As we were leaving the dining facility, Laura turned to me and asked, "Will you be cooking a big meal for Thanksgiving tomorrow?"

"Yes, I'll be in the kitchen most of the day. My mom is here visiting, and our son is home from flight school. But I'm making breakfast for the ten soldiers who guard our house on the morning shift, and then I'll cook a turkey dinner for the soldiers on the evening shift and for us."

"You sure have a lot to do!"

I was thinking the same thing when President Bush interrupted my reverie. "Would you and the General like to ride in our vehicle to the parade?"

Dick and I responded in unison, "Sure, that would be nice."

We got into the official presidential car and sank into luxurious leather seats embroidered with the presidential seal. The doors closed, and there we were, just the four of us, face-to-face: Dick and I and our new best friends, George and Laura Bush! Dick and President Bush started talking, and Laura put on some lipstick, so I followed suit. Then she brought out a little tin of Altoids breath mints and offered them to us, while I thought, *She is so normal!*

They were both gracious and sincere, and they looked right at us with their beautiful blue eyes. We rode out with them to the parade field, where fifteen thousand soldiers and thousands of family members were assembled, including Clint and my mom. There were congressmen, senators, and the governors of both Kentucky and Tennessee. There were civilians and VIP guests from our communities. As we approached the field, I saw the look of awe and wonder on the president's face; I don't think he had ever seen such a large formation of soldiers. As many times as I had seen formations, that sea of green camouflage and black berets never ceased to amaze and move me as well.

When we exited the vehicle and lined up behind the stage, the chants and cheers from the crowd were deafening. Dick gave the president a 101st Airborne Division flight jacket to wear, and as we walked out onto the stage, I felt as if I were in a dream as I sat next to Laura while Dick gave the introduction and then the president spoke. He turned to Dick and said, "I want to thank Commander Cody for his hospitality and his leadership. I took a good look at him . . . I'm glad he's on my side!" The crowd erupted in cheers.

Afterward, when we went backstage, Clint and my mom and about ten other people got to meet the president and the First Lady. It was the chance of a lifetime for all of us. Pictures were taken of each of us with the First Lady. It all happened so fast, yet I remember every single moment.

When it was time for them to leave, we rode out to the airfield with them and then exchanged a flurry of good-byes. I hugged Laura and shook the president's hand, and then they were climbing the steep stairway to Air Force One. Dick and I stood there and watched them taxi and take off. Holding hands, we turned to walk back to our vehicle. I felt like skipping as I turned to Dick and said, "Holy shit, we just spent the day with the president of the United States!"

I also caught a rare glimpse of George W. Bush the man that day. When we were in the car heading to the airfield, Dick was talking to the president, thanking him for his leadership during such a difficult time for our country. President Bush said he had surrounded himself with some really smart people and how important that was, and Dick and I both told him he was doing a great job as president.

He looked out the window, with a wistful look on his face, and said, "I had a really good teacher. . . . [*Long pause.*] My dad." There was something in the way he said it, something in his look, that told me I had just witnessed something very private, a very human side of him. I saw him not just as our president but as a man who deeply respected his father, a former president.

When I got home that afternoon, Clint and my mom were at the house, waiting for me. They had CNN on and had been watching replays of the coverage of the president's visit. It was weird and exciting to see Dick and me on TV. Family and friends called throughout the afternoon and evening. It was my fifteen minutes of fame, but it was so much more than that—it was yet another moment in time that is now forever etched in my mind.

The fame and glory were short-lived, however, because I had so much to do to get ready for Thanksgiving—casseroles and pies to make, and a huge turkey to prep for the next day's dinner. Just like that, I was back to my real life as mother, daughter, hostess, cook, and CG's wife.

★ ★ ★

Right after Thanksgiving, Dick was briefed on upcoming operations in Afghanistan. The 101st deployed a brigade combat team, the first conventional unit to deploy troops to Afghanistan in support of the war on terrorism. At the same time, Clint got his official orders for the 101st. He would be living near us for the first time since he had left home for college, but my excitement was tempered by the reality that the division could deploy. Still, at that point, I told myself just to wait and see, because maybe it would not come to that.

I busied myself with all the usual preparations for the holidays, but nothing felt normal. There was still so much heartache in our country, my dad's death was fresh in our minds, we had soldiers deploying, and there was a possibility that combat operations would begin in Afghanistan.

We spent Christmas in Vermont. My family was experiencing all the sad "firsts" without my dad, but it felt good to be together, especially in light of all that had happened in the last year.

As uncertain as those times were, we also had much to look forward to. Tyler had just one semester left at Texas A&M and would graduate in May. He and Brooke were talking about getting engaged, so for all the heartache of the previous year, life presented us with blessings, too.

PS: The events of September 11 changed the course of so many lives, not just those who lost loved ones in the World Trade Center or the Pentagon or on the planes that went down, or the firefighters and policemen who died trying to save people. The terrorist attacks changed the life of anyone serving in the military or who had loved ones serving. For all of us, it was the beginning of a war on terrorism that would mean multiple deployments, in different countries, for the next decade. And for me, having a husband and both sons in the Army just got even more dangerous and stressful.

20

A New "Band of Brothers"

The first weeks of the new year were busy ones for all of us in the 101st. First Lieutenant Clint Cody signed in to the division and the 101st Aviation Brigade. My hopes of seeing him and having Sunday dinners together didn't exactly pan out. I resigned myself to the fact that at least he was close by and we saw more of him than we had in the last six years, but Clint was one busy lieutenant, going through integration into his unit and the division, learning the local flying area, and getting mission qualified. Typically, all of that would have been spread out over four to six weeks, but that January, time was of the essence and Clint got qualified in just two weeks. He also had all the responsibilities of a brand-new platoon leader. He worked hard to blend in and tried to be like any other new lieutenant, pilot, or platoon leader in the division, but that still wasn't easy, given who his father was.

One of the companies from Clint's battalion had deployed to Afghanistan in December as part of Task Force Rakkasan, and the rest of his battalion was on alert. Not yet ready to face reality, I ignored the fear that was trying to surface.

One night over dinner, Clint and his roommate, Matt, asked Dick when he thought they should "get their motorcycles out of the garage." We all laughed over the fact that we were still using the same code words that we had been using since the kids were little.

Dick turned serious and said, "Clint, I think you'll need your motorcycle before me."

I looked at all of them and felt the old, familiar sinking feeling in my gut. "Dick, what do you mean by that?" I asked.

"So far, the requirements from US Central Command [CENTCOM]

have been for specific company and battalion size units, to be attached to the task force already there." He went on to explain, "They have not yet asked for my division headquarters. This is different from what we were used to when the entire division deployed for Desert Storm."

On March 1, Operation Anaconda began in Afghanistan, involving Task Force Rakkasan of the 101st Airborne Division. When Dick wasn't at his office, he was on his special secure phone at the house. Almost immediately after the operation was underway, Dick got calls from the command center in the combat zone that more Apaches were needed.

As soon as it was daylight, Dick went into his office. When he came home that afternoon, he found me in my rubber gloves, washing windows, cleaning—what I always did when I got scared. He walked right to me, and in an instant I knew what was coming.

"I'm sending the rest of 3-101st to Afghanistan. Clint's battalion is leaving . . ." He paused. "I'm sending Clint to combat."

"Clint is going? You're going, too, aren't you?"

"No, Vick, I'm not. They still haven't asked for our division headquarters."

"What do you mean? You have to go with him! He can't go without you!" I felt as if someone had punched me in the stomach. My mind was racing: *This is* not *part of the plan. I thought Dick and Clint would go together.* I wasn't thinking straight.

I ripped off my rubber gloves, flung them onto the floor, and walked away, muttering, "I never signed up for this!"

Later, when Dick recounted the story, he told people that I said to him, "You go!" But I never said that. I said, "You go *with him.*" There's a difference.

I was a mess. You would think that I would have been prepared, but it still blindsided me. It was no longer a possibility that *our* son was going into combat—it was a reality.

Meanwhile, Dick was standing there with a scared look on his face. I went to him and hugged him and said, "I know it's not your fault; I'm just so scared."

"I know, Vick. I am, too."

"Does Clint know?"

"His unit is being called right now. Give him some time, and then he'll call us."

Clint called within the hour and said simply, "Mom, I'm getting my motorcycle out of the garage."

I was determined not to cry. Clint was already in preparation mode and had so much to do to get himself and his platoon ready. I didn't want to be a drag on him or add to his already-full plate. Plus, I was in shock. I just kept thinking, *There is* no way *Clint is going to Afghanistan without his dad.*

For the next three days, I felt as if I were in no-man's-land. Clint sounded exhausted whenever he called, but he said he still had much to do. I felt powerless—it wasn't anything like helping him pack for college. When we met with a JAG officer (an Army lawyer) so Clint could give me power of attorney to handle things that might come up in his absence, the deployment became a reality. I could not stop the tears that day. But after a brief meltdown, I was ready to do what I always did for his dad in those situations: be a sounding board and supportive in any way I could.

Tyler was calling daily from Texas A&M. He was worried about his brother and couldn't believe Clint was deploying so soon after he'd gotten to the division and when he was just months out of flight school. He and Clint talked frequently.

One night at about midnight, I heard Clint's car pull into our driveway. Dick was asleep, and I ran downstairs to see my boy. His platoon was packed and ready, and he was heading to his house to gather up the rest of his personal gear. He looked exhausted, physically and mentally. I went to hug him, but he winced and pulled away. He had gotten six shots in his arms that day and could barely lift them. I also noticed his shaved head. He and his guys had gotten haircuts, just like his dad used to do.

We went into the kitchen, and I made him soup and a sandwich; he hadn't eaten all day. We sat there in the quiet of the night, and I kept looking at my boy, who seemed to have grown up overnight yet also still looked so young and vulnerable. I was working on my game face, and I did pretty well that night. I had to, not just for me, but for Clint. I just kept thinking how lucky we were that we lived there at Fort Campbell and I had those days with him. I will never forget that night, not because of anything special that we said to each other but because I had him all to myself for a brief time, before he left the next day.

When I woke up the next morning, Dick was sitting on the side of the bed, just staring into space. I reached over to him and said, "I can't say good-bye. I can't let him go."

"I know, Vick. It's killing me, too." In that moment, Dick wasn't a division commander; he was a father.

"How are we going to do this?"

"We don't have a choice. We just have to do it."

A few minutes later, after Dick had shaved, he said to me, "Think about all the people, all the kids out there, who go through life and never get to do something they want to, never test themselves, never get to see what they're capable of. . . . Clint is doing what he always dreamed of doing."

"I know you're absolutely right, but it doesn't make it any easier."

That morning was our scheduled monthly information meeting with all the commanders' spouses. Dick wanted to brief them, so he accompanied me and talked to the group of about seventy-five spouses. Before turning it over to me, he told them, "Vicki and I are on our way out to the airfield to say good-bye to our son. He is leaving on the next flight to Afghanistan."

At that, the room let out a huge, collective gasp. Things had happened so fast in the short time that Clint had been in the 101st, many of them did not realize that our son was even in the division, much less deploying.

I would like to tell you that I was totally in control of my emotions, but the minute I stood before the roomful of my fellow Army spouses, I caved. My game face totally failed me. But as Dick stood there, I curtailed my crying and kept my comments brief, knowing that if I let go I would not be able to stop.

I looked at their concerned faces. I knew them all so well, and most of their husbands, too. "I'm pretty scared," I told them. "But if our son has to go to combat, I'm glad he is with your husbands. I can't think of better commanders and leaders for him. We'll get through this together." I meant what I said. I knew that I would get my strength from them in the coming months and that, in turn, Dick and I would support them.

On the way out to the airfield, we were both pretty quiet. I had no questions to ask—or, rather, none for which I wanted to an answer.

Back then, there was no fanfare, no sending-off ceremony. The units had been deploying in bits and pieces, as needed. I was allowed to go because I was the CG's wife; otherwise, no other family members were there. I was so glad to finally meet Clint's copilot, Mike, whom I'd heard much about. Mike was in his mid-thirties and had flown in Operation Desert Storm, so his experience gave me reassurance. He was soft-spoken and polite, and he told me that Clint was already a great pilot and gunner.

"I'll look after him," he assured me. "Try not to worry about him—he'll be okay."

I was grateful for his kind words and reassurances, and I told him so. After that, we just sat on some hard wooden benches and didn't have much more to say. Clint's crew chiefs were there, too, and I thought about how young every one of them looked, just as I had thought about Clint the night before. Now, my son had his own game face on as he handed me his Aggie ring, his cell phone, and his wallet. We took a few pictures, and I was struck by the fact that we were posing and smiling as if it were any family occasion. Old Abe was in the background, as always.

I hugged Clint as long and hard as I could. I wanted to hang onto him forever, but I also knew it was time to let go. I didn't really cry, just a little sob, but no big tears, which was good. I didn't want to embarrass him.

We left the airfield, and I dropped Dick at his headquarters. He had a full day of work, and I had things to do. I drove the short distance to our house and was relieved when I pulled into the driveway and saw that our enlisted aide wasn't there. I was planning on having a nice little "pity party," and I didn't want anyone around. If I felt like crying, I was going to let loose, once and for all. I was tired of being strong and holding it in. I lay on my bed and thought about getting under the covers and just staying there indefinitely. I felt like quitting my life as an Army wife and mom, if only for a while. It was just getting too hard.

Then the phone rang and I forced myself to get up. It was Lisa Preysler, whose husband was one of the infantry battalion commanders in Afghanistan.

"Vicki, I've been thinking about you. Are you okay?"

"I'm okay. It's just scary. It's so different than sending Dick off." It was such a new feeling for me that I had trouble finding the words to describe it as I continued. "Lisa, it was like sending a part of me away. I don't worry about Dick the same way I worry about my sons. Clint just seems so young—I don't know how else to say it."

We chatted for a few more minutes, and she tried to reassure me that Clint would be all right. "We'll get through this together, Vicki."

When I hung up the phone, I thought of all our spouses who had someone deployed, and I knew they were worried like I was. And that evening, when I called Mike Wells' wife, Sarah, I felt an instant connection with her. By the time we hung up, I felt better than I had in days, and maybe I helped her, too. In the coming days and weeks, I got phone calls, notes, and messages from spouses telling me that they were thinking of me and praying for our son, and each one meant the world to me.

The hardest part of Clint's deployment was our lack of communication and not knowing what he would be facing when he got to Afghanistan. When he called about a week later, I was so relieved to hear his voice and to know that he was safe. I was then able to start moving forward, one day at a time, but I woke up every morning thinking about Clint and praying that he was safe, and I went to bed every night doing the same.

When Clint deployed, the roles that Dick and I had been playing, as the commanding general and his wife, became intertwined with our identities as the parents of a deployed soldier. It happened the first time we attended a family readiness group (FRG) meeting with the families of the aviation task force. That first time, it felt strange, but after a few more meetings we were comfortable in our dual roles. I also had the same feeling I'd had in the past, of knowing there was a reason and a purpose for our being there at that point in time. If we had been living somewhere else, we would have had no connection to the people our son was deployed with. By the same token, because Dick and I were living what they were living, we were able to truly support them during a difficult time. Once I looked at it that way, I felt better.

On the way home from an FRG meeting, Dick finally said what he had been trying to verbalize for days: "Vicki, I look at all those young moms with their kids, and I realize that's how it was for you every time

I left. I see how hard it is for them. I now know what it's like to be the one left behind."

"Hallelujah! Finally, after all these years—validation!"

"Vick, I knew it was hard for you whenever I went away; I just never saw it from this point of view until now. I'm sorry I put you through so much when our kids were young."

★ ★ ★

Given the instant gratification of cell phones and the Internet that the modern era offers, I was used to talking to both of my boys on a daily basis. Those early weeks of Clint's deployment in Afghanistan, he didn't even have e-mail, so that was one of the hardest things for all of us. But it forced us all to get back to basics: writing letters. Like his dad, Clint was a good letter writer—insightful and usually funny. I lived for the mail again, just as I had when Dick was gone.

In early April, Dick made an official trip to Afghanistan and Kuwait to check on his soldiers. I was in Vermont with my family for the one-year anniversary of my dad's death. It was also Clint's birthday, and I missed him especially during that time, but I had sent a birthday goodie box over with Dick.

Dick called from Afghanistan and said that Clint was doing great. "Hey, Vick, guess what? I got to fly a mission with Clint. We flew from Kandahar up to Bagram with Clint as flight lead and mission commander. I flew behind him in another Apache. It was great!"

"That is so neat, Dick. I wish I could've seen it."

Clint called later to give me his rendition of their flight. He said that while they were flying in formation, his dad veered off and left the formation. Clint told me he got right on the radio and said, "Eagle 6, this is Blue Max 26. Say your position!"

"Mom, I have no idea what he was doing, but he was shooting at something in the mountains. I ordered him to get back in formation, as briefed! Mom, I've waited my whole life to be able to give Dad an order!"

We had a good laugh over the whole incident, but I was glad I hadn't known in advance that they would be flying together, or I would have been really worried. And by the time Dick got back to the States, the story of Lieutenant Cody's having given General Cody a direct order was already circulating the halls of the Pentagon.

Once Dick returned, I hung on his every word and pumped him for any information pertaining to Clint. He told me Clint was doing well and had flown great in Operation Anaconda.

"He was in combat?"

"Well, of course, Vick—that was the whole idea of his going over there."

"But I thought you said he would have time to get oriented!"

Dick just shrugged and proceeded to tell me all about his visit and how nice it was to see not only Clint but all of his other Screaming Eagles. He had awarded air medals to Clint and most of the pilots in his unit, and had also awarded the soldiers of Task Force Rakkasan their coveted Screaming Eagle combat patches, which they would wear on their right shoulders forevermore.

Dick told me, "That evening, when I went around to visit my soldiers, I found them in their tents, sitting on their cots, sewing on their new combat patches. Vicki, it was so poignant to see those tough, gritty, battle-tested soldiers trying to sew."

"Is that what you did when you got your combat patch in Desert Storm?"

"Yes, and I remember it like it was yesterday. We sewed them on before we went to bed that night. It never changes—each generation of soldiers so proud of what they've accomplished, so proud of their unit, so proud to be a Screaming Eagle."

I thought, *A new "band of brothers" has emerged, and Clint is among them. He now wears the same combat patch as his father.*

★ ★ ★

While all that was going on, Tyler got his orders for flight school. He wanted to fly Apaches like his dad and his brother. He also told us he was going to request the 101st Airborne Division for his first assignment after flight school, so he could serve with Dick and Clint. Tyler proposed to Brooke that spring, and we looked forward to their wedding the following year.

My life consisted of attending a series of FRG meetings; addressing

all the usual needs of the soldiers, both the deployed and those back
in garrison, the spouses and the families at Fort Campbell; and at the
same time trying to get through Clint's deployment. Dick had said all
along that the deployment would most likely be six months, but there
was no concrete return date. I was thankful for my busy schedule and
for being surrounded by spouses who inspired me every day.

As Tyler's graduation was almost upon us, I made his scrapbook,
and, as with Clint's, it was so gratifying looking back on Tyler's life and
putting it into a book for him. It just reinforced for me what a great kid
he was.

During a phone call with Clint, I sensed a weariness in his voice.
The living conditions were getting old and the heat of summer had
kicked in, and when they weren't flying missions, they were bored and
had a lot of downtime. I felt guilty that our lives went on while Clint's
was on hold in Afghanistan. I hated that he wasn't with us, doing all the
normal things. He said he had no way to get a graduation gift for Tyler,
but he had an idea.

"Mom, I know what I want to do for Tyler. Go over to my house,
go in my footlocker, and get Dad's flight wings, the ones you pinned
on me, and also Dad's old flight bag. I want Tyler to have them; it's his
turn now."

Dick had given Clint his original wings and flight bag before Clint
left for flight school. The flight bag was old and outdated, but it was
full of history and it bore the patches of all the aviation units Dick had
served in. I was so touched by Clint's thoughtfulness that I cried as I
rummaged through his footlocker. I loved that Clint had thought of
the gift all on his own, and I loved that he wanted to hand down to his
brother what his dad had given to him.

When we headed out to College Station for the last time, I again
felt that tug on my heart that I always had when we were closing a
chapter. We got to meet more of Brooke's family and enjoyed our time
with them—although Tyler and Brooke were going to wait until the
following summer to get married, and I sensed that Brooke's parents
were concerned about Army life and what their daughter was marrying into. I thought, *How in the world can I explain this way of life to
them?* During that initial visit, I didn't even broach the subject—we
were busy with all the graduation festivities—but Brooke's mom talked

to my mom at one point that weekend and my mom told her, "I know how hard it is to have your daughter move away, but Vicki and I are as close as any mother and daughter can be, in spite of the distance." I was so proud of my mom for sharing that with Brooke's mom. And who better than she to talk about that?

When Tyler signed in to flight school at Ft. Rucker, I went down to help him get settled in his apartment, as I had with Clint. He was mentally preparing himself for what lay ahead for him.

"Mom, do you realize I have not only the pressure of being Commander Cody's son but also the pressure of being Clint's brother?"

"I can't imagine what that must be like, Ty." I was nervous for him, as I had been for Clint, and I thought, *What if he can't do it—like, what if he isn't cut out for flying?*

Dick's advice to Tyler had been simple: "Do the work, study hard, and give it all you've got. You'll be fine."

But I understood what Tyler was saying. I knew it was tough on both our boys because of who their dad was, and Tyler did have more pressure on him than anyone. I was so relieved when he got through the first weeks and started flying. He took to it like just his father, his brother, *and* his mother.

★ ★ ★

Our time in the division was almost up, and Dick's replacement had been named: Major General David Petraeus. It was an emotional time as we prepared to say our good-byes to the place and the people who had been such an important part of our lives and of Dick's career. We were certainly richer for having spent all those years at Fort Campbell, Kentucky, especially 2000-2002, but it was hard to think that such a big chapter in our lives was coming to an end. When we left Fort Campbell that summer, it would be for the last time. It would also be Dick's last time in a unit with soldiers. Even if he were lucky enough to go further rank-wise, he would most likely be in staff positions.

The division change of command was festive yet poignant. It took place on a perfect summer evening, and I hated that our boys couldn't be there, but we had a large number of family and friends to share the moment with us. Wynonna came and sang the National Anthem, which made it even more special. As the sun was setting behind Old Abe on the parade field, we watched the magnificent sight of fifteen thousand soldiers of the 101st Airborne Division and the other tenant units pass in review. I watched Dick's back as he stood at parade rest, and I knew exactly what he was thinking: he would not be with these soldiers on their next rendezvous with destiny. We both knew the deal, but leaving was harder than we had thought it would be—even harder because we still had US soldiers deployed, including our son.

Right before the change of command, General Shinseki called Dick to tell him that his next assignment was at the Pentagon and that he would be getting promoted to lieutenant general. We had much to look forward to because of the promotion and our move back to Washington, DC, but until Clint returned home safe, none of that mattered.

PS: The day Clint deployed, I felt the harsh reality of Army life up close and personal. If I thought that sending Dick off to war was the hardest thing I would ever do, I was wrong—so very wrong. I had come a long way since my early days as a new Army wife—I had grown and learned to face the challenges of Army life head-on, and not much scared me— but being the mother of a deployed soldier frightened me more than anything I had ever faced.

Thoughts on Deployments

Whenever Dick walked through the door wearing his desert BDUs (battle dress uniform), the reality of his upcoming deployment hit me like a punch in the stomach. It was no longer an abstract notion, something we had been talking about for weeks or months; it was really happening. The change in uniform was but one of the many physical reminders—like a fresh high-and-tight haircut, arms hanging limp after receiving the multiple shots required for overseas travel, a meeting with a JAG officer to get a power-of-attorney form, kit bags lined up by the door—that signaled the beginning of the actual deployment and meant that the good-bye and the departure were just days away.

Not quite as subtle was the game face that showed up one to two weeks prior to a deployment. For Dick, it was kind of a vacant or distracted look, like he was not really listening to or with me. The first time I noticed it was when he and I were engaged and he was stationed in Hawaii. At that time, I was clueless in the ways of the Army and had no idea what a game face was. Years later, when Dick explained it to me, I thought back on that very first deployment and clearly remembered the look in his eyes. The game face is a state of mind, not unlike what a superstar athlete uses to win at his sport; fueled by adrenaline, it gives soldiers the courage to go into combat. Dick's game face got better with each deployment. As he once told me, "The game face gets you through the tough times; it helps you keep the edge. Pilots, especially, never want to lose that edge. Once the game face is on, you've pretty much already left."

When they first leave, you feel a sense of relief—relief from the stress, the buildup of emotions, the dread of actually saying good-bye. But that relief is short-lived, because what follows is fear. For me, it was fear that something would happen on the long flight to where he was going, then fear for his safety and what awaited him and his soldiers at the other end. Then it was loneliness and the overwhelming feeling: *How will I get through the months without him?*

Sometimes these scenes merge and my memories of Dick's leaving are intertwined with Clint's and Tyler's departures. Certainly, there are different emotions attached to sending my husband off and sending a son or sons off to combat. But what never changes, no matter how many times I've experienced a deployment, is the overwhelming sense of helplessness and fear mixed in with love and pride. You see, the men in my family don't just go on business trips or paid sabbaticals or adventures for pleasure; they go on combat missions or, at the very least, training exercises that are almost as dangerous.

I pride myself on being strong before a departure, but right after he leaves, whether it is Dick, Clint, or Tyler, it's a whole other story—I find myself crying over anything and everything. Recently, I was grocery shopping and my bag of groceries fell off the self-checkout stand, with all the contents smashing and spilling on the floor, creating a big mess. The man next to me immediately started picking things up and then the janitor came and they were both so kind. I stood there bawling like a kid. It wasn't just embarrassment; Tyler had left for Afghanistan that morning.

Within a week or so, though, my emotions are back in check and my normal routine continues. The first phone call from my soldier is a relief and a turning point. From that moment on, I know I can get through the months.

During Dick's many deployments, we did not have e-mail, cell phones, Skype, or FaceTime. We had good old-fashioned letter writing and an occasional phone call. When that is all you know, you make it work. I once had the honor of meeting the wife of Medal of Honor winner Colonel Bud Day, who had spent six years as a POW in Vietnam, one of the longest held in captivity. It was the year after Desert Storm when I met Doris Day (same name as the actress), and we chatted about our husbands' war experiences. When she told me that the POW wives sometimes went two years without a letter, I was speechless. I was amazed at her strength and realized how good I had had it when Dick was in Desert Storm. I'm sure the current generation looks at mine and thinks, *How did you get by without e-mail and daily FaceTime?* I've always said that it's all relative and you do what you have to do to get by.

When the boys were young and their dad was gone, I knew that keeping our routine and providing my sons with a sense of normalcy and familiarity was essential to our well-being. Being surrounded by other families going through the same thing was the other key ingredient, because no one else understood like other Army families did. I relied on all my usual comfort zones, too; my hobbies and volunteer work served me well, and the care packages and goodie boxes that I sent were as gratifying for me as they were for Dick. They always made me feel useful.

Operation Desert Storm was the first time I felt the impact of instant news coverage. It was a double-edged sword. It was great when I got to see Dick being interviewed when he first arrived in Saudi Arabia because it gave me, our family, and our entire unit such peace of mind. The downside was that we also knew the minute something bad happened. Terms like "breaking news," "101st Airborne Division," and "Apache helicopter" would stop me in my tracks, and my heart would pound until I heard the rest of the sentence. The weeks after the ceasefire were even more stressful because Dick's unit was still conducting combat operations deep inside Iraq. Helicopters were shot down; accidents and all kinds of other incidents made the news and sometimes were reported incorrectly. A journalist calling a helicopter by the wrong name can be devastating to the people back home who are waiting and watching the news.

It seemed like I had just gone through all of that with Dick, and then the terrorist attacks on September 11, 2001, brought that same reality back into my life all over again. Off and on for the next thirteen years, both of our sons would be deployed, often together. The news arrives even more quickly now, and still the triggering words for me are the same ones. As I stand there staring at the TV, holding my breath, for a moment I think the worst. Then it passes and I move on.

I've talked about compartmentalizing my emotions throughout my journey. Over the years I perfected the skill, which continues to come in handy now that Clint and Tyler have begun deploying. It started out as a coping mechanism but became a matter of survival. The compartments were like rooms in my mind, each one for a different fear. I kept the doors shut most of the time because I knew that if a door opened, the fear would consume me. I couldn't allow myself to give in to it because I had too many people counting on me. It was exhausting, though, keeping those doors shut.

Dick and I now live through the deployments together, both of us waiting for phone calls, e-mails, sometimes a letter. When something happens, it is Dick who gets the first word about it because of his position in the Pentagon. During a visit to the combat zone, Dick spent time with Clint and even flew with him before he flew on to Kuwait for more briefings. During the briefing, Dick got word that an Apache had gone down just outside Bagram, where he had left Clint just hours earlier. Dick said it was the longest seven minutes of his life while he waited to get the tail number of the downed aircraft. He said it was as if time stopped, and for those few minutes he was convinced it was Clint's aircraft. When he found out that it wasn't Clint, his relief immediately turned to concern for someone else's son. Dick confided in me that most days in his office, he lived in fear of a phone call about one of our sons. He finally knew what I had lived with all those years.

One of the hardest things for a mother is not being able to control or fix what your kid is going through. I fixated on the living conditions the first time Clint deployed to Kandahar, Afghanistan. I knew they were primitive; the soldiers slept on cots in tents with no electricity, no running water until later. His first deployment to Iraq was pretty much the same thing. It was so hard for me to block that out of my mind that it took all of my resolve not to obsess about it when I lay in my comfortable, warm bed at night.

But by the time the boys started deploying, I had found my safe haven in my writing. Writing a booklet for parents of soldiers was a hugely therapeutic venture for me. At one point during that process, I kept getting ideas for song lyrics that swirled around in my head, and I ended up taking a little detour. With the help of Wynonna Judd's manager and a talented songwriter, I ended up cowriting a country song in Nashville. Who would've thought that writing would become my passion and my way of coping with the stresses of deployments and Army life?

And then one day I wake up and it is *the* day. The deployment is almost over, and my soldier is on his way home. The excitement and joy of seeing him walk down the steps of the big plane melts away all my earlier stress and fear. The homecoming represents that piece of Army life that makes the waiting, the worrying, and the sacrifices worth it. The homecoming is a little slice of heaven.

21

Inside the E-Ring

When we left Fort Campbell in summer 2002, while Clint was still in Afghanistan, I felt as if we were leaving a piece of us behind. I felt that as long as Dick was the division commander and we were stationed at Fort Campbell, Clint would somehow be safer.

The weeks leading up to Dick's change of command had been hectic and emotional. When it was over, we were spent and needed to decompress, so we went to Florida. We were still waiting to hear when Clint would be returning, hoping that we could stop on our way back from Florida to welcome him home. But the flights from Afghanistan were delayed, so, after our trip, Dick went up to Washington, DC, to prepare for his new job and I stayed with friends at Fort Campbell to await Clint's arrival. Dick would fly back down as soon as Clint was inbound.

I had no sooner unpacked my bags and gotten Barkley and me settled in our friends' house than Dick called to tell me that General Shinseki wanted to promote him the next day.

"He wants to promote you *tomorrow*?"

"Yeah, Vick. I need you to come up here. Can you get packed up and drive up to DC? I can hold it off for maybe another two days."

"Of course I can—I wouldn't miss your promotion for anything. But what about Clint? What if he comes in the next few days?"

"The minute we hear his plane has left Afghanistan, we'll fly back down there. It takes at least twenty-four hours for them to get to the States, so we can make that, easy."

For promotion to three- and four-star general, you don't go before a promotion board; rather, you are nominated by the secretary of defense and the president and then have to be confirmed by the Senate and the House. Dick's confirmation had gone through quickly, and his new position would be G-3 of the Army.

I was on the road bright and early the next morning and made it to DC before dark. The next day, I stood beside Dick in a small reception room in the Pentagon and, along with General Shinseki, I pinned on his third star. It was so spur-of-the-moment that there was no way our family could come down from Vermont. Dick's fellow Army staffers, some generals, and a handful of friends were in attendance. We were excited about his promotion, but it happened so fast, and without our sons and family there, that it felt anticlimactic.

We would move into quarters at Fort Myer again, and since we still had no confirmation on Clint's arrival, Dick set up our move for Monday, August 13, which would also be his first day in his new job. We asked ourselves what the odds were that Clint's flight would come in on that particular day.

Of course, that's exactly what happened. We got the call that Clint had left Bagram Airfield and after a couple of stops was due at Fort Campbell on or about August 13. Six months of stress and worrying about our son came tumbling out, and I had the meltdown of the decade, complete with a migraine. At first we didn't know what to do, how to make it work. It was the weekend, and the movers were on their way; there was no way to stop them. Yet there was no way we were going to miss seeing Clint come in from Afghanistan. We were staying with friends, Mike and Barbara Oates, and Dick and I were going through all the scenarios, trying to figure out what to do. Barbara and their daughters offered to go to our quarters on Monday to accept our shipment so we could fly down to Fort Campbell. What a blessing—for the rest of my life, I will be grateful to them. Dick had to at least report to his new job Monday morning, and then we would catch a flight to Nashville and Fort Campbell.

Monday morning, Dick reported in as the new G-3 of the Army, and by 10:00 a.m. we were driving to Baltimore to catch our flight. The past twenty-four hours had been such a whirlwind that Dick and I hadn't even had much time to talk. Once we were on the road and I let go of the fact that the movers were at our house, I began to breathe again and allowed myself to feel the excitement of Clint's coming home.

I looked at Dick and asked, "How in the world did you get out of there on your first day as the G-3?"

"I gathered my staff in my office—all the colonels, the one- and two-star generals, and my aides—and, after quick introductions, I told them that I was leaving in about thirty minutes to catch a flight to Fort Campbell, Kentucky, because my son is coming in from Afghanistan. Vicki, it was pretty crazy, with everyone talking at once, reminding me who I had a meeting with, where I needed to be, who was waiting to see me, and on and on."

"What did you do? What did you say?"

"I went around the room and delegated tasks to each general and then told them, 'There is not one thing going on in this Pentagon today that is more important than me welcoming my son home from combat. What are your questions?'"

"Wow, Dick, I can't believe you pulled that off. I am so proud of you!"

We couldn't get to BWI Airport fast enough. The entire forty-five-minute drive, I just kept thinking, *We're on our way to welcome Clint. He's finally coming home.*

There was no welcome-home ceremony, no fanfare, no band playing—just us and some other families waiting for our soldiers. Those last minutes before the plane arrived were agonizing. I couldn't sit still, and Dick went outside to pace. Finally, he came back in to tell us the plane had landed and the buses were on their way. The next thing I knew, Clint was walking toward us and I was running and hugging him and crying all at the same time. It was one of the greatest moments of my life. I had never felt such relief.

While we waited for him to turn in his weapon, I just kept staring at him. He was still the same handsome boy, a bit thinner but more grown-up. *I can't believe we made it through our son's first deployment,* I thought.

Dick needed to go back to the Pentagon, but I stayed another day. Then Clint started his reintegration classes, so I headed back to DC, knowing that he would come home on leave the following week.

I flew back to DC feeling at peace, but the minute I landed, I had to face the reality of unpacking fifteen thousand pounds of household goods from wall-to-wall boxes. By the time Clint came home on leave, the house was livable and I forced myself to stop obsessing about the remaining boxes and just to enjoy the time with him.

One day while we were in the car, he said, "Mom, I know this sounds weird, but . . . I miss *it*."

"What do you miss?"

"I miss being with my guys and what we went through. As awful as it was over there, it became home to all of us; there were no outside distractions, just all of us together, flying and doing missions. Since we've gotten back, everybody's gone their separate ways and I miss what we had."

"You know, Clint, I don't think it's that weird. I remember your dad saying the same thing after Desert Storm. I think I get it. You bond and become so close in those situations; then the dynamics change when you get home." Clint didn't have a wife or girlfriend waiting for him when he returned, and I realized it was lonely for him.

"Has Dad mentioned anything to you about another deployment? There's talk of a deployment to Iraq—like, maybe a war. Our unit is already making plans to get all the equipment and aircraft ready when we come back from leave."

"Clint, you just got back from Afghanistan. . . . I'm trying to live in the moment!" I paused. "But, to answer your question, Dad has talked about the plans for the next phase of the war on terrorism, and of course I hear about it on the news."

Dick had in fact talked to me about it. He had already been briefed and was preparing the Army for a massive deployment to Iraq. I didn't know the particulars, but that day with Clint, I didn't want to think ahead; I just wanted to enjoy having him home safe.

After Clint returned to Fort Campbell, I got the rest of the boxes unpacked and Quarters 2 at Fort Myer began to feel like home. Just down the street from where we had lived previously, it was again a big, historic house with large rooms, and perfect for entertaining. We had the same beautiful view of Washington, DC, and we were just up the hill from the Iwo Jima memorial. I was happy to be back in a place where I still had friends—including Nancy, who was at Fort Meade, Maryland, just a short distance away—and I loved our neighborhood.

★ ★ ★

Clint readjusted well to his old routine at Fort Campbell. When we talked on the phone, it seemed as if he had never been gone. Tyler was doing really well in flight school and whenever possible, drove up to Fort Campbell to spend time with Clint.

Dick was extremely busy, even more so than he had been at his previous job in the Pentagon. The G-3 role had a huge scope: running day-to-day operations, which included the overall readiness of the Army, leader development, force structure (the makeup of the units), war-plan strategy, and all of the Army requirements worldwide. His office had to man, equip, train, mobilize, and deploy the National Guard and Reserves, too. I think Dick would have worked himself to death if I hadn't been there for him, with a home-cooked meal and a shoulder to lean on when he came home at night. We attended a lot of official-type functions that went with Dick's position and title, but I made sure we had date nights on Saturdays whenever possible.

Working inside the E-Ring was like a whole different world. We wives joked that the guys had what we called "Pentagon pallor": their hair became grayer, and they looked pale because they never saw the light of day; they went in before the sun was up and left long after dark most days.

Dick spent much of that fall and early winter preparing to move half of the Army around the world, something that had not been done since World War II. He made a lot of trips to Central Command (CENTCOM) in Tampa, Florida, for briefings. Based on the requirements for the war, he had to prepare the Army for the actual deployments and still maintain the requirements for the rest of the forces in the US and abroad. At the same time, he and his staff had to anticipate the second and third orders of effects of a war in the Middle East and the impact on the entire Army. By November and December, tens of thousands of soldiers, Marines, and Airmen began amassing in Kuwait.

During one of our many discussions on the subject, Dick told me, "The entire 101st Airborne Division will deploy—not just part of it, but all of it. Based on the timeline, I think Clint's battalion will leave in February."

"I can't go through it again. And what about Clint? He's been back only six months!"

"We don't have a choice, Vick. This is just the beginning of a pro-longed period of deployments for our military."

When the boys came home for Christmas, it was pretty much a given that the United States was headed for war in Iraq. It was hard to ignore, but I wanted to enjoy having my family together for the holi-days, so I compartmentalized—something I was still quite good at.

When the boys left to go back to their respective places, the familiar feelings of fear crept back into my consciousness. I had taken a break from it for a couple of months, but to me, the new year meant uncer-tainty and letting go of my son again. It was just a matter of time before we would head to Fort Campbell to say good-bye.

That January, Dick and I went out to Keystone, Colorado. We had not been skiing since 1999; we hadn't even had time to stay in the condo that we had bought. I knew that life would get even busier when the war started, so I felt that we needed to get away from the Pentagon and DC for a bit. Dick always listened to me. It was a short trip, since we knew Clint would be deploying soon, but three days of skiing was better than nothing. We loved staying in our own condo, and, as always, the trip served as a healthy distraction in the midst of the chaos that was on the horizon.

When we returned, Tyler drove up to Fort Campbell in early February to say good-bye to his brother, and that was when the reality hit me. We were one step closer to Clint's leaving. Up until that point, I had kept hoping something would change the course of events.

Dick had flown out to Fort Leavenworth, Kansas, to speak at the Command and General Staff College, and, wouldn't you know it, Clint called that day and said the Air Force planes were on their way to pick them up. He would be gone within twenty-four hours.

"Clint, we'll be there. I promise."

My heart was pounding as I called Dick's office to see when he would be home. I was prepared to leave without him if I had to. I asked his XO (executive officer) to get a message to him the minute he landed. By the time Dick landed at Andrews Air Force Base, I had booked us on the last flight out of Baltimore and had our bags packed. I called Clint and told him we'd be there later that night.

We went right to Clint's house, and I'll never forget the first thing he said to us: "Thank you for coming."

"Of course we would come! Did you for one minute think we wouldn't?"

His appreciation melted my heart. He looked exhausted, so we left him and checked into our room at the guesthouse, hoping to get some sleep ourselves. I was mentally fatigued but also keyed up with that familiar, scary adrenaline rush that always came before a deployment.

We had most of the next day with Clint. He and his roommate, Matt, were all packed up. Their small house was full of kit bags, flight bags, and gear. Dick spent the afternoon talking to Clint and Matt about flying in the desert, what to expect in Iraq, and anything else he could think of that might keep them safe. In each of their green Army logbooks, he wrote his Commander Cody's "Ten Commandments," his thoughts on leadership and safety. As I watched Dick with Clint and Matt, noting his thoughtfulness as a leader and as a father, I knew that he wanted to go with them; I knew how hard it was for him to say good-bye to his son again.

We headed out to the airfield that night. It was freezing cold, and there was snow on the ground, but it was aflutter with activity, reminiscent of those times when Dick was leaving with his battalion. Dick helped Clint carry his bags to the loading bay; then we gathered in the battalion headquarters with all the other soldiers and family members. Clint still had the same commander, LTC Jim Richardson, and we were so thankful for his good, caring leadership. Jim was the best commander we could have asked for for our son. That, plus the fact that Clint would be flying with Mike Wells again, gave me some comfort. Clint was in a great unit, and I just had to keep telling myself that the rest of it was in God's hands; there was nothing more that Dick and I could do.

There were some tearful scenes, but most of the families were smiling and posing for pictures with their soldiers. I got to talk to some of the parents, who, like we had, had dropped everything to be there. They had come from all over; some had driven all night, others had flown in, as we had, and some had been there for days, waiting in hotel rooms, all for the sole purpose of saying good-bye to their soldiers. It didn't matter whether it was a son or a daughter, enlisted or an officer; how long they had served; where they had come from—we were spouses and parents who shared the same fears about, pride in, and love for our soldiers. When Clint had left for Afghanistan twelve months earlier, I'd had no one to share it with, just Dick. But that night I felt comforted just being with other Army families.

I hugged Clint as long as I could and told him, "I love you so much and am so proud of you." I forced myself to let go, but all the while I was thinking, *I'm almost out of courage.*

PS: There were times that fall when I felt unsettled. I was used to being a commander's wife, which was a clearly defined role, a role that I knew how to play, but as the G-3's wife, I didn't really have a role or any responsibilities, and I missed that sense of purpose. As it had so many times before, I knew that something would present itself to me. But I wasn't just looking for something to amuse me and to take up my time; with war on the horizon and my son deploying again, I needed something to occupy my mind and at the same time help others in the same situation.

22

Operation Iraqi Freedom

When Dick got back to work after Clint left for Iraq, the Pentagon was in full preparation mode for the upcoming war there. When the air attacks on Baghdad began on March 21, 2003, it was déjà vu for me, watching a war unfold on live TV, but the big difference between Operation Desert Storm and Operation Iraqi Freedom was that Dick was watching it with me, and it was our son we were worried about.

There had been a lot of political controversy in the weeks leading up to the war. General Shinseki, who testified before the Senate Armed Services Committee that it would take "several hundred thousand" troops to effectively do what needed to be done, including the postwar occupation, was heavily criticized for saying as much (though, in the end, it proved to be true). The war started with units still arriving in Kuwait and equipment still on ships out in the Mediterranean Sea. So that night, when General Tommy Franks' "shock and awe" campaign began, Dick was as surprised as I was. He was under the assumption that the war would not begin until April and was concerned about the premature start. He was making phone calls, trying to get information, when Clint called from Kuwait. It was only the second time we had heard from him, and I waited anxiously while Dick talked.

"Dad, what's going on? We heard that the Air Force has begun bombing. We don't have any way to get the news, so tell me what is going on."

"Clint, I'm watching it on TV. This is not what I expected."

It was weird to think that Clint was calling us from Kuwait, asking for information. He told us they were packed up and ready to move north into Iraq but didn't have any orders yet. Now that the Air Force was paving the way, Dick told him they would probably be moving out soon.

I talked to Clint briefly, but the connection was bad and he assured me he would call again before he moved anywhere. Dick and I were nervous all night because these events signaled the beginning of combat operations in Iraq—combat that would involve our son.

I had thought this mission would be similar to Operation Desert Storm or even Clint's previous deployment to Afghanistan: a buildup of troops, some waiting; then, after the Air Force bombed and paved the way, the Army would go in and work its way up through Iraq, take over Baghdad, and capture Saddam Hussein, and then it would all be over, all neat and tidy. Our troops would come home; life would get back to normal. I thought Clint would be gone maybe six months. Now I realize it wasn't so much that I was naive as that I was just scared. I needed to dream up my own version of what I thought would happen, because that made it easier to handle, easier to sleep at night, and easier to get through the weeks and months. I could handle my version better than I could handle the reality of war.

Wynonna Judd called right after the war started. She was watching it on TV and worrying about Clint. She told me she had been sitting there with both her kids next to her, all safe and warm, and she had thought of me.

"How do you deal with this?" she asked me. "How do you let your son go, knowing how dangerous it will be? As a mother, I can't imagine how hard it is."

"It is the toughest thing I've been through. But we did the best we could to raise our sons, and now we have to let them make their choices and allow them to follow their dreams. I just never envisioned their dreams would lead to this!" Then I continued, "I feel like I've spent my whole adult life waiting by the phone. In the beginning, I was waiting for word from Dick that he was safe, and now I'm waiting for the same from my son."

"Hmm . . . That sounds like a country song, Vicki."

We both chuckled. Wynonna lifted my spirits that night. There was something about verbalizing my feelings to her that helped me see the situation for what it was. I had no control over what was happening in Kuwait and/or Iraq. I knew the worst was yet to come, when Clint and his unit would leave the relative safety of Kuwait, and that I had better gird my loins for that.

Clint called a few days later. "Mom, I just wanted to say good-bye."

Then we got disconnected. I stared at the phone, ready to cry, so afraid that that was it. After two more attempts, he got through and said quickly, "I just wanted to say I love you, Mom."

"I love you, too." And then, as I had done so many times in the past with Dick, mustering all my courage, I told him simply, "Be careful, fly safe, do what you need to do, but don't do anything foolish. We are already so proud of you."

★ ★ ★

The following weeks were some of the toughest I had ever experienced, certainly as a mother. Once Clint and everyone else began moving forward through Iraq, there was no word from him, just what we saw on TV. There were nights when we couldn't sleep, nights when I told Dick to go to the Pentagon and see if he could find out something, anything. I didn't care what information he could gather; I just needed some indication that Clint and his unit were okay. One night, while pacing in front of the TV, Dick turned to me and said, "I never knew how hard this would be—being back here, waiting and watching. How difficult it must have been for you all those times I was gone." I had never felt closer to Dick than I did during those long, scary nights at the beginning of the war.

About that time, a huge sandstorm blew through the desert of Iraq, just when Clint and his unit had made it halfway to Baghdad. I had been so worried about the Iraqi army, Saddam Hussein, chemical weapons, weapons of mass destruction, and Clint's helicopter getting shot down, I hadn't considered or anticipated the fury of Mother Nature. For three long days, Dick and I did not sleep. I had never felt such fear in my life; it was worse than anything I had ever felt for Dick, and I honestly didn't think I could take the stress. You see, on those scariest of nights, we were just ordinary parents, like all the other parents out there. It didn't matter who we were or that Dick was a three-star general and the G-3 of the Army; nothing could guarantee that our son would be safe. The only advantage we had was that Dick could go to his office at the Pentagon and check for updates on all the units in the Army. For that, I was grateful.

Whenever the phone rang at night—and it rang a lot because of Dick's position—I held my breath, waiting to hear him say something that would clue me in to what the call was about. It was never good news—soldiers wounded or killed. I lived in constant fear that the phone call would be about Clint. Sometimes it was about someone we knew, and then, while I felt relieved that it was not our son, I would lie in bed and think about some parent or spouse who was receiving the most dreaded news.

When I was so beside myself with fear that I wondered how I would get through the war, life presented me with an opportunity that led me down the path that I had been looking for. The Army set up a toll-free hotline for family members, and one day a week that winter and early spring, I answered phones at the Army's Community and Family Support Center (CFSC). I had a big binder full of information, phone numbers, anything and everything you could think of that might be relevant to a family member who had a soldier deployed. We were there not to answer questions about the specifics of the war but rather to answer more basic questions about the Army in general and to steer the callers in the right direction.

After a few weeks of taking phone calls, I realized that it wasn't just technical information I was giving out to the strangers on the phone; it was reassurance and comfort. I was living what they were living, I understood their worry and fears, so I was able to connect with them. Answering their questions made me realize how much I knew about the Army from my years as an Army wife. I would go home from my volunteer work feeling good that I was possibly making a difference, and that helped me get through some difficult times. Still, it wasn't enough. And then the seed of an idea began to form in my head.

One night while Dick and I were walking Barkley, I relayed my thoughts to him. "There has to be a way that I can reach more people. I feel like I have so much more to give—thirty years' worth of experiences that I want to share."

"What are you thinking, Vick?"

"What if I wrote down all the basic information that I'm giving out on the phone—information about the Army and deployments, my personal experiences—and got someone to publish it? We could hand out the book to parents and family members. We have a lot of information for spouses, but there's nothing for parents of soldiers."

Dick thought it was a great idea, so I began with an outline and told myself I would just see where it led me. For me, once again, the writing gave me something to focus on besides worrying about Clint and the war. Even so, it was hard not to dwell on what was happening in Iraq. I couldn't avoid the news; we were inundated with images and headlines that made it difficult not to freak out. Private Jessica Lynch was captured; an Apache helicopter was shot down and the two pilots captured for a brief time; there were sandstorms; the tanks of the 3rd Infantry Division were rolling through the desert toward Baghdad as the 101st provided air support; US casualties were mounting in the battles of Fallujah, Nasiriyah, and Najaf; and so on and so on. How could I sleep at night with all those images swirling around in my head? I would greet Dick every night with the same question: "How is Clint's unit? Have you heard anything at all?"

He would always reply, "They're fine, Vicki." But that was never enough. I always needed more.

★ ★ ★

We went down to Fort Rucker at the end of March for Tyler's graduation from flight school. Like his father and brother before him, Tyler took his wings off the board at the Officers' Club the night before graduation, and the next day Dick and I and Brooke pinned the wings on him—the very same ones that Dick and Clint had worn. We had a little party back at our guesthouse, and Tyler's buddy and his parents came over for refreshments. It was a very special occasion, but at the same time I was filled with worry because we had not heard from Clint in weeks.

While we were celebrating, Dick got a call on his special satellite cell phone and went outside to answer it. When he came back in, he rushed over to me.

"Clint and his unit are fine; they've been involved in quite a fight in the city of Hillah, but everyone is okay."

"What do you mean? What can you tell me?"

"That was the Army Operations Center [Dick's office]. I was given the status of all the units that had been involved in combat. Clint and his unit are fine—that's all I know."

The fact that he looked so relieved indicated to me that Clint had been in real danger. To be celebrating with one son while our other son was in harm's way was more than even *I* could compartmentalize. But I was good that day and hid my feelings from everyone except Dick, who knew me all too well.

★ ★ ★

April 9, 2003, was a day of celebration for the United States, as the Army rolled into Baghdad and officially took control of the city. I watched on TV as the statue of Saddam Hussein was toppled. It was also Clint's twenty-sixth birthday, the second one in a row that he had spent in a combat zone. I had sent him a birthday box but didn't know then if he'd gotten it.

We got sporadic mail from him, and in one letter he described a little bit about flying his Apache helicopter through the desert. He never mentioned what the combat had been like; instead, he talked about having been on the move for weeks and how they had finally settled at an airfield near the city of Mosul. He detailed his living conditions in a very matter-of-fact way, never complaining about the lack of hot showers, hot meals, phones, or Internet. His letters were always upbeat and funny. Reading them, I thought, *I am so glad both our sons inherited our sense of humor.*

On May 1, President Bush declared the end of combat operations in Iraq and the beginning of an "occupational" force. I believed that my son would be coming home by the end of the summer.

Finally, on Mother's Day, I got my first call from Clint. Dick and I were walking down by the Iwo Jima memorial when his cell phone rang. I sat down on the steps of the monument and talked to Clint. Tears streamed down my cheeks when I heard his voice for the first time in six weeks. It was the best Mother's Day gift I've ever received. He sounded good, so normal, and that was all I needed.

Clint said they were being told that they would stay just long enough to get things stabilized, and then the National Guard and Reserves would come in to replace them. That was what we had all been hoping for.

★ ★ ★

In June, we gathered in Texas for Tyler and Brooke's wedding. As we celebrated with family and loved ones, I thought back to when Dick and I got married and all the excitement of the new adventure awaiting us. The joy I felt for Tyler and Brooke was tempered by the fact that there was a war going on and I didn't know what that would mean for them. Dick took Clint's place as Tyler's best man, and when he read the letter that Clint had sent, there wasn't a dry eye in the crowd. I hated that while we were celebrating such a big event, two important people were missing: Clint was in Iraq, and my dad was gone.

Tyler had already begun a Longbow (the newest version of the Apache) course at Fort Rucker and had about two more months before he and Brooke moved up to Fort Campbell. He had orders for 1-101st Aviation Battalion, the Expect No Mercy battalion, the very unit that Dick had commanded during Desert Storm. Tyler and Clint would be in the same aviation brigade, just different battalions.

Just days after the wedding, I watched Dick on the news, giving a Pentagon briefing about extending the length of deployments, as the situation in Iraq was not nearly stable enough to allow our troops to leave. When he came home that night, I knew what he was about to tell me. He looked more fatigued than usual, weighed down by the world.

"Clint's unit will be staying in Iraq for another eight months."

Just when I'd thought it couldn't get any worse, it did.

"You know what this means: when Tyler signs in to the 101st, he will join Clint's unit in Iraq."

The dream world that I had been living in exploded. My version of reality had the 101st coming back before Tyler got to Fort Campbell. I felt the bottom drop out of my stomach. I just looked at Dick. When he hugged me, I sensed that he was as overwhelmed as I was. All I could think was, *How in the world are we going to get through this one*—both *of our sons in Iraq?*

Clint called almost immediately and talked to his dad. I heard Dick say, "No, Clint, probably not by Thanksgiving . . . longer than that."

When I got on the phone, I could hear the despair in Clint's voice. He had begun his countdown and was down to ninety days. Eight more months was pretty significant. I couldn't control my crying, which I knew was upsetting for Clint, and I hated myself for doing it on the phone.

"Mom, calm down. It's no big deal. I'll be fine." And then, in an upbeat voice, he said, "This means Tyler will be coming, so we'll be together. That will be great! Tell Tyler I'll be waiting for him when he gets here."

We talked to Tyler later that night. He asked how Clint took the news. And then he said, "With me going, it will give Clint something to look forward to. We'll get through it together." *I love these boys for thinking of each other*, I thought.

Tyler was trying to explain everything to Brooke, who was trying to explain it to her parents. My heart ached for them; they were new-lyweds and would have to make some adjustments and decisions that they hadn't planned on. While there had always been the possibility that Tyler might have to deploy, we had figured, like many others, that since combat operations were over, the troops would start coming home. Dick and I spent the rest of the night on the phone with our parents and family members, who wanted to know what it all meant.

I desperately needed some quiet time. I had so many distractions in my life that I was having trouble hearing my inner voice. I needed to listen to and follow my instincts, and I was certain that if I began writing again, my purpose would become clear. It seemed like every-where I turned, I saw signs that pointed me in the right direction. As I finally put pencil to paper, I thought back to 1975, when Dick deployed right before our wedding, and how I had nothing to guide me or my parents—or Dick's, for that matter. I thought about Tyler preparing to leave his brand-new wife. I thought about Brooke's parents and how confused and worried they were, as no one in their immediate family had served in the military, and I thought about all of our friends who had sons and daughters serving. It was for them and all the other moms and dads out there who had someone serving that I wrote my book. I designed the chapters around the needs of the people in my life and the ones I had been meeting and talking to on the phone. Suddenly, it was all clear to me.

I had already pitched my idea to the Association of the United States Army (AUSA), a professional nonprofit association that represents the US Army on Capitol Hill and in the local communities. They liked my idea and, thankfully, said they would get the funding to publish my booklet so that it would be free to everyone, as I didn't want anyone to have to pay for the information I wanted to share.

Meanwhile, in Iraq, the insurgency was growing and the country was becoming more dangerous and unstable. Dick was working day and night to keep up with the demands and requirements of an army at war. The second and third orders of effects of invading Iraq proved more challenging than the actual invasion. The war planners at CENTCOM had not counted on a sustained occupation force. The vacuum that was created when the US military toppled Saddam Hussein's regime and took control of Iraq enabled sectarian violence between the three main religious groups, and the presence of al-Qaeda thwarted any efforts at nation rebuilding. It was total chaos, which made the country too unsafe for the nongovernmental organizations (NGOs) to come in and provide support and assistance. It was up to our military to do all of that. Dick explained to me that it was just the beginning of a very long and protracted mission in Iraq.

★ ★ ★

Clint's letters continued to be upbeat, in spite of his pitiful living conditions and the intense summer heat in Iraq. His unit had settled into what would be their "home" near Mosul for the remainder of the deployment. He started a new countdown: to when his brother would arrive. My only pleasure was sending him goodie boxes with anything I could think of that might make his life a little bit better. He started writing a monthly newsletter to keep up with all the packages and letters he was receiving from so many family and friends. His newsletters were entertaining and often hilarious, and they got even funnier once Tyler arrived and gave Clint more material to write about.

Tyler signed in to the 101st Airborne Division at Fort Campbell. He was given a few weeks to get in-processed and get Brooke settled before he left for Iraq, sometime around the end of September. Time passed quickly for them, as they had a lot of ground to cover. Tyler, having grown up in the Army and having spent much of his youth at Fort Campbell, knew his way around the Army and the area, but for Brooke, it was all new. I was reminded of my first year in Hawaii, trying to learn everything about Dick's job and the Army. I knew Brooke was overwhelmed and that her experience was much more difficult because her new husband was leaving for a combat zone. Dick and I spent a lot of time on the phone with them, answering their questions, listening to their concerns, and supporting them in whatever they decided to do.

Suddenly it was time and we were heading back down to Fort Campbell to say good-bye to Tyler. It was the first time I saw Dick struggle with his game face, I think because of the realization that *both* of our sons would now be in a dangerous combat zone.

Dick left to go back to DC, as he had an already-planned trip overseas to Iraq. I had a few days alone with Tyler and Brooke, and then her parents arrived from Texas. I was glad for their company; I didn't feel so alone with my fears. I could only imagine what they were feeling and thinking. I tried to be strong and reassuring for everyone, but my heart was breaking and I had no game face left. Saying good-bye to Tyler was agony; there is no other way to describe it. I was scared for both my boys and our new daughter-in-law; my worries had tripled.

I had the eleven-hour drive back to DC all by myself to collect my thoughts and get my head straight. I talked to my mom, my sister, and Nancy at various times during the long drive. I cried some, but by the time I pulled into Fort Myer, Virginia, my eyes were dry. I felt empty from head to toe. All three of my men—my whole world—were halfway around the globe, in either Kuwait or Iraq. Dick would be gone about two weeks; he was visiting as many camps and bases as he could.

When Dick finally got home, I was full of questions about everything. I was so glad that he had gotten to spend some more time with Clint and his unit. And, as it turned out, Dick and Tyler had run into each other, albeit briefly, at an airfield in Kuwait. I was especially thankful that Dick had gotten to lay eyes on Tyler one last time. I knew how lucky we were that, because of Dick's position, he had the opportunity to see our boys.

During Tyler's first call to me, he told me that Clint was there to greet him when he arrived, took him around the airfield, and showed him where everything was. For the first time in months, I actually felt some peace of mind just knowing that the boys were together. I knew that they would look out for each other, and that was all I could ask for.

Tyler was busy integrating into his unit and doing all those things Clint had done when he got to his first aviation unit. Tyler's battalion commander was LTC Doug Gabram, a wonderful officer who had been a company commander for Dick during Desert Storm. There were still a couple of warrant officers and crew chiefs that had remained in the unit since Dick had commanded it. Tyler's copilot was CW3 Tim "Vinnie" Vincent, who had flown the Task Force Normandy mission with Dick in Desert Storm. I was so relieved as I thought, *How weird that our boys are flying with pilots who also flew with their dad.*

Eventually, my life settled into a new normal with both boys in Iraq. I've always believed that the good times in life offset and balance out the tough times, and it wasn't all doom and gloom during those months of war and deployments; there were also great moments and happy times for Dick and me.

We celebrated two other weddings that year. My sister, Chris, whose marriage to Jim had ended in the mid-'80s, had finally found her soul mate. She and Tom were married that summer, and I was overjoyed to see my sister so happy. The highlight of that fall was Wynonna and D.R.'s wedding in Nashville. We met the rest of the Judd family, who all showed us warmth and kindness. We were honored to be included in all the festivities surrounding the big event.

Brooke adjusted to Army life. While it was difficult in the beginning, she made some good friends, and, like Army wives past and present, they got through the long days and lonely nights of the deployment, learning from and supporting one another during plenty of scary times that fall and winter.

Tyler called one day and in an excited voice told me that he had just flown his first real combat mission.

"Mom, you'll never guess what aircraft I just flew: Dad's old Apache, tail number 977. Vinnie and I flew *Rigor Mortis!*"

"Wow, Tyler! I had forgotten that *Rigor Mortis* is still in the unit."

"When we formed up before the mission, LTC Gabram handed me the key and said, 'This is your dad's aircraft that fired the first shots of the Gulf War—don't crash it!' Mom, it was so awesome!"

As he continued talking, memories of Dick and Desert Storm came flooding back to me and my eyes filled with happy tears.

"Mom, I always knew what Dad had done, but I didn't feel the significance until I saw his name on the door with the original tail number. When I strapped into my seat, I saw the brass plate on the dashboard that read AT 0238 ON JANUARY 17, 1991, LTC DICK CODY FIRED THE FIRST SHOTS OF THE GULF WAR, and I felt the full impact of what my dad had done. I was honored to be flying his aircraft."

Dick had flown tail number 977 from 1989 to 1991, while he commanded 1-101st Aviation Battalion during combat in Iraq and Kuwait. Dick and Brian Stewmon had been shot at in that aircraft and defied all kinds of odds the night they flew 977 through the desert to take out the radar sites and open an air corridor into Baghdad. They wreaked havoc on the enemy with their hellfire missiles and rockets, whereupon tail number 977 had been aptly nicknamed *Rigor Mortis* and remained in the unit after Dick left.

"Tyler, I'm so proud of you! Just fly safe and be careful." I smiled as I hung up the phone. It was just so unbelievable—and yet so *meant to be*. When Brooke and I talked about it, we both agreed we felt better just knowing that Tyler would be flying Dick's old aircraft. And when Dick came home from the Pentagon that evening, he was grinning from ear to ear. "Can you believe it, Vick? Tyler is flying *Rigor Mortis*! I feel like it is a passing of the torch." There was something strangely comforting in that. Again, I felt the hands of fate holding us close.

★ ★ ★

I dreaded the holidays that year. Dick didn't think he could take leave and be away from the Pentagon at such a critical time, so we didn't go to Vermont. It was probably the loneliest Christmas we had ever experienced. Luckily, my mom and sister came down to DC for New Year's, so we managed to get through the season. That was all I wanted at that point, because I knew that if we could do that, we would be on the downhill side of the deployment and I could begin to count the weeks until the boys redeployed.

Once the end was in sight, it was all I could think about. I knew that Clint and Tyler were doing dangerous things. I knew that every mission they flew, every time they went up in their Apaches, they were defying the odds. I prayed that they would be safe, just a little bit longer.

Tyler got home first. We flew down just for the day to welcome him. As Brooke and I stood there, waiting for the plane, shivering in the cold rain, holding our sign, I was lost in my thoughts, processing the fact that it was my boys who were returning from war. I couldn't stop thinking, *Where have all the years gone?*

We were on our tiptoes, scanning the faces in that sea of desert camouflage coming toward us, hundreds of soldiers. Luckily, Tyler is very tall, and all of a sudden, Brooke said, "There he is!"

He was walking right toward us. I stepped back while he and Brooke hugged, waiting for my turn. "Welcome home, Tyler!" I was shaking as I continued, "We are so proud of you!"

Clint was coming in the following week, and we would head back down to greet him. My mom had never experienced the joys of a "homecoming," and since she couldn't be there for both, we decided to have her come for Clint's so she could see Tyler and Brooke, too.

We all gathered at Fort Campbell, including my cousin Toby, who drove down from Ohio. I couldn't wait for them to experience the homecoming. When Tyler met us out at the airfield, we were all running on adrenaline and didn't mind that it was 4:00 a.m., cold, and dark. Clint was almost home! And, as with so many times before waiting for Dick or for Tyler, I thought the big plane landing and taxiing toward us was the most glorious sight I had ever witnessed. In those moments, nothing else in the world mattered. Dick was up near the plane, shaking the hand of every soldier as he got off. Mom, Toby, Tyler, and I kept waiting and watching for Clint. Those last minutes seemed like an eternity. Then he was walking toward us and the tears came. We all just kept hugging each other as my mom and I sobbed with relief. I was so glad she was with us and got to experience such an indescribable event firsthand.

As we celebrated for the next few days, I felt like the luckiest person in the world. When I watched Clint and Tyler together, I wanted only to hold on to the moment a little longer. Dick went back to DC, and I followed a few days later. Clint spent a week with us, and then, all of a sudden, life seemed normal again, as if nothing had ever happened. It was baffling how quickly the fear and stress subsided, and also wonderful to finally go to bed at night without having to worry.

PS: Even in retrospect, I'm still amazed at the irony that Dick was in that rank and position in the E-Ring of the Pentagon at that very point in time—responsible for so much of what went on in the Army and making critical decisions every day. But who better to be making those decisions that affected so many hundreds of thousands of soldiers than the father of two of them?

Thoughts on What Goes Around Comes Around

I've often thought that life's greatest rewards are the blessings that you don't even ask for, the ones that come along when you least expect them. Dick and I went about our life trying to do the right thing, leading by example for our sons and the people in our units, hoping that our actions had an impact on those around us. Being in the military gave us plenty of opportunities to give to others and hopefully make a difference. So many times, we got tangible feedback, both verbal and written, that validated our hope that we were making a difference. But sometimes it wasn't until years later that we realized we had impacted someone's life or, even better, that what we had done for someone was reciprocated for our family.

I loved being a mother figure to the spouses in our units. I never forgot what it was like to be newly married, new to the Army, and far from home. All of the senior wives who showed me the way, took me to functions, and taught me how to be an Army wife served as my role models when my turn came to pass on the traditions.

The year that my dad was sick with cancer and I made numerous trips to be with my parents, I had so many responsibilities as a division commander's wife, I wasn't sure how I could divide my time, do all the things I was so used to doing, and still be there for my family. I had always been the one in charge, the strong one, the one ministering to others. Now, suddenly, I was in a situation out of my control and I had to depend on those around me, not just to help with my responsibilities but also for emotional support. All the times I had done that for others came back to me that year, and I was surrounded by the love and support of my fellow Army wives. And when Clint deployed that first time to Afghanistan, the spouses of the soldiers with whom he was serving were the ones who gave me the strength I needed to get through it.

When Dick was deployed to Desert Storm, I mailed a monthly newsletter to all the families, including the parents of our single soldiers. I met many of those parents at the homecoming, and they thanked me and told me how much they appreciated my having included them. I never dreamed that one day I would be in their shoes, so grateful for a newsletter from Clint's or Tyler's unit.

In Dick's travels to the combat zones in Afghanistan or Iraq, he went to as many outposts and camps as he could, to talk to the soldiers and let them know how much he cared about them. He sought out anyone we had a connection to—a friend of Clint's or Tyler's, or the son or daughter of someone we knew—and always reported back to their family how that soldier was doing. When Tyler was in Iraq, his company was attached to the 4th Infantry Division for a short time, and he moved to Tikrit. He left the familiarity of his battalion and his brother right around Christmas. I hated that the boys weren't together; it made the holidays even more difficult for all of us. And then Tyler called us on Christmas Day and said, "You'll never guess who woke me up this morning to wish me a merry Christmas—General Odierno!" Our good friend Ray Odierno, the commanding general of the 4th Infantry Division, who had served with Dick a couple of times and whose wife and family were close friends of ours, had found our son that Christmas morning. It meant the world to Dick and me. For all the times Dick had done the same for someone's kid, it had now been done for us.

On that same Christmas Day in Iraq, Clint had guard duty in Mosul and was away from his unit. He later told us that the Peshmerga soldiers he was working with brought him a home-cooked meal of chicken and rice on Christmas night. I thought about all the holidays I had fed soldiers who were alone or single. It warmed my heart to know that there were people out there looking out for our sons, just as we had done so many times.

After September 11, when Dick was commanding the 101st Airborne Division, we had soldiers guarding our quarters around the clock. On Thanksgiving, I made breakfast for the soldiers on the morning shift. That evening, I made a full turkey dinner for the soldiers on the evening shift. We set up tables on our carport, complete with tablecloths and candles. I had gotten permission from their company commander for them to take a short break to eat. Clint was home from flight school and helped us serve dinner. A few years later, Clint was in Iraq, standing in line at the mess hall, when a soldier came up to him. After saluting, the soldier said, "Sir, you probably don't remember me, but I was one of the soldiers who guarded your parents' house after September 11. I was one of the soldiers who had Thanksgiving dinner there. I remember you."

Clint was shocked that the soldier recognized him. He said something like, "Yes, I remember that evening."

The soldier went on to say, "I will never forget what your parents did for us. When you talk to your mom, will you tell her how much it meant to me, to all of us?"

Clint called me that day from Iraq and said, "Mom, you'll never guess who I ran into today." When he told me the story, I felt warm inside. I knew it was one of those special blessings that had come back to me. I also knew it was good for Clint to have heard that from a perfect stranger, because he, too, had made a difference.

While Clint and Tyler were growing up, I never knew how much of our way of life they absorbed. But when each of them became a company commander, I saw that they had the same caring, compassionate leadership style as their dad, but it was not something Dick had consciously taught them; it was something they had observed.

In 1990, right before Dick deployed to Operation Desert Storm, a team of engineers from the Army's night-vision labs came to Fort Campbell to brief him on the night-vision system in the Apache helicopter. The head engineer was a Vietnamese woman, and after the briefing, Dick approached her, curious to know how and when she had come to the United States. She told him that she and her family had evacuated to Guam in 1975, before they had immigrated. He smiled and told her that he had been a lieutenant then, working on Guam. She stared at him and his name tag as he continued, "I used to hand out popsicles to the kids. . . ."

Before he finished his sentence, she exclaimed, "You were the popsicle man! I remember you!"

She had been ten years old at the time, and now, fifteen years later, as a highly educated engineer working for the US Army, she just happened to be briefing Lieutenant Colonel Cody. She followed Dick's career for the next ten years, and when he was at the Pentagon, their paths crossed occasionally. He had told me all of that, and I already thought it was remarkable, but it wasn't until she came to his retirement in 2008 that I realized the impact Dick had had on this young woman. She and I cried as we hugged each other.

She gave Dick a card that day, which was also his birthday, and we were amazed at her eloquence when she wrote, "Commander Cody, you melt my heart and strengthen it too whenever I think of you and see you in action. I'm very glad to be one of the children you helped in Guam and inspired forever. With love and respect, Trang Bui."

What goes around comes around, indeed.

23

A Fourth Star

The spring and summer of 2004, while the war was raging in Iraq and Afghanistan, Dick and I had much to be thankful for. Both our sons were home safe and enjoying their lives at Fort Campbell, Kentucky. Dick was nominated for his fourth star and a promotion to vice chief of staff of the Army. After an easy confirmation, Dick was promoted to the rank of general on July 2, 2004, in the Pentagon auditorium. (We had definitely moved up from the basement room where he got his second star.) Although throughout his career, I had been the one to have the privilege and honor of pinning on each of his new ranks, Dick had recently promoted each of the boys to captain and I decided it was time for them to promote their dad. They stood on either side of him and pinned on those beautiful, gleaming four stars.

I held the Bible as Dick was sworn in as the thirty-first vice chief of staff of the Army, and, standing before the crowd, next to my husband and sons, while listening to the chief of staff talk about Dick, I had another one of those "who would've thought?" moments. I mean, consider the odds: Dick Cody, just an ordinary kid from small-town Vermont who graduated at the bottom of his West Point class and began his career as a transportation officer, went on to become a respected Army aviator and test pilot and, through hard work and determination, made it to the number-two position in the entire Army—and was the first Army aviator ever to do so. As I looked over the audience, filled with family, friends, and soldiers, I thought, *How did we, two kids who fell in love and began a journey not knowing where it would take us, knowing only that we wanted to make it together, raise a family, and watch our sons follow in their dad's footsteps, ultimately make it to this pinnacle of power?*

That whole weekend was a celebration with our loved ones. The night before the promotion, Clint and Tyler had presented their dad with a very special gift: a framed collage of photos of them as young boys with their dad and again as Apache pilots. Each of their flight wings, including Dick's original ones, were mounted underneath the photos. The engraved brass plate at the bottom read: WE ARE PROUD TO FOLLOW IN YOUR FOOTSTEPS AS SOLDIERS, AVIATORS, BUT MOST IMPORTANTLY AS YOUR SONS. It was the best compliment and gift they could have given their father.

As Dick and I began this new chapter in his career, we also reached a personal milestone as we began our thirtieth year of marriage. The next four years would prove to be some of the most exciting and enriching, but also some of the most stressful, that we had ever experienced as an Army couple. Everything that we had learned along the way—all our knowledge and skills, our faith, and, above all, our solid marriage— would come into play during that time.

Dick's job as the vice chief of staff of the Army (VCSA) included both overseeing the day-to-day operations of the Army and executing long-term strategic plans: restructuring, rebasing, growing, and deploying. He worked on the budget, equipping the Army, and so on and so on. It was a huge job involving a vast scope of decisions that would affect the Army for years to come. Given all of that responsibility, I knew that Dick needed me, more than ever, to be his sounding board. And I liked that role. The Army was in uncharted territory during those particular years, 2004 to 2008. Nation building, ongoing counterterrorism opera-tions in two different countries requiring humanitarian assistance, and the training of Iraq and Afghan forces meant there was no end in sight for deployments of US soldiers. At the same time, on domestic soil, a string of natural disasters required more National Guard and Reserves units to be called up than ever before. What was being asked of the all-volunteer force and their families was unprecedented.

Dick felt that the best way to support and to assess the needs of the soldiers was to get out of the E-Ring in the Pentagon and visit as many posts, camps, and stations as he could, both in the United States and in the combat zones. I completely agreed with him. Where I came into the picture was to travel with him, whenever possible, to meet with spouses and families to see what could be done to meet *their* needs. All of the top military leadership agreed that changes were necessary in family support; we just needed to get the ball rolling.

Over the next four years, Dick and I would travel all over the United States, wearing many hats: we were the VCSA and his wife, we were husband and wife, and we were parents. While we listened and talked, Dick's aides took notes for us. There were times when we comforted and times when we laughed with these amazing Army families. We took it all back to Washington with us, and Dick vowed to make things easier and better in any way possible. Sometimes that was all they needed to hear.

The other part of the job that I enjoyed was our regular trips to Fort Leavenworth to speak at the training courses for the newest Army leadership: battalion and brigade commanders, brigadier generals, and their spouses. Dick was such a great mentor and had so much leadership experience to offer them, and together we shared our experiences as an Army couple and family.

We entertained a lot, and I was glad to have the two enlisted aides who worked at our house. We hosted monthly dinner parties for a variety of guests: Department of Defense officials, diplomats, ambassadors, congressmen, senators, journalists, think-tank people, authors, an occasional celebrity, and always some fellow generals and their wives. The conversations around the dinner table were interesting and lively as Dick and I shared stories with them, hoping to give them a snapshot of the men and women and their families who make up the Army. We loved sharing our beautiful home with so many different people. While the Strolling Strings from the US Army Band played in our dining room, I often caught Dick's eye at the opposite end of that long table and knew we were thinking the same thing: *Can you believe we get to do this?*

One of Dick's responsibilities as the VCSA was to plan, schedule, and synchronize all of the Army units for deployments, based on the needs of the war in Iraq and the ongoing mission in Afghanistan. Dick had warned me that many of the Army's ten divisions would be on regular rotation cycles, possibly for the next five to ten years.

"I don't understand, Dick. How can this war go on that long?"

"Now that we're so embroiled in this, there will be no easy way to exit. It's going to drag on for the foreseeable future."

I couldn't help but think, *When Clint and Tyler entered the Army, I never imagined it would be like this.* At the end of the summer, Clint left Fort Campbell to attend the Aviation Captains Career Course at Fort Rucker. And then, that fall, we were thrilled to discover that Brooke was pregnant and we were going to be grandparents. It was a bright spot in the midst of all the talk of war.

As the months flew by, in spite of our busy schedules, Dick and I made time for each other and our kids. Just having everyone together for Thanksgiving or Christmas was a blessing; Army life had taught us to make the memories now, not to wait for tomorrow.

When Clint requested to go back to the 101st after his course at Fort Rucker, the aviation branch assignments officer went to see Dick.

"Vicki, he asked me if we were okay with Clint going back to the 101st, knowing that the division is deploying to Iraq this summer. He also told me that Clint requested 1-101st Aviation Battalion—Tyler's unit. He was concerned and wanted to make sure we are in agreement."

"What did you tell him?"

"I told him that Clint had talked to us and we are fine with it. He was a little surprised, considering the fact that Clint already has two deployments and it would mean our two sons would be in the same unit in a combat zone."

Dick and I had come to realize that if our sons had to deploy, we would rather they be together. The fact that they would both be in Dick's old battalion, the Expect No Mercy battalion with LTC Doug Gabram, seemed to be their destiny.

★ ★ ★

I was almost finished with my booklet for Army parents and was pleased with how it had turned out. I took it in to AUSA and was assigned an editor, and we began the process of getting my manuscript ready for print. My dream was about to become a reality.

As the politics of Washington and debates over the justification of the war raged on in the media and in households throughout America, I was reminded of the turmoil of the late 1960s and early '70s. The

war in Iraq had become as controversial as the Vietnam War. All of
the background noise served only to motivate Dick more. He was on a
personal mission to make life in the Army better for *all* soldiers and to
lighten the load in their rucksacks. There was so much that kept him
awake at night, but he just kept moving forward.

Clint finished his courses and moved back to Fort Campbell. While
Clint and Tyler prepared to deploy, Brooke prepared for the baby and
Dick and I prepared to be first-time grandparents. That summer of 2005
was certainly a time of contrasts—so much excitement on the horizon,
and yet the old fears resurfaced as we got closer to the deployment.

Our first grandchild, Austin Marshall Cody, was born that July, at
Fort Campbell, Kentucky. Dick and I and Brooke's parents were in the
waiting room, beaming with pride. Many of our friends had told us
what it was like to be grandparents, but it is one of those monumental
experiences that you don't understand until it happens to you.

Just weeks later, while we were in Hawaii celebrating our thirtieth anniversary, we were thrown a curveball. During Baby Austin's
checkup, the pediatrician discovered a problem: the bone plates along
the back of his head were actually fusing together, creating a ridge. Tyler
called us and said they were going to Vanderbilt Children's Hospital
in Nashville to meet with a pediatric neurosurgeon. That doctor confirmed that Austin had craniosynostosis of the sagittal suture, a defect
that occurs in about one in every two thousand births and is twice as
likely in males. Austin would need surgery soon, as there was a short
window of opportunity to correct the condition, between eight and ten
weeks of age. My heart ached for Tyler and Brooke and what they were
facing with their newborn baby. I had never felt so helpless.

While we all tried to reassure each other, at the end of the day, neu-
rosurgery on our ten-week-old grandson was the scariest thing we had
ever faced. Not to mention that we had another deployment hanging
over our heads.

When Tyler explained the situation to his company commander,
everyone in his chain of command agreed that Tyler could stay back
until after Austin had recovered from the surgery, and he could join his
company in Iraq afterward. In the midst of all our stress and fear, we
were relieved that Tyler could at least be with his wife for their baby's
operation.

PS: I made my summer visit to Vermont that year, and the day I left, I was standing in my sister's driveway, crying while saying good-bye to her. Chris had never seen me like that and wasn't sure what to do. As I hugged her, I said, "I don't want to go back to DC, because I have so many hurdles to face. I don't know if I can do it: say good-bye to Clint, get through Austin's surgery, and then say good-bye to Tyler."

She hugged me and said, "You always handle things, Vicki. It's just tougher this time, but you'll do it."

24

More Deployments

August 2005 signaled the beginning of a series of rapid-fire hurdles for Dick and me. Clint was leaving for Iraq at the end of August. As emotional as the good-bye was, at least I had been down that road before. I figured I could get past that and through another deployment. What I was fearing and dreading most was Baby Austin's surgery and its emotional impact on Tyler and Brooke. That was a road not previously traveled, and I didn't know how to prepare myself, or any of us, for it.

While we were facing uncertainty as a family, our country was facing one of the deadliest and costliest hurricanes in decades. Hurricane Katrina hit the US Gulf Coast with a devastating blow. I had not thought about the storm's impact on our military, but by the time we got back to DC, Dick had just days to make preparations for the units that were returning to Louisiana from a recent deployment and to activate the National Guard.

The week we spent at Vanderbilt Children's Hospital elevated our fear and anxiety to a whole new level. I don't know which was more agonizing: Austin's surgery or the aftermath. We prayed a lot in that waiting room and in the days after the operation. But the procedure went well, and the doctor was optimistic that Austin would be fine, so I tried to live in the moment.

My book, *Your Soldier, Your Army: A Parent's Guide*, was presented at AUSA's Annual Meeting at the Washington Convention Center while I was at Vanderbilt. It exceeded AUSA's expectations and mine. We started getting feedback immediately: notes, letters, and e-mails from parents, grandparents, and even soldiers. I knew then that my book was doing exactly what I had hoped it would do, and that wonderful feeling kept me going.

The next hurdle was saying good-bye to Tyler when he left for Iraq. As a mother, I felt my heart breaking for him, as he had to leave his wife and baby right after the surgery. I was relieved that Brooke was going to live with her parents in Texas, knowing that she and Austin would be well cared for, but I still worried about them. And, once again, I experienced the strain of having both of my sons in a combat zone. As with the time before, my only comfort was knowing that they were together.

That winter was one of the rare times in my life when I was burdened with even more stress than I was used to, and there were times when I couldn't see my way out of the dark tunnel I was in. During Austin's follow-up appointments, his doctor was concerned that he might have to do a second surgery. It was not the news we wanted to hear. Then I hit rock bottom when we had to put Barkley down right before Christmas. At the same time, we were caring for Tyler's dog, who was a real handful. I lost weight, which at any other time I would have welcomed, but I was losing it for the wrong reasons. I felt like more and more anxiety was being heaped onto my already-full plate. I got up each day and put one foot in front of the other and forced myself to focus on what was in my control. I prayed for the strength to face the rest, and I relied on Clint and Tyler to look out for each other.

Dick was just as worn out as I was. He had not only our personal worries, but also the weight of the entire Army on his shoulders. One night after a long day at the Pentagon, I met him at the door and literally hung on him. I was crying as I tried to tell him, "I can't do this anymore, Dick. I'm too overwhelmed; I'm not used to feeling this way."

"We don't have a choice, Vick. We're going through what so many others are going through. It's going to be okay. The boys are doing fine and looking out for each other. If Austin has another surgery, we'll get through that, too." He was my rock in that moment; I felt as if he was the only person in the world who understood me.

★ ★ ★

What definitely helped me during that time were my role and duties as the VCSA's wife. Dick and I continued our travels to posts throughout the Army and were amazed at the strength and resiliency of the spouses we met. They were so inspiring that just being with them got me through some tough times.

Living on Fort Myer, however, meant there was no avoiding the realities of war. Arlington National Cemetery, with its endless rows of white headstones, so much a part of the landscape, was right there. On all my morning walks with Barkley, I had watched the riderless horse and the caisson as they made their way to the chapel and the cemetery. Our first years at Fort Myer, while the sight of the procession always gave me pause, I didn't think too much about *whom* the caisson was carrying. But in 2003, we started seeing funeral processions carrying soldiers from this war. By 2004, we had friends whose sons and daughters were among the injured and the casualties. Suddenly, those funeral processions took on a very real and personal meaning.

Dick was right, however: we did get through those months. I was twelve pounds lighter and had a few more gray hairs, but I still found laughter and blessings in everyday life. The bright spot during that time was the feedback that I continued to get for my book; I had never expected that my little sixty-four-page manuscript would connect me with so many people, so many of whom shared that they found comfort in the fact that I was living what they were living. For all those people whom I helped with my book, they were helping *me*, too, even if they didn't realize it.

★ ★ ★

Finally, it was August and Tyler was on his way home. We went down to Fort Campbell for his homecoming. Each one was unique, but that particular one was special because we got to see our son reunite with his wife and baby. We were all apprehensive about how Austin, just one year old, would take to his dad, who had been gone for nine months. That first night, as we sat at their kitchen table eating pizza, Austin, in his high chair, very nonchalantly reached over and put his chubby little hand on Tyler's arm. It was such a meaningful gesture for a one-year-old that something inside me just melted. I looked at Dick and said,

"It's time to go home; all is well here." Then when Clint arrived a week later, I felt as if most of my prayers had been answered: both boys were home safe.

Within weeks of Tyler's return, Austin had his second surgery; he was just thirteen months old. It was another agonizing week at Vanderbilt Children's Hospital. Again, the doctor was optimistic that he had corrected the problem, so we were hopeful and prayed that it would be the last surgery for our grandson.

By that fall, I felt as if some of my burdens had been lifted. My family was safe, healthy, and happy, and I savored that sweetness because it felt so hard-won. I was also so proud of Dick and all that he was doing as the VCSA. His unique leadership style was just what the Army needed during those years. He was a champion of the soldiers during a difficult and tumultuous time of war. He knew what to focus on and which battles to fight, inside the E-Ring and the halls of the Pentagon and on Capitol Hill. He was never intimidated by red tape or politicians, or anyone else for that matter; he was tough with the bureaucrats and gentle with the soldiers. He took on some high-profile and unpopular issues, but never wavered in his commitment to solve problems and improve conditions within the Army. Soldiers knew they could count on General Cody for just about anything; he was known as the GIs' General, and rightly so.

★ ★ ★

On December 30, 2006, Saddam Hussein was executed by hanging. For many, it meant closure of some sort, the end of a bad chapter in history, the end of a tyrant. Osama bin Laden was still on the run, and to me he was the "bad guy" we needed to bring to justice. Iraq was in the throes of a civil war, although that was the subject of much debate both in the United States and in Iraq. I got tired of hearing all the rhetoric on TV and in the media. The death toll continued to rise, helicopters were being shot down and crashing, and IEDs were killing and maiming our soldiers. Talk of a surge and more troops being sent to Iraq, of extending deployments to fifteen months, dominated the news. It was a difficult time in our country, and a very scary time to be a spouse or parent of a soldier. What made it more difficult was all the fighting

between political parties; the nitpicking, hair-splitting semantics; and the antiwar protesters' second-guessing every decision. I understood freedom of speech, but, as a mother of two soldiers, I found it hard to hear all of that played out in the news, especially when Clint and Tyler were deployed. To me, it undermined what our brave men and women were being asked to do. I think we Army families wanted to know that what our soldiers were doing in Iraq and Afghanistan was appreciated and worthy of their sacrifices. I *had* to believe in the mission; otherwise, how could I get through the deployments?

When former president Gerald Ford passed away, Dick filled in for the chief of staff as one of the honorary pallbearers at the state funeral in Washington, DC. As I walked into the National Cathedral that morning, I had no idea what to expect, or, rather, how the day's events would move me. At a time when our country seemed so divided, the sight of three former presidents—Carter, Bush, and Clinton—alongside George W. Bush gave me a warm sense of peace. What struck me was that this city where the politicians, the pundits, and the media rule, a city that runs on cynicism and partisan politics, suddenly didn't seem so divided.

After the service, while riding in the motorcade to Andrews Air Force Base behind the flag-draped casket and the Ford family, Dick and I noticed people lining the city streets and all along the route on I-295. Everyday people, ordinary Americans—men, women, and children from all walks of life—had stopped what they were doing and were standing in front of 7-Elevens and Dunkin' Donuts, on the hillside, along the curb. As we passed by, they took their hats off, saluted, or put their hands over their hearts in a spontaneous and beautiful tribute to a former president. I turned to Dick as he looked out his window and said, "These are real Americans; this is the America that I love."

The Army was definitely stretched but not broken, as Dick reminded Congress and the Senate whenever he had the opportunity. The problem with the repeated, back-to-back deployments was that the units spent most of their dwell time training and resetting for the next deployment, and Dick worried about the toll all of that was taking on the Army.

During that time, Dick began walking home from the Pentagon whenever possible. It served a couple of purposes: First, in combat boots, with a rucksack on his back, he knew it was good for him physically. Also, mentally, the walk home gave him a chance to reflect without anyone around—no entourage, no aides, no one briefing him, no phones ringing. He told me that those walks helped him keep his perspective and focus after a long day in the Pentagon. He told me that as he crossed the Arlington Memorial Bridge and rounded the bend along the cemetery, the sight of those white headstones served as his motivation and gave him his sense of purpose. He would ask himself, *Am I doing everything I can to live my life in a way that's worthy of the sacrifices our soldiers are making?*

Oftentimes I met him halfway, at the bridge, and made the rest of the walk with him. We came to love those evening walks by the cemetery and up the hill past the Iwo Jima memorial, catching up on the day's events, whether significant or insignificant. They were little stolen moments in the midst of our busy lives.

★ ★ ★

We spent the Fourth of July at the National Training Center (NTC) at Fort Irwin, California. After all those years of listening to Dick's stories about thirty-day rotations, training in extreme desert conditions, and being in "the box," I finally got to experience and see for myself what it was like to be a soldier, and how they trained for deployments to Iraq and Afghanistan. After a tour through mock villages, complete with real Afghan and Iraqi role-players, we ended up in the big mess tent for a special Fourth of July dinner. We dined with hundreds of soldiers who would be leaving for Iraq as soon as they finished their training. I had met so many soldiers throughout the years, and in all kinds of settings, but never like that—in 116-degree heat in the middle of the desert, with dust and sand everywhere, sweat dripping off all of us. What spirit, what camaraderie they had, young men and women from all parts of our country, ordinary-looking on the outside yet anything but ordinary on the inside, and all heroes to me. I prayed that they would be safe in their travels and would return home to their families.

In fact, Dick and I had been surrounded by heroes for the past thirty-six years. Arlington National Cemetery and cemeteries throughout the

United States are full of heroes, but heroes are not just the wounded and the fallen; they are the men and women who wear the uniform, who continue to deploy, who say good-bye to their loved ones time and time again, sacrificing so much. Heroes are the wounded warriors at Walter Reed in Bethesda, the Center for the Intrepid in San Antonio, and all the other military hospitals. Heroes are the doctors, nurses, and therapists who take care of them, and the chaplains who minister to the soldiers in combat and the families back home. A hero is the young soldier's wife with two little kids, seeing her severely wounded husband for the first time at Walter Reed and realizing the full extent of his injuries, or the sister who quits her job and moves to Walter Reed to care for her seriously wounded brother. Heroes are these families who stand beside their soldiers and serve their country, too, from the sidelines.

★ ★ ★

The day the new chief of staff of the Army was announced, Dick came home from the Pentagon with a defeated look on his face.

"It's not that I expected to be the chief, Vicki, but, let's face it, when you're in the number-two position, it's hard *not* to think about the number-one position. This means there's no other job for me and that at some point I will have to think about retiring."

I went to him and put my arms around him. Unlike me, Dick had never been one to give in to his emotions, but that night I knew he was about as close to tears—or at least a quivering lip—as I had ever seen him.

Dick had always said to those around him, "Work every job as if it is your last one." Dick had always done just that, pouring his heart and soul into every role, no matter how big or small, from platoon leader to vice chief of staff of the entire Army. But I don't think either of us thought this was his last position.

"What does this mean? What will we do?"

"I have a meeting with the SECDEF [Secretary of Defense Bob Gates], and we'll see what he says. But, Vicki, you know me. I'm not going to hang on, hoping for some job down the road. I love being the vice, and I can still make a difference. If he asks me to stay on, I will. But after that, I'll retire."

All I could think was, *Retire? We're not old enough to retire. That's for other people—not us!*

Secretary Gates did ask Dick to stay on for another year as the vice. We then had a timeline. We told ourselves to put smiles on our faces and move forward, and we continued to remind each other that it had been a great ride. Dick had gone further than we had ever dreamed he would. It just took some time to wrap our heads around the concept.

Dick had a lot of things he wanted to accomplish, and we both wanted to enjoy the time we had left. Our life was an amazing series of unbelievable happenings and moments. I would be lying if I said it wasn't exciting traveling with an entourage, flying on a Gulfstream jet, meeting some pretty famous people, attending all kinds of fun events. The power of those four silver stars on Dick's uniform and the way people reacted to him was at times a heady experience. Yet what I remember most were the small, intimate moments. At an event honoring Stevie Wonder, we were backstage with Wynonna Judd when we ran into Smokey Robinson. When he saw Dick in his uniform, his mouth literally dropped open. In his signature soft voice, he thanked Dick for his service and then asked if he could hug him. I stood there in awe as Smokey Robinson, *the* Smokey Robinson, whose music we had grown up listening to, hugged my husband with tears in his eyes. He told us that he, too, had served in the Army. Every bit as emotional was the severely wounded soldier trying to stand and salute my husband from his hospital bed, or the little boy and his dad riding in an elevator with us, looking up at Dick with wide-eyed wonder. And when Dick knelt down and gave him one of his General Cody coins, I thought the little boy was going to cry.

One beautiful spring day, Dick and I went to the White House for Military Spouses Day on the south lawn. Dick just happened to be briefing President Bush right after the event, and since I was going to be with him, we were told that I could wait in the West Wing while Dick had his meeting. After the reception, Dick and I were ushered into the waiting room just outside the Oval Office. I sat down in a chair, put on my reading glasses, and was signing one of my books for Dick to give the president, when suddenly the door opened, and with absolutely no pomp and circumstance, no trumpets blaring, no entourage, in strolled George W. himself.

He walked up to Dick, and they shook hands. Then Dick turned to me, and the next thing I knew, the president was walking toward me with his hand outstretched. I was startled, as I had not expected to see him. I froze, and as I stood up, my book fell off my lap and I fumbled to take my glasses off. I put the pen and my glasses in my left hand so I could shake hands with him. I was wondering if he remembered meeting us at Fort Campbell back in 2001, but he and his wife crossed paths with so many people every day, there was probably no way. His staff must have briefed him, though, because as he shook my hand, he asked how our sons were and if they were deployed. He then put his arm around me, and the photographer started snapping pictures. I still had the opened Sharpie pen in my hand, which was now behind the president's back because I didn't know where else to put it. He was talking to me, and I was answering and smiling for the camera, all the while worrying that I was going to get black permanent marker on my beautiful pale yellow suit or, worse yet, on President Bush's suit! When no one was looking, I gently laid the marker and my glasses on the antique credenza behind us and hoped that the surveillance cameras and the secret service didn't think I was up to something! All of that was going through my mind while the president was talking to me. After a few minutes, President Bush said, "Dick, are you ready to brief? Vicki, are you coming in with us?"

"No, thanks, Mr. President. I'll just wait outside."

As I sat in the reception area in the West Wing, I saw all kinds of important people coming and going with their briefcases and their entourages. I tried to look important; little did they know, I was actually writing a grocery list. And that's how it was in a nutshell: talking to the president of the United States or to George Clooney at the White House Correspondents' Dinner one minute, doing daily errands or speaking with Army wives whose husbands were in combat in Iraq the next.

So, if we ever began to feel special because of Dick's position, everyday life always tempered the glamour and glitz, and the soldiers and families we met always humbled us and brought us back to reality. We knew how blessed we were, and we tried to never take it for granted that both of our sons had lived through combat deployments. Every time we visited Walter Reed or attended a funeral at Arlington, we remembered our good fortune.

Our sons were making names for themselves in the Army and doing it on their terms. Clint was commanding an Apache company in Dick's old unit in the 101st and doing a great job. He was preparing his unit for yet another deployment to Afghanistan. Tyler went to the Aviation Captains Career Course at Fort Rucker, then got accepted into the Instructor Pilot Course, and became an instructor pilot. Dick and I were so proud of them for the leaders they had become and for handling everything else that went with being General Cody's sons.

Meanwhile, I was still worried about the day-to-day stresses of Dick's job. The traveling, the long hours, the late-night phone calls, and all the attendant responsibilities concerned me. Many a Sunday after church, he would go in to his office, or up to Walter Reed to visit wounded soldiers. I once asked him why he didn't take Sundays off. He reminded me, "Soldiers in the combat zone don't get Sundays off." I never mentioned it again.

Still, I became even more relentless about scheduling time off for him. I often met with his schedulers and entourage to ask them to work with me to carve out some down time for Dick. He had more energy than anyone his age, and because he loved what he was doing, he rarely said no to anyone. But I also knew there was a limit to how much he could take on before something had to give, and he usually listened to me. Date night became more important than ever, since we spent so much time at large functions and were always with his entourage. I scheduled ski trips, often meeting up with Tom and Gail Greco at our condo in Keystone, Colorado. While Tyler, Brooke, and Austin were at Fort Rucker, we made annual trips with them to the beach along the Florida panhandle. But there were times when Dick needed alone time, and as someone who cherished my own solitude, I certainly understood and made sure he had that, too. If he had any free time, he either played golf or drove up to his hangar at the Carlisle, Pennsylvania, airport. He would fly the plane when the weather permitted or just putter around. I was so glad he still had his passion for flying. He needed that more than ever.

PS: I remember thinking at one point that Dick and I were on a fast-moving train that would pull into the station for a brief stop and then start rolling again, leaving us barely enough time to unpack and repack our bags. Between our responsibilities with Dick's job and our family, I just wanted the train to stop for a while. I wanted to relish and appreciate the people and places and things that we were experiencing. Sometimes I just wanted to stop and smell the roses.

Thoughts on the Nature of the Business

When we pulled up to the brigade headquarters, Father Di Gregorio, our Catholic chaplain, met us. I practically ran to him. "Is it Dick?"

"Dick is fine, but there's been an accident." I was relieved, but it was short-lived, because I knew that meant someone's husband had been injured.

My mom just happened to be visiting me at Fort Campbell when two of Dick's Apaches collided during training in the California desert. Mom sat with me in the brigade commander's office that day while I waited for the details and figured out what was needed of me. At one point, my eyes met my mom's and she looked stunned. Nothing had prepared her for what was happening. One minute she and I were shopping for yarn for a knitting project, and the next we were waiting to hear the fate of four pilots in Dick's unit. And as many times as I had been through it myself, I was never prepared for the reality. I was so glad for my mother's company those days after the accident. I remember at one point, she said to me, "Vicki, I don't know how you live this way."

I replied, "I don't know, either." But then I thought, *It's just the nature of the business.*

Many times throughout Dick's career, I found myself struggling to explain our way of life. How do you describe the unique, unusual, sometimes bizarre, often challenging, acronym-filled roller-coaster ride that we call Army life? How do you justify the long hours and low pay, the years spent apart, moving eighteen times in thirty-three years, or the ache in your heart each time your husband or son deploys? My husband didn't just work in a nice, safe office building: his office was a hangar at the flight line or the cockpit of a very complex helicopter; it was the firing range; it was a tent in a frozen, muddy field in winter, or in the desert of California or Egypt in the heat of the summer; it was an airfield in Georgia or Florida. And his workday didn't end at 5:00 p.m. if there was still work to be done. It extended to Saturdays after our kids' soccer games, Sundays after church, holidays, birthdays, and anniversaries. Life revolved around training cycles.

Dick and his fellow soldiers worked, ate, slept, and survived together, as a team. Working in such close proximity, often in adverse conditions, forges a bond and closeness that separates the Army profession from most others.

For Dick, it was never enough to be just a pilot; he wanted to lead soldiers, too. He seemed born to do so, as he possessed an uncanny ability to motivate and inspire young men and women. Commanding a unit is what most officers strive for as soon as they get commissioned into the Army. Company command is the first level of command, then battalion or squadron, brigade or regiment, and ultimately division. An officer is lucky to be selected for one command at each level, but Dick got more than his share. He commanded twice at each level and then went on to command a division. Some say he had more commands than any other officer in his generation.

If soldiering is an affair of the heart, then commanding soldiers is an affair of the soul. Command takes every bit of your mind, your heart, *and* your soul. Commanding soldiers involves so many human dynamics. It's not just about high-tech equipment, expensive helicopters, gee-whiz machinery and gadgets; the Army is a melting pot of men and women from all backgrounds, socioeconomic levels, religions, and races. When you strip away everything that is the Army, when you peel away all the layers, at the very core, deep in the heart of the Army, you have human beings—soldiers and the families who love them. To Dick and me, whether it was his company, battalion, brigade, or division, that unit became our family. We were like parents who had two years to raise our entire family, two years to make a difference in their lives.

I can't think of any other profession that affords a person the opportunity to be the CEO of the equivalent of a midsize company, and at a fairly young age. Dick was not quite thirty-nine when he took command of his battalion, which included 335 soldiers and officers (pilots, crew chiefs, mechanics) and approximately $500 million worth of helicopters and other equipment. But it wasn't the dollar amount that was so daunting; it was the human assets.

"If I do nothing else in life, at least I got the opportunity to command," Dick often said. He treated his soldiers as he would his own sons and provided them with the best leadership he could, and he exacted the same leadership from the commanders below him.

While Dick was commanding the 101st Airborne Division, as we drove through the main gate after a long holiday weekend, he said to me, "I think I'll go work the main gate and check IDs with my MPs. They didn't get the weekend off, and besides, I want to see my soldiers coming back in from leave." He put on his uniform and walked over to the main gate and worked for the next few hours. You can imagine the reaction of the soldiers and anyone else who came through the gate. There was Commander Cody, their CG, checking IDs!

So it was only natural that the nature of Dick's business became my business, too. My role as the commander's wife was to be strong, positive, and reassuring, much like a mother. I was a coach, mentor, cheerleader, and support system for the spouses and families. I helped form up and run the family support groups within our units. It was something I chose to do and enjoyed every aspect of.

We Army wives formed the same special bonds that our soldier husbands enjoyed. My friendships were as important to me as my family. And unlike friendships that are based on the amount of time spent together and on living in close proximity, where you can nurture and tend to the relationship, Army friends don't always have that luxury. We make new friends each place we live, doing it quickly, oftentimes with very little in common besides the fact that our husbands are serving together. We form connections out of mutual respect and sometimes out of adversity, like getting through a deployment together. We pack a lot of history into our time together, knowing that we will have to say good-bye at some point but, all the while, hoping that we will reunite somewhere down the road. Our friendships are able to withstand great distances and months or years apart, but none of that matters when we see each other again. I am lucky to have a handful of these friends whom I carry with me, even today. And while there are many other friends with whom I may not be in constant contact, I know they're out there, always part of my Army family.

I'm sure some people see my life as an Army wife as trivial, perhaps insignificant. I'm sure some must wonder why I didn't go out and get a paying job, how I could have been content to spend my life in support of my husband's career, and how I could have felt fulfilled doing volunteer work. It's hard to explain a way of life in which my husband's job and position did define my role, but having the opportunity to take part in and impact his units was exactly what I wanted to do. I was part of a generation of Army wives who accepted the role, the responsibilities and duties, willingly. Some would call that old-fashioned, and in many ways it was. Maybe I was part of a dying breed of women, but everyone I knew did it, and like our husbands, we saw it as a privilege to be in a leadership position.

We wives didn't get paid for what we did, at least not in money, but the rewards were far greater than any amount of income. For me, the pay was the gratification and satisfaction of knowing that I had made a difference in the lives of soldiers and their families. Because of Dick's numerous command positions throughout the years and all the various positions I held, I gained an understanding of the Army and learned so much about people and about myself. I took advantage of what the Army offered to commanders' spouses and attended all of the courses and classes at Fort Leavenworth and Carlisle Barracks. By the time Dick became a four-star general, I felt like I had a Ph.D. in Army life.

Dick and I experienced every kind of trauma in the units he commanded. When tragedy struck or someone died, it was like losing a family member. It wasn't always aircraft accidents, although there were plenty of those. We dealt with all the other life experiences, like car accidents, training accidents, suicides, and illnesses, too. There were times when we faced something the schools or books hadn't prepared us for, times when I turned to Dick and asked, "How in the world do we deal with this?"

I've often thought how strange it is to have a profession that affords you the opportunity to command soldiers, but just when you've gotten things running well—you've built your team, led them, guided them, trained them, taken them as far as you can, all the while having the time of your life—you have to hand it all over to your replacement. It's a heartbreaker. In most other professions, you work your way up, and when you get to the top, you get to stay as long as you are capable. If you are a doctor or a lawyer, you build your practice and run it for as long as you want. But not in the Army.

Dick was doing a great job as the VCSA, but when his time was up, it was really up. There is always someone waiting to replace you, no matter how good you are. The thought of retiring from a way of life that Dick so believed in and loved was overwhelming. I realized that he and I had been going through a grieving process in the months leading up to his retirement. It came over us in stages, much like any kind of grief. At first we were angry about the fact that there was not another job waiting for Dick and that he would have to retire. Then we confronted a fear of the unknown and what we would do at ages fifty-eight and fifty-five, a scary time in our lives to begin anew. And then a variety of other emotions kicked in as we both thought about Dick's actually taking off his uniform and leaving the Army. House hunting and sorting through thirty-six years' worth of memorabilia and mementos was part of the process of letting go; I spent an entire evening crying as I looked through all of my recipe boxes and realized the recipes I had collected from my fellow Army wives were like a chronicle of my life. But ultimately, planning Dick's retirement reception and other family gatherings to celebrate his career served as a form of therapy and helped us reach a point where we began to feel excited about the future.

25

The Last Chapter

If we learned nothing else from our years in the Army, we learned to value the important things in life, which aren't a fancy house, a big income, first-class trips, or material wealth. When we visited our siblings and civilian friends and watched them build their dream houses, raise their kids in one place, or buy time-share vacations because they could predict their lives, sure, it was enviable. But oh, the benefits Dick and I had accumulated—the experiences, the people, the places we had seen; the challenges and fears we had faced; the joys and love we had shared with our two sons—made us feel like the richest couple on Earth.

One evening in 2006, we were sitting around our dining room table with the Judds—Wynonna, Naomi, and Grandmother Polly. They were in DC for an event, and we had invited them for dinner. Having spent a lot of time together over the years, we were all very comfortable with each other and the conversation flowed easily. The table looked beautiful, with candles lit and fresh flowers, and our enlisted aides served us a delicious meal. Naomi looked around, taking in everything, and then turned to me and said, "You must be so happy now; Dick is a general, and you live in this beautiful house."

"Actually, Naomi, I've always been happy. Even when Dick was a captain and we lived in crappy little quarters, I was happy." I paused, then continued, "I was just sitting here thinking, *Who would've thought that one day we'd have the Judds at our dinner table?*"

Without missing a beat, Naomi replied, "And I was thinking, *Who would've thought the Judds would be having dinner at a general's house?*"

Times like that, and there were plenty of them, were priceless. But it was all coming to a close, now that Dick was thinking about his

retirement. Where had the years gone? One minute Dick was a lieutenant with his whole career in front of him, and now, as his was ending,
his sons were beginning their own. I would be lying if I said it was easy
and that we were ready; we were anything but.

I know plenty of people look forward to retirement—people who
don't love their job, people who are tired or bored and can't wait to play
golf and relax. But we didn't feel that way, neither one of us. You see, I
had come to realize that being a soldier is more than a job, more than a
career; it's an affair of the heart, a way of life. For Dick, it was his *raison
d'être*, and because my life was so intertwined with his, being an Army
wife had been *my* career, along with raising our kids. So the thought
of its being over was traumatic for me, too. Neither one of us could
imagine any other way of life.

Seeing Dick among soldiers—whether it was one or two, or a crowd
of hundreds or even thousands; whether he was on an Army post or in
a combat zone, on the wards at Walter Reed Army Medical Center, or
serving chow in the mess tent at the National Training Center on the
Fourth of July; whether he was pinning on medals and awards or pro-
moting soldiers, swearing in new recruits at Times Square in New York
City, leading West Point cadets in cheers at the annual Army-Navy
game, checking IDs at the gate at Fort Campbell, or just stopping to
talk to a soldier in the halls of the Pentagon—never ceased to be won-
drous. He just had a way about him that was unlike that of any other
general or leader, and it was consistent from the beginning, even when
he was a second lieutenant. Dick had a gift for relating to any soldier,
anywhere. In a gathering of them, Dick was always in the center. I had
witnessed that for over thirty years, and now, as much as he would miss
being among soldiers, I would miss watching him with them. How in
the world could we leave that?

Because for the past thirty-six years the Army had pretty much
decided Dick's job, where we lived, and his pay, the thought of that big
world out there and having all those decisions to make, at our ages, was
daunting and intimidating, to say the least. Things that most people
do in their twenties and thirties, like deciding where to live, buying a
house, and beginning a career, Dick would be facing at fifty-eight. There
were no maps to guide us; it was going to be the mother of all moves.

During one of our many discussions on the subject of where we wanted to live, I told Dick, "I really want to stay in the DC area. It's felt like home since the first time we lived at Fort Myer. No other place has felt like this to me."

"I know, Vick, but the cost of living is so high that I would need to get a very good job in order for us to afford living here."

"Well, just think about it. I've followed you everywhere for the past thirty-five years and had little say in where we lived. I'm just putting my vote in early for the DC area."

"I understand. Trust me, if I can get a good job, we'll stay here."

We had watched many other friends and peers retire from the Army in recent years. Some had taken jobs and bought a house, only to find they had made a mistake and had to change jobs and relocate all over again. We didn't want to find ourselves in that position.

One of the groups Dick played golf with was a group of retired four-star generals, former chiefs and vice chiefs of staff, many of whom he had served with while they were on active duty. He had watched them over the years as they navigated and enjoyed civilian life. They assured him that they would help steer him and guide him as he made the transition, giving up not just a job but also a whole way of life.

In the meantime, Dick stayed busy making things happen for the Army. The war in Iraq was dragging on, and the mission in Afghanistan had reemerged. The famous "troop surge" in Iraq put more demands on the Army, and deployment lengths increased from twelve to fifteen months. Dick and I continued our travels to Army posts, and by 2008, when we revisited some of the posts we had been to earlier in the war, there were spouses whose soldiers were on their second and third deployments. The questions they posed to us were more about their soldiers downrange than for themselves. That was a shift from what we had seen on previous visits. They worried about battle fatigue, low morale, and PTSD, not to mention the mounting casualties. They were even concerned about equipment and the training of their soldiers. They were counting on Army leadership (including Dick) and the Pentagon to resolve these issues.

At Fort Carson, Colorado, in a meeting with spouses whose soldiers were on their second and third deployments, a spouse told us she was concerned about her husband's mental state; he was depressed, and she was worried for his safety. She was sitting right in front of me, tears rolling down her face. I was so worried for the young woman and all that she was trying to cope with—not only the dangers of combat but also the fear that her husband was mentally unstable. I was worried about her soldier, too. It warmed my heart to see the spouses on either side of her put their arms around her. I couldn't wait for the session to be over so I could hug her myself. Before the day was over, Dick had contacted the chaplain in the soldier's unit in Iraq, and the chaplain had already reached out to the soldier. Still, for every time we made a difference, there were many other times when circumstances were simply out of our control.

During those sessions, the line between my family and those families became blurred. We were living the stress and the worry of having sons deployed, and, like those other families, I was tired of it. The spouses we met—their faces, their concerns, and their fears—stayed with us long after we left them, and I was haunted by the fact that some of them would lose their husbands in combat.

Dick made one last trip to Iraq and Afghanistan to check on the troops, talk to the commanders, and make sure they had everything they needed. For his own peace of mind, he wanted to make sure the soldiers were okay as he prepared to leave the Army. He needed closure. He even got to see Clint. I was thankful for that and, as always, couldn't wait to hear how our son was doing.

"He's doing great, Vicki," Dick said. "He's so much more mature than I ever was at that age, and he's a great commander; he always takes care of his soldiers. I'm so proud of him!"

During those years of frequent deployments, I realized that each of our boys, like their dad, had the heart of a soldier and had truly found their calling. They had always been good sons to us, better than any parent could have asked for, but what was just as wonderful to see was each of them maturing into such good, caring leaders.

★ ★ ★

With the help of his mentors, Dick began to think about job opportunities. It was important for both of us to stay connected to the Army, and he knew he wanted to continue to serve soldiers, and there were lots of opportunities for him to do that in the DC area.

We started house hunting in DC and northern Virginia in late 2007 and early 2008. We were in no position to actually buy a house until Dick had a job offer, but he couldn't accept one until he retired the following August, so it was a real catch-22. After experiencing the initial sticker shock of the housing prices in the area, we set a limit for ourselves and used those months to narrow our search. Dick was pretty sure a couple of job offers would come his way, so knowing those two pieces of the puzzle made the thought of retirement palatable. We had so much fun looking at neighborhoods and houses that we felt like kids again, excited for the future.

Once we found our dream house, it was like we turned a corner—we began to look forward, rather than back at what could've been or should've been. I already knew I wanted to write another book, possibly a memoir. I had made an outline and had written some chapters during a self-imposed sabbatical to Florida earlier that year. I had never gone on a trip completely by myself, but I knew that if I was going to try to write, I had to get away from my real life, to clear my head and center myself. I went down to Pompano Beach and sat by the sea, collected my thoughts, and began writing. There were no distractions, no temptations, nowhere I had to be. It was just me, myself, and I, and the ocean, for seven days, and my ideas started flowing. It was exactly what I needed, but I couldn't stay there forever; my real life was calling to me. When I left Florida, I promised myself that even if I had to put my book on hold temporarily once Dick retired, that would be *my* time to write. It gave me something to look forward to as the weeks and months flew by and Dick's last day on the job approached.

Dick went down to Fort Rucker to take his last flight in an Apache Longbow. Tyler was the instructor pilot in the front seat; Dick was in the back seat. Brooke and Austin were on hand as well. When they landed, Dick emerged from the cockpit and found, as is the tradition when a pilot takes his last flight, a fire truck there to hose him down. The pilot holding the big fire hose was CW5 Brian Stewmon, Dick's former copilot from Desert Storm. Brian had been a brand-new pilot fresh out of flight school back in 1991, when he flew the Task Force Normandy mission with Dick. He went on to achieve the highest rank of a warrant officer and by 2008 was an instructor pilot serving alongside our son at Fort Rucker.

What a way for Dick to end his Army flying career. Later, when I talked to Tyler, he said, "Dad flew really well. I'm amazed by how good he still is!"

And Dick told me, "Tyler is a great pilot, better than I was at that age."

Dick has gotten to see each of his sons excel, and the mutual respect they have for each other warms my heart. Not every father and son get to experience that, I thought. That was the other piece of closure that Dick needed, I realized—his sons were the future of the Army, and he was now ready to leave it to them.

I hated to miss his last flight, but there was no way I could fly down to Fort Rucker for the day. It was just a week before his retirement, and I was up to my eyeballs in making arrangements, accommodations, and menus for all the relatives and friends who were coming in for the ceremony. It was like planning a large wedding. Dick and I had sat at many a retirement dinner and ceremony and watched people cry at their own events, but we didn't want to do that—we had too much to be happy about.

Clint came in from Afghanistan, and Tyler, Brooke, and Austin were all able to be with us for the week. Clint, Tyler, and Brooke presented us with a quilt that told the story of our life in the Army, complete with family photos, all the unit patches, and a beautiful poem transferred onto the fabric. It was the most meaningful gift they could have given us.

Dick's retirement dinner was a wonderful celebration with all the old friends who had made the trip—people we hadn't seen in years, as well as friends and colleagues from all over the DC area—and for that reason, it wasn't as sad as I had thought it was going to be. And as our family and more friends began arriving for the actual retirement ceremony the following week, the event turned into a big reunion for my whole family as well as Dick's. For the first time, all of Dick's aunts and uncles were able to make the trip. They had been huge supporters of Dick throughout his career, sending cards, letters, and prayers every step of the way, but they had never been able to attend any of his ceremonies. Having so many relatives with us definitely made it easier.

We didn't have much alone time once our relatives showed up, but one night, as we lay in bed, Dick and I took a few minutes to relive all the wonderful things that had been done in our honor in the past few days.

"Are you doing okay?" I asked him. "It's pretty amazing, having so many people make the trip here just for us."

"I know. Just seeing my dad with all his siblings for the first time in a long time is wonderful."

"I feel like your retirement has been the best reason for our family and friends to gather. I'm not dreading it like I thought I would. Are you ready?"

"I guess I'm as ready as I'll ever be."

★ ★ ★

The night before the ceremony, our family and closest friends, about forty-five people, came to our house for dinner. I kept thinking it was like a rehearsal dinner and that the ceremony the next day would be the equivalent of a wedding. We gathered around our dining room table, and Dick and I welcomed everyone. I always knew how much our families meant to us, but it was never more evident than that night before Dick's Army career ended. As I looked around the room, I felt full of love for my family and Dick's, and all our extended family members.

I thought about the young Dick Cody, just shy of his eighteenth birthday, who left his home in Montpelier, Vermont, to attend the US Military Academy at the height of the Vietnam War. I'm not sure his grandfather, his parents, or his siblings ever dreamed that the Army would be his career, his life, for the next forty years.

Whether they were sending goodie boxes and letters to Dick while he was deployed; calling the boys and me; or understanding when we missed family gatherings, weddings, birthdays, and anniversaries—our families were the reason we were able to do what we did all those years. As we moved all over the world, they were the constant in our lives; they were the ones we came home to. I knew without a doubt that we could not have done what we did without their love and support. It takes a family to raise and support a soldier, and they were our biggest fans, always cheering us on from the sidelines. And now they were doing that for our sons as they made their own way through Army life. Our experience had come full circle.

★ ★ ★

On the morning of August 1, 2008, I woke up feeling almost as nervous as I had been on my wedding day. And if *I* was nervous, I could only imagine what Dick was feeling. The ceremony itself was a big deal, carefully orchestrated and rehearsed, not to mention that he had to keep his emotions in check and give what was probably the most important speech of his career to a huge crowd. He was out of bed long before I was, working on it.

It was a picture-perfect day—not a cloud in the sky, eighties and low humidity—and for that, I was thankful. I had been worrying about our older relatives and the soldiers out on the parade field suffering in the heat.

After a quick breakfast, everyone began congregating at our house. Shuttle buses would take us to Summerall Field, just a few blocks away. I was upstairs getting ready and, as usual, was down to the last minute.

Dick called upstairs, "Vicki, it's time to go! Everyone is here; the bus is waiting."

"I can't find my new lipstick! I'll be down as soon as I find it."

"Come on, Vick—never mind the lipstick. We've got to go!"

"But I bought it to go with my outfit!"

"Everyone is waiting!"

I finally found my lipstick, applied it quickly, took one last look in the mirror, and started down the stairs. Then I stopped on the landing and took in the sight below. In that moment, my life with Dick flashed before me. I looked down and saw the foyer and living room packed with people. I scanned the crowd, and in a second I took it all in: my mom, my sister, my brother, and their spouses; my cousins; Brooke and Austin; Dick's mom and dad; his sisters and brother and their spouses; his aunts and uncles and nephews; Wynonna and her son. And then, in the middle of all the faces, I saw the three loves of my life: Dick, Clint, and Tyler in their dress blues. It was the last time the three of them would all be in uniform together.

My breath caught, and I felt as if my heart would burst. *Where did the time go? It's been thirty-nine years since that June night when I bounded down the stairs in my cutoffs and T-shirt to meet the boy of my dreams. For my entire adult life, there has not been one day when I have not felt Dick's love for me. Whether he was in Korea or Kuwait, the deserts of California or Saudi Arabia, Iraq, or Afghanistan, even when we had nothing but written letters to connect us, I always felt it. No matter where he was, he was always in my heart.*

It was like herding cattle, getting everyone on the shuttle bus to Summerall Field. On the way to the parade field, I turned to Wynonna, who was sitting behind me. She had been wearing her sunglasses the entire time. She lowered them and revealed her red, puffy eyes.

"I've been crying since I woke up. I'm not ready for this, Vicki. I can't imagine him not in the Army. The entire time I've known him, he's been in uniform."

"I know, Wy—me too. It's hard for me to imagine life after the Army."

"What if it changes things? What if it changes our relationship?"

"Wynonna, I can tell you without a doubt that this will not change your relationship with Dick. He will still be the same man we all love; he just won't be in uniform."

The parade field looked beautiful, filled with the Third US Infantry Regiment (the Old Guard), the United States Army Band (Pershing's Own), and the Fife and Drum Corps. Flags from all fifty states lined the perimeter. It was so spectacular, I almost forgot why we were there; I kept thinking, *Maybe this is someone else's ceremony.*

At the ceremony, Dick and I were recognized for our years of service and our contributions. We were each given awards and medals. Standing before the huge crowd, listening to someone talk about me that way, made me want to fidget; it was so humbling that I felt almost embarrassed. But I also thought about how great it was that the Army recognizes its spouses' contributions as well. Standing there next to Dick, I knew he was thinking the same thing I was: *It's not about the awards, it's about the* rewards, *and we've been given enough of those— every step of the way, at every duty assignment—to last a lifetime. They weren't always tangible, but they're memories that we'll always carry in our hearts. How lucky we are.*

I watched Dick and imagined how heavy his heart was as he made his final salutes and "trooped the line." After the other speeches, it was his turn to talk. After he acknowledged me, the boys, our families and friends, and all the dignitaries, he got down to business. The GIs'

General did what he did best: he talked about soldiers and soldiering. "Being a soldier is a privilege and honor few will ever know," he shared. "I have been trained by, led by, and inspired by soldiers my entire adult life. There is no end to being a soldier. I will take off the uniform, but I will always be a soldier."

He put into perspective his thirty-six years of service to our country without taking credit for himself; instead, he gave all the credit to the soldiers he had served with. I was never more proud of Dick Cody than I was that day.

As the sun beat down on us in the front row and the ceremony wound down, I looked at my husband and thought, *He did something few could ever do: he touched the soul of the Army. Through tireless, endless days at the Pentagon, as he fought for anything and everything that would make a difference in the lives of the soldiers, they all knew how much he cared. I watched him work until he was bone tired and had nothing left to give but a salute, a hug, or a coin. This man is my hero.*

Clint and Tyler were up on the podium with Dick for the Pass in Review, the final act of a military ceremony or parade, when all the units pass by and render honors (a salute) to the reviewing officer—in this case, Dick. For this particular occasion, the ceremony was performed by the Old Guard at Fort Myer, Virginia, where those units and other soldiers carried the flags of all fifty states. After that, the band played the Army song, signaling the end of the ceremony, and everyone stood and sang along, just as we had done at every Army ceremony and parade for Dick's entire career.

When we stood up, I turned to Brooke and said, "Let's go up there and stand with our guys."

"Can we do that? Are we allowed?"

"Of course we can." I took Austin's hand, and the three of us walked over to the podium and up the steps, stood next to Dick, Clint, and Tyler, and sang the Army song together, one last time. What a moment; what a day.

And then it was over. Dick and I walked off the parade field together, hand in hand, just as we had begun our journey back in August 1975. We looked at each other, and without a word, our eyes said it all: *no regrets.*

PS: I read somewhere that one of the keys to a strong marriage is sharing new adventures and discovering new things together as a couple. Dick and I didn't have to pay to go off on expensive and exotic adventures; we got those courtesy of the good old US Army! Every time we packed up, loaded up, and set out on the highway or the airways for a new location, it was us against the world. We discovered new places together and made a new life, first as a couple and, later, as a family. Knowing we had each other comforted us and bonded us eternally, no matter whether we were in Hawaii, lower Alabama, or Korea. It was all part of the greatest journey we would ever go on.

Epilogue
McLean, Virginia, 2015

It sure is quiet here in suburbia. We live just fifteen minutes from Fort Myer, fifteen minutes from our former life, and yet at times it feels surreal that Dick's career in the Army has come and gone. We still go to Sunday Mass at the Fort Myer Chapel; I go to the Fort Myer fitness center; and sometimes when I drive by our old house, I feel almost as if that was someone else's life. Each of us misses Army life off and on; the nostalgia comes over me or Dick at the strangest times, not always when we expect it.

Obviously, both of us went through an adjustment period after Dick's retirement. Dick's transition to civilian life was far greater and more traumatic than mine. There were times in the beginning when we had no one but each other. Together we sorted through, downsized, reminisced and grieved, and eventually we let go of the past. In doing so, we discovered new aspects of our relationship, as we had more time for just the two of us than we'd had in years. The first time we went on a trip and Dick didn't have to sign out on leave, we felt like kids skipping school. We realized we could go skiing for ten days if we wanted to, we could go on date night any night of the week, we could visit our kids and grandkids or go up to Vermont as often as we wished. I could actually accompany Dick on business trips to places like Paris, or ride the train to New York City for a night out. All these things may sound trivial to many in our age group, but to us, it was as if a whole new set of freedoms and a new world of adventures had opened up.

After six weeks of "quiet time," Dick began a second career in the corporate world. His job is the perfect fit for him, and his mentors played an important role in helping him find just the right position.

Dick needs to work, not for the money but for a sense of purpose. He is not one to sit around the house, hanging out with me all day.

I, on the other hand, was perfectly content to decorate and set up our new home, and I frequently reminded Dick, "This is the last time I intend to move!" And once everything was in order, I was able to begin my newest journey: writing my memoir.

Our family has grown in the past few years. Clint finally met his soul mate at Fort Campbell, Kentucky. Kimberly, a West Pointer, had deployed twice to Iraq with the 101st Airborne, but in all that time, their paths had never crossed. When they met, at a mutual friend's party, they both agreed it would probably never amount to anything, as Clint was on his way to Afghanistan for yet another deployment and Kim was in the process of getting out of the Army. But isn't that how it usually works—when you least expect it? For them, it was just meant to be. Two years later, they married at West Point, and in 2012, they blessed us with another grandson, Connor. Clint deployed again to Afghanistan and returned safely. They had a second son, Dillon, in November 2014.

Tyler and Brooke had another son, Zachary, in 2009. When they got stationed in DC, we were able to watch Austin and Zac grow, and to enjoy their company for a blessed three-year period.

Our lives have come full circle, as we are now on the sidelines. We have watched with pride as our sons have commanded aviation companies and completed military and civilian schooling; they continue to honor our country with their service. We agonize and worry when they leave their wives and young children to deploy, but we cherish our time with our grandchildren and continue to wonder how we got so lucky. Above all, we understand the joys, the challenges, the ups and the downs of *their* Army lives.

We have stayed connected to the Army and have had plenty of opportunities to attend ceremonies, black-tie events, and galas. At first it was strange for me to see Dick in a tuxedo, rather than in his dress blues. But so many of his friends are in tuxedos now, I don't give it a second thought.

We love living in the DC area for a number of reasons. We have a network of old Army friends who retired here, too, as well as a continual flow of friends who are still serving and are always coming back to our city. Dick's office overlooks the Pentagon, and he is a frequent visitor there for meetings. We attend promotions and all the usual events that include retired four-star generals, and we watch with pride as this generation of officers and soldiers, men and women who were young when they served for and with Dick, become the leaders of our Army. I think we would have missed too much of this if we had packed up and moved back to Vermont.

Clint recently got stationed at the Pentagon, so we now have the joy of spending time with him and Kimberly and watching their young boys grow, too. Tyler is back in the 101st Airborne Division and deployed to Afghanistan.

And the circle of Army life continues.

Acknowledgments

Writing this memoir has been one of the most gratifying things I have ever done. It was therapeutic, and at times very emotional, to go back in time and examine every aspect of my marriage and motherhood. I relived every move, every joy and sadness, every challenge and triumph. In the end, I still wouldn't change a thing about my life.

Thank you to Brooke Warner, Crystal Patriarche, and their wonderful teams at She Writes Press and Spark Point Studio for taking me on. You make it easy for brand-new authors.

I would like to thank A.J. (Tony) Tata who was my first mentor and believed I had a story worth telling. A great big thank-you to my editor, Annie Tucker, who read my manuscript and, through the too many words and too many pages, saw the potential. You "got it" from the beginning, and with your gentle guidance and prodding, you brought out the best in me. I can't thank you enough!

I want to thank my family, Dick's family, and my friends, who have been so understanding and supportive for these last eight years while I plodded along on this project. I'm sure many of you didn't think I would ever finish. Sometimes, *I* didn't think I would finish. A special thank-you to Nancy, who read my drafts repeatedly, listened to me complain, procrastinate, and continued to encourage me.

Thanks to my mom and dad for their unconditional love, always believing in me, and being my biggest fans; I would not be who I am today without you. To my sister and closest confidante, and to my brother, thank you for always being there for me, even as I came in and out of your lives all these years.

To all my fellow Army spouses, past and present, thank you for showing me the way when I was a brand-new Army wife and for passing on to me all of the wonderful traditions of Army life. To this generation of Army spouses, including my daughters-in-law, thank you for teaching me even more about resiliency and strength during a very difficult time for our military. You have shouldered far more burdens than my generation ever had to. You all inspire me each and every day.

To Clint and Tyler, thank you for being the best sons a mother could ask for. It has been nothing but joy to raise you and watch you grow into such fine officers, leaders, and pilots—and, most important, wonderful husbands and fathers. Thank you for your service and all the sacrifices you continue to make for all of us. I couldn't be more proud. You and your wives and beautiful sons are such a blessing to our family.

Thank you to the most important person in my life, Dick. I have never once regretted the journey we have taken. You were the inspiration for me to write this story. It is to you, our sons, and all the men and women who wear the uniform, that I dedicate this book. Thank you for being my biggest cheerleader all these years, especially during the writing of our story. I could not have done this without your guidance and unfailing support. The fact that we are still in love, still rockin' the slopes at A-Basin, doing date night, laughing at each other's jokes, and enjoying life together, is a miracle that few people know.

About the Author

© Rebecca Cullinan

Vicki Cody grew up in Burlington, Vermont and graduated from the University of Vermont with a BS degree in education in 1975. For the next thirty-three years she was an Army wife, supporting her husband in his career. While raising their two sons and moving all over the United States and overseas, she served as a coach and mentor for other Army spouses, and as an advocate for Army families.

Her first book, *Your Soldier, Your Army: A Parents' Guide* was published by the Association of the United States Army in 2005. Her articles have appeared in numerous military magazines and publications. This is her first memoir.

She and her husband of forty years live in the Washington, DC area.

SELECTED TITLES FROM SHE WRITES PRESS

Accidental Soldier: A Memoir of Service and Sacrifice in the Israel Defense Forces by Dorit Sasson $17.95, 978-1-63152-035-8
When nineteen-year-old Dorit Sasson realized she had no choice but to distance herself from her neurotic, worrywart of a mother in order to become her own person, she volunteered for the Israel Defense Forces—and found her path to freedom.

Make a Wish for Me: A Mother's Memoir by LeeAndra Chergey
$16.95, 978-1-63152-828-6
A life-changing diagnosis teaches a family that where's there is love there is hope—and that being "normal" is not nearly as important as providing your child with a life full of joy, love, and acceptance.

Renewable: One Woman's Search for Simplicity, Faithfulness, and Hope by Eileen Flanagan $16.95, 978-1-63152-968-9
At age forty-nine, Eileen Flanagan had an aching feeling that she wasn't living up to her youthful ideals or potential, so she started trying to change the world—and in doing so, she found the courage to change her life.

The Longest Mile: A Doctor, a Food Fight, and the Footrace that Rallied a Community Against Cancer by Christine Meyer, MD $16.95, 978-1-63152-043-3
In a moment of desperation, after seeing too many patients and loved ones battle cancer, a doctor starts running team—never dreaming what a positive impact it will have on her community.

The Shelf Life of Ashes: A Memoir by Hollis Giammatteo
$16.95, 978-1-63152-047-1
Confronted by an importuning mother 3,000 miles away who thinks her end is nigh—and feeling ambushed by her impending middle age—Giammatteo determines to find The Map of Aging Well, a decision that leads her on an often-comic journey.

Warrior Mother: A Memoir of Fierce Love, Unbearable Loss, and Rituals that Heal by Sheila K. Collins, PhD. $16.95, 978-1-938314-46-9
The story of the lengths one mother goes to when two of her three adult children are diagnosed with potentially terminal diseases.